THE SURREY INSTITUTE OF ART

Smart books are the essential p~~~~ 499 I bus005 people.
They are practical guides designed to give killer business subjects,
and deliver sound principles in a style that is both informative and has attitude.
They are the perfect resource for time-starved business people everywhere!

The newest **Smart** titles are:

Smart **Leadership**	JONATHAN YUDELOWITZ
Smart **Marketing**	JOHN MARIOTTI
Smart **Finance**	KEN LANGDON
Smart **Strategy**	RICHARD KOCH
Smart **Business**	JAMES LEIBERT
Smart **Risk**	ANDREW HOLMES

Also available in the Smart series:

Smart Things to Know About	**Brands and Branding**	JOHN MARIOTTI
Smart Things to Know About	**Change**	DAVID FIRTH
Smart Things to Know About	**Consultancy**	PATRICK FORSYTH
Smart Things to Know About	**CRM**	DAVID HARVEY
Smart Things to Know About	**Culture**	DONNA DEEPROSE
Smart Things to Know About	**Customers**	ROS JAY
Smart Things to Know About	**Decision Making**	KEN LANGDON
Smart Things to Know About	**E-commerce**	MIKE CUNNINGHAM
Smart Things to Know About	**Growth**	TONY GRUNDY
Smart Things to Know About	**Innovation and Creativity**	DENNIS SHERWOOD
Smart Things to Know About	**Knowledge Management**	THOMAS KOULOPOULOS
Smart Things to Know About	**Lifelong Learning**	ANDREW HOLMES
Smart Things to Know About	**Managing Projects**	DONNA DEEPROSE
Smart Things to Know About	**Mergers & Acquisitions**	TONY GRUNDY
Smart Things to Know About	**Motivation**	DONNA DEEPROSE
Smart Things to Know About	**Partnerships**	JOHN MARIOTTI
Smart Things to Know About	**People Management**	DAVID FIRTH
Smart Things to Know About	**Scenario Planning**	TONY KIPPENBERGER
Smart Things to Know About	**Six Sigma**	ANDREW BERGER
Smart Things to Know About	**Managing Talent**	STEPHANIE OVERMAN
Smart Things to Know About	**Teams**	ANNEMARIE CARRACIOLO
Smart Things to Know About	**Technology Management**	ANDREW HOLMES
Smart Things to Know About	**Your Career**	JOHN MIDDLETON

CAPSTONE

work smarter

smart

•➔ marketing

JOHN MARIOTTI

First published in 2000

This edition published in 2004 by
Capstone Publishing Ltd (a Wiley Company)
The Atrium
Southern Gate
Chichester
West Sussex PO19 8SQ
England
www.wileyeurope.com

CIP catalogue records for this book are available from the British Library and the US Library of Congress

658·8 MAR

ISBN 1-84112-585-7

Typeset by Forewords, 109 Oxford Road, Cowley, Oxford

Printed and bound by T.J. International Ltd, Padstow, Cornwall

10 9 8 7 6 5 4 3 2 1

This book is printed on acid-free paper responsibly manufactured from sustainable forestry in which at least two trees are planted for each one used for paper production.

Contents

Preface

How to start a book on such a huge topic as Marketing is a daunting question, but then anyone who is intimidated by such a question has no business writing Smart books –especially about Marketing! So here we go – hang on!

This is not a book you need to read through from start to finish like a novel. It may help a bit with terminology if you do, but each chapter and many of the subheads are intended to be useful – "Smart Things to Know about Marketing" – on their own. So read on, or find something that interests you and just open it anywhere and start reading until you feel like stopping. Between the quotes from learned authors, the advice from experienced practitioners, a few quotes that are timeless, and a lot of questions (and some answers) you should be "smarter" about marketing – and maybe about life too!

Where should I start? How about, take everything you know or have heard about marketing and set it aside. Don't forget it entirely; just put it on trial for its credibility, applicability and usefulness in today's environment. It may not be wrong *per se*, but it is certainly in need of major updating since the world of marketing is undergoing cataclysmic changes almost daily! Most of the old knowledge about marketing is still useful, valuable, and important – so I'll go through it as we progress. *But* – this is a big revolution.

To be really smart about marketing in this era of accelerating know-ledge, information avalanches, the ubiquitous internet, and exploding e-commerce you have to do "smart things", and make "smart decisions" faster and better than ever before. If you don't you'll be a "smart job hunter", because your company will get beaten or bought by competitors who do!

To start with, a smart thing to know is that marketing is one of the most overused and least understood words in the business vocabu-lary. It is also one of the most powerful and far-reaching disciplines influencing the success of companies and organizations in the world today. As I just pointed out, those first few sentences in this chapter would have been true decades ago. But maybe, just maybe, this *is* the big *one*. Since 1995 the global explosion of the Internet and the World Wide Web have added millions of pages of marketing informa-tion every week so the value of putting the "Smart Things to Know about Marketing" in a single book is an even greater benefit.

The more people you talk to and the more material you read, the more opinions you will find about what's smart and what's not. You see, there are a lot of things that were "smart things to know" in the past that aren't quite so smart any more. At least that is the case according to no less an authority than Peter Drucker who recently stated that *"everything you know is obsolete or out of date"*!

What a relief that is for me! It means I can start with a clean slate, and tell you what I think the smart things to know about marketing are – *as of now*. And I can do it with very little fear of being too badly second-guessed.

Over the course of this book I will enlist the help of many "experts and authorities". I will confer with people who are doing real mar-keting every day – where the competitive game is played for real money, and draw some of the wisdom out of their minds. These opinions and insights are tremendously valuable. As the book (and you) progress, I will include numerous real world examples of marketing – both good and bad, smart and not so smart – with observations about what went right or wrong, and what the "smart thing to do" might have been.

When I am done – and when you are done – with this book. I hope five central themes will have stuck in your mind. With that brief introduction and these five recurring themes, let's get into *Smart Things to Know about Marketing*.

The Five Smartest Things to Know about Marketing

- The strategy of marketing has to match the strategy of the business, so *you must have a plan* – clear, concise, well communicated and then take action based on it.

- Marketing is all about serving the customer, and to serve the customer, you must understand the customer in all respects, so *get close to the customer*, and preferably get "inside their minds".

- Always *do your homework*; do it fast and as well as you can in, the time you have.

- Marketing is especially must *remember relationships*; first look outside-in, but don't forget the inside relationships either.

- The Internet doesn't change everything, but what it does change is the ability and ways to *use the speed and reach of technology* in marketing.

Marketing and the Business

1 The Past and Present of Marketing

This chapter will frame today's marketing environment in a historical perspective, and introduce you to some of the things that are different amidst many that remain the same. Look for recurring ties to the Five Smartest Things to Know about Marketing, which will appear at the start of each chapter.

> **The five smartest things to know about marketing**
>
> - You must have a plan
>
> - Get close to the customer
>
> - Do your homework
>
> - Remember relationships
>
> - Use the speed and reach of technology

Experts everywhere – outside of marketing

I can't begin to count the times that I have been in meetings either with my own employees or with employees of one of my clients that the subject of marketing hasn't been the primary topic. Surprisingly, most of these meetings were not even with marketing people. There were no marketing people in the room – or even nearby! For most of the meeting marketing was the big discussion topic although these were meetings with manufacturing people, engineers, or those folks who were supposed to be marketing's closest allies, sales.

It seems in nearly every problem we talked about involving manufacturing or engineering is perceived to have been caused by a decision made in marketing (or so they seem to believe). It was as if the only goal of marketing was to make all these decisions that make life more difficult for the engineers or the manufacturing plant. Worst of all, it appears to these people outside of marketing that the decisions were made arbitrarily! The same kind of feeling goes for sales, who has, the toughest job – facing the customer and bringing home the orders!

"Trust is a peculiar quality. It can't be bought. It can't be downloaded. It can't be instant – a startling fact in an instant culture. It can only accumulate slowly, over multiple iterations. But it can disappear in a blink."

Kevin Kelly, *New Rules for a New Economy*

If marketing is populated with such uninformed, arbitrary and capricious people it's a wonder they get anything right. The answer, of course, is that marketing people are not fools! They don't take important decisions lightly nor do they make all that many of them arbitrarily. The simple fact is that marketing is a business of interpretation and communication, both of which are fraught with peril. Marketing's job, in the words of noted marketing authority Dr Roger Blackwell, *"is to have what will sell"*. What a simple task. Or is it?

If you don't go where you don't go, you won't know what you don't know!

"People fall into comfortable patterns and habits. Marketing people cannot afford to do this. Patterns and habits are inhibitors of discovery and wonderment. A card-carrying, bone-deep, streetwise marketing pro has the following tendencies:

1. Never rent the same kind of car twice in a row.

2. Get down on the floor and play with kids (and really watch them to see how they think and discover).

3. Go left when everybody else goes right.

4. Go to the magazine stand and page through the magazines they think they don't like!

5. Introduce themselves to people they don't know at a party or conference and spend time with them instead of the comfortable old cliques.

6. Constantly connect dots that other people don't even see.

You get the idea. Marketing pros are explorers, not followers."

Steve Goubeaux, Partner and Principal, Visual Marketing Associates

Helping the non-marketing experts . . .

This book will help countless marketing people by providing them with just the *handout* they need for their partners in all of the non-marketing disciplines – engineering, manufacturing, sales, and even in the executive suite and boardroom. The old saying goes, *"A little knowledge is dangerous"*. My view of this is that *a little knowledge can be highly beneficial,* because it creates a greater appreciation for the difficulty of the job that marketing must do successfully. You can be smart by making information deposits in your personal "partner accounts" with these people. The more they feel "in the know" and part of what is happening, the more they will help make things happen, and reciprocate with information of their own.

In the days before the Internet, the judgement calls that marketing made were usually made on far less than complete information, and may have seemed arbitrary to other parts of the organization, and even information on the Internet is not perfect. With everything moving at warp speed, and with the volume of available information increasing exponentially, the need for quick, insightful and accurate marketing decisions is greater than ever. And making them is harder than ever! Information, flowing freely and openly among the various parts of a company, is the best tool for making faster and better decisions. The time for deliberation that might have been days, weeks, or even months is now reduced to hours or minutes. A week or two to make a decision is a luxury.

> "Manufacturing productivity has risen steadily, but marketing is just getting more expensive and less effective."
>
> Dr Philip Kotler

This book is intended to be useful for all you smart (or wannabe smart) marketing types, because it will help you explain (and/or defend) your decisions to the other parts of the organization. It's the smart thing to do – see, it says so right here! Not only might the others stop thinking that you are arbitrary in making those decisions, they may even provide some useful information (along with their opinions) that will help improve your decisions.

And to all you folks in R&D, engineering, manufacturing, purchasing, finance and sales, *listen up*! You can help marketing by reading this book and giving them your informed input on what you think is practical, possible, and imaginable – before they are caught in the bind of having to make an on the spot final decision. When you do that, and then you are behaving like "smart people" who know a lot of smart things about marketing, and everybody wins! Let's start on the journey!

"Don't hide your light under a bushel"

This biblical phrase is apt for this situation. Once you have made the hard decisions – what to sell, to whom, where, etc. – then it is time to communicate them! The right action is to communicate these decisions in two directions – internally and externally. There must be excellent communications internally, within your company – to the engineers, to operations people and to sales partners – why this product or service will excite customers sufficiently that they will buy it. The smart marketer builds relationships that make this communication effective and natural, and not a surprise. A later chapter is devoted to this topic of relationships.

Everything has changed – but not quite

Most people, including many "experts", say that marketing has entered a new era thanks to the Internet, e-commerce, and the explosion in communications and computing infrastructure around the world. They're probably right but the smart thing to know is that the new era does not eliminate or invalidate all of the fundamentals from previous eras. The fundamentals are mostly as true as ever – it is just the pace and potential brought about by the digital era that makes marketing different.

What has changed more than anything else is the speed and global reach of marketing thanks to developments in technology – espe-

- 1980s – Ready, Aim, Fire

- 1990s – Ready, Fire, Aim

- 2000s – Fire, Fire, Fire!

Dr Philip Kotler

cially information, computing and telecommunications. What has not changed is that people are still people and relationships matter a lot – especially in marketing. Customers are people with motives, emotions, needs, and wants. Understanding those motives, emotions, needs and wants, and communicating them to your organization is your job if you are in marketing!

> "We now stand on the threshold of a new age – the age of revolution . . . it is going to be an age of upheaval, of tumult, of fortunes made and unmade at head snapping speed."
>
> Gary Hamel

Crafts become people's names

To see what I mean by this let's go back in time to prior centuries. The markets of that era weren't nearly so specialized as this field we call marketing today. In fact, marketing was simply a byproduct of earning a living. Most people were employed in either agrarian work (farming, raising animals, etc.) or in crafts and trades necessary in the manufacture of things people used in the day-to-day life, or in the conduct of commerce. These craftsmen created some of the earliest brands in the form of the marks they put on their work to identify whose product it was. Some of the earliest forms of marketing were no more complicated than the sign in front of their shop, which announced their name, their craft/trade, or both. This was all they needed at that time.

It shouldn't be surprising that many of the surnames of people we find in much of the Western world are based on the crafts or trades of their family predecessors. Think about the fact that in times gone by people might be known as "John the Baker" or "Charles the

Shoemaker". This was all of the identification they needed. In later times these names would be shortened to "John Baker", "Charles Shoemaker", and so forth. Marketing was pretty straightforward. If you wanted some grain milled, you probably went to "Edward the Miller", and later on to Ed Miller and maybe even later to Miller's Grain Company!

> (!)
>
> Everything we know is from the past, yet everything we must decide will be in the future. How will the future be different from the past?

If you go back far enough, to the era before the invention of the printing press, most of the written word was in the form of books, created by monks in monasteries, laboriously hand copying the text. Most people did not even know how to read and write. Thus traditional written forms of marketing we consider commonplace were not even used. People made plans and communicated their purchase intentions via word of mouth. If the craftsman's work was worthy and good value, then the word of it spread from purchaser to purchaser. A smart marketer can learn a lot from this age-old lesson.

The printing press

Johann Gutenberg, 1455

Now let's continue our journey through time from the past to the future. When the printing press was invented a whole new way of reproducing text-based information came into being. The invention of mass-produced paper made it possible for the word to be spread far and wide by the circulation of printed material. At this point in history, the slow forms of transportation still limited the spread of printed information. While wandering vagabonds might carry printed material with them, it was often very difficult to purchase goods from faraway craftsmen. As always seems to happen, a few breakthroughs altered the landscape of marketing and commerce.

Communications at the speed of . . . a horse

The Pony Express, 1860

Communications of a century ago were very slow – usually limited to the distance a person walking or riding a horse could travel in a given amount of time. Because transportation was limited to walking or riding a horse (or a horse and buggy), people would seldom travel further than necessary from their home to obtain the necessities of life. This made marketing of that era a decidedly local, word-of-mouth practice. Handbills were one of the first forms of distance marketing, but these also had to travel by riders on horses, or overland carriages (often called stagecoaches in the US). Then there was the problem of travelling to make the purchase and bring it back with you.

> How can we use speed to gain an advantage over our competition and better serve our customers?

There is still nothing like word of mouth testimonial to spread the knowledge and desirability of a product service. There is another side to this, however, because studies have proven that failures of products and services are passed on by word of mouth at least five to ten times as often as successes. Therein lies the opportunity and the challenge for smart marketers. The next major event that dramatically influenced marketing was the application of the steam engine to the development of railroads and trains.

Railroads and telegraphy

Stockton & Darlington Railway, England, 1825, B. & O., USA, 1828; Samuel Morse, 1844

The railroads made possible a giant leap in the speed and distance a person or goods could travel in a given amount of time. They provided a means of conveying products to purchasers in faraway places.

"Over the course of a few years, a new communications technology annihilated distance and shrank the world faster and farther than ever before. A worldwide communications network whose cables spanned continents and oceans, it revolutionized business practices and gave rise to new forms of crime."

The subject: not the *Internet*, but the *telegraph*, in 1840.

The first message: "What hath God wrought?"

Around the same time that the railroads developed, the second part of that revolution came into widespread use – the telegraph.

The telegraph was the first means for information to travel further and faster than a person could travel (well, with the exception of homing pigeons which were not particularly reliable and had a very limited payload). This meant that information could be at the person's destination before they got there. While the Morse code used in the telegraph was unwieldy for use as a marketing tool, the sheer magnitude of this leap in communications changed the world of commerce dramatically.

"E-commerce is to the Information Revolution what the railroad was to the Industrial Revolution – a new, unprecedented, and unexpected development."

Peter F. Drucker, "Knowledge Work", *Executive Excellence*

Telephones and automobiles

Alexander Graham Bell, 1876; Karl Benz & Gottlieb Daimler, 1885–6

At the turn of the last century, the third major marketing and communications breakthrough was taking shape – the telephone. Anyone who answers a telemarketing call now, and is annoyed by it, can hardly imagine how great a breakthrough the telephone was for the people and businesses of its early years. The unwieldy and slow Morse code of the telegraph could now be replaced by the spoken word.

Around this same time, in 1908, Henry Ford created the mass-produced automobile, the Model T, which made transportation more affordable, faster, and far more flexible. While Ford's Model T was far from the first automobile produced, it was perhaps the most important automobile ever produced because it was affordable to a much larger part of the population. The combination of the telephone and an affordable automobile ushered in a whole new means of marketing, on which the smart marketers of today still rely.

"Security is mostly superstition – it does not exist in nature. Life is either a daring adventure or nothing at all."

Helen Keller

During the first half of the 20th century the telephone and the automobile, in combination with the printed word in the form of newspapers and magazines, were joined by yet another new invention, the radio. This combination truly revolutionized marketing again. For the first time ever large, widespread groups of people were economically accessible to marketing communications. This fact led to the development of larger "stores" and the concept of mass merchandising was born.

The birth of mass marketing – mail order catalogs

The combination of the United States Post Office (founded in 1913), the telephone, railroads, and the automobile (in the form of trucks) permitted early retailing pioneers like Sears, Roebuck (1886) and Montgomery Ward (1872) to build their catalog mail-order businesses on a much broader scale. Their catalogs were among the most effective and legendary marketing tools ever created.

Remnants of this era remain today as specialty catalogs and are now being replicated digitally on the World Wide Web. As highways were built and transportation improved further, larger retail stores – first for groceries and later for general merchandise – began to spring up in urban and suburban areas of major cities.

Television (BBC, 1936) and marketing's "golden age" (1950–2000)

Concurrent with this infrastructure development was the next great leap in marketing, the development and rapid spread of television. Advertisers everywhere now depend on television so heavily that imagining an era without it is hard to do. Television made it possible to animate the catalogs, to merge the spoken word of radio with the animated pictures and creativity of advertising. Many would say that the heyday of television, essentially the last half of the 20th century, was the "golden age of marketing". If that is so, then a smart marketer would call this the "platinum age", because never before has so much been possible in the form of media tools for the marketer.

> "Just as surely as the Industrial Revolution invaded every sector of society in the 18th and 19th centuries, the e-revolution is creating changes so pervasive and profound that they have the potential of invading every avenue of life in the 21st century. Yet, the more things change, the more they stay the same."
>
> Roger D. Blackwell and Kristina Stephan, "The Retail Paradigm", *Retail Merchandiser*, July 2000

"What goes around comes around"

Mosaic and Netscape web browsers, 1994

There's an old saying, *"What goes around comes around."* It's true! History does tend to repeat itself, with some adaptation to current conditions. The refined version of the Internet that fills the popular news media is only a decade old. The Mosaic browser which evolved into Netscape Navigator made the World Wide Web a tool for the masses – and for marketing's new era.

Every time you read about the incredible revolution that the Internet has made possible, just remember those previous revolutions such as the invention of the printing press, the telegraph, the telephone, and television had similarly huge impacts on society – and on marketing. Each successive evolutionary or revolutionary advancement in the speed and reach of communications through the history of man has moved marketing to a new level. The Internet is just doing it again. A smart marketer gleans what s/he can from the lessons of the past

"The ability to communicate readily, at great distances is embodied only in angels. Distance is a fundamental premise of a material world. It fell not to the telegraph, the telephone, the television, or the airplane. None of these achieve true action at a distance. Transmitting a few words, a few minutes of voice, even the few filmed spectacles that broadcasters deign to bounce around the globe, serves only to remind us how bound and gagged we are.

. . . These gags and ties are now giving way. When anyone can transmit any amount of information, any picture, any experience, any opportunity to anyone, or everyone anywhere at any time, instantaneously, without barriers of convenience or cost, the resulting transformation becomes a transfiguration.

George Gilder

and avoids the marketing mistakes of a prior era. In doing so, the basis is formed for better marketing decisions in the future.

The need for better, faster decisions is the one aspect of the speed and reach of the Internet-era that surpasses the prior upheavals – the speed and reach of the Internet are unprecedented. Nothing in our human experience compares to the blinding, instantaneous, asynchronous, global speed and reach of the Internet. What that means to all of you smart marketers is that you have far less time than ever before to make decisions, launch a marketing plan, develop and sell a product or service, and make some money at it before competitor half way around the world beats your brains out. But if you do it well, the entire earth can be your market, faster than ever. How exciting!

The age of mass customization, 2000–2010

As if the potential for spanning the globe isn't impressive enough, the Internet provides the potential for mass customization. Marketers have always dreamed of the ability to reach out and touch individual customers with their message and their products/services. In the era of mass merchandising, mass media was a sufficient and effective way of marketing. Market research could deal with averages aggregating demand and preferences with only occasional large errors. It's not that way anymore.

"Marketing needs a new paradigm and new skills for the New Economy."

Dr Philip Kotler

The challenge now is that you *can* reach out and touch individual customers. But how? And who? And to do what? *Time's up!* That's about how long you have to decide! While you were reading last two sentences some competitor was beating you to the customer. Scary? You bet! Exciting? Absolutely! The Smart Things to Know about Marketing in this era are infinitely more fascinating and powerful than in any prior period of time, and the time you need to know them is *right now!*

The power of brands – past, present, and especially the future!

There's one more topic I want to touch briefly before moving on to a whole different set of issues. If I can take you back to the early part of our travel through time I commented on the brand the craftsman used to mark his work. All through the evolution of marketing from a local, craft-based effort to today's lightning-fast global Internet marketing, brands continue to be one of the most important assets of a smart marketer. A brand is a shorthand description of a complex package of value, which has made an impression on the mind of the consumer. There's no telling how valuable that impression can be to a marketer. Many brands were built over decades – names like Coke,

> "A powerful brand frequently provides the source of a company's wealth for many generations. The best brands improve with age, developing clearly defined personalities, as well as the affection and loyalty of the public. The best become parents to sub-brands and brand extensions, which give the owner a chance to exploit their values and names in new areas."
>
> *The World's Greatest Brands*, Interbrand Group

Marlboro, Mercedes-Benz, AT&T, and so forth. Some brands were created more recently. Now familiar names like Nike, Lexus, Lucent, Cisco, Intel, and Microsoft are all products of the past 25 years or less. The Internet and its explosion on the World Wide Web in the last five years have permitted brand building with unprecedented speed and on a previously unimaginable scale.

America Online (aol.com), Yahoo.com, amazon.com, eBay.com, Google.com and many others were unknown, unheard of, and in many cases nonexistent less than ten years ago. They're almost household names today and the "picture of the package of value they form in consumers' minds" is extremely valuable in itself. Every smart marketer must understand brands and brand building – but then I wrote another whole book in the Smart series devoted to that topic, so I will only touch on it in this one where it is an important part of the overall marketing topic.

Before consumer products come the industrial products

Although it is easy to get caught up in the popular, easy to relate to area of consumer marketing, retailing, advertising, etc., one fact remains true. Before any of these products or services can exist, someone upstream has to produce an industrial product or service from which these consumer goods and services are made. Plastic containers for food, cosmetics, and everything else come from molds. Someone must make the molds, and the molding machines that run them. Someone else must maintain it all and provide infrastructure services like electricity, water, transportation, and so many more. Others must produce the plastic resins from the byproducts of petroleum refining. Someone must sell the mold-makers and machinery-makers steel and cutting tools and lubricants and controls. Marketing to this sector is the great forgotten area of marketing. Smart marketers would be wise to pay attention to it. It is *huge!*

Marketing is important in both industrial and consumer products and services, and the new economy of e-commerce recognizes both with the terms B2C (business to consumer) and B2B (business to business). Some distinctively different issues, and many of the same issues, influence marketing in these different arenas.

Don't forget "not-for-profit" marketing

One of the most often overlooked and most powerful areas in marketing is marketing for non-profit endeavors. This is perhaps the fastest growing and most dynamic field of marketing in the world today. Did I say marketing in religion? You bet – check out televangelists like Pat Robertson and The 700 Club, or remember Jim and Tammy Faye Baker? How about Oral Roberts and Dr Robert Schuller? Or how about selling students on attending a given college? Have you seen the Red Cross or American Cancer Society campaigns lately? How about the local United Way campaign? Is there any doubt that the election campaigns for major governmental positions including the presidents and prime ministers are not some of the world's most highly developed and expensive marketing programs?

If you think this isn't marketing, then you're not being a "smart marketer". But pay attention and you can be. Even history has been altered by smart marketing – some for good; some for evil. Certainly the Red Cross emblem is a sign of hope around the world during wars and natural disasters. But do you think the Nazi Germany's swastika was a brand icon for a marketing campaign? I do – and an extremely powerful one! I'll explore some of these different kinds of marketing in a chapter to come.

> "Marketing actually begins with an idea for a product or service and ends only after the consumer has had sufficient time to evaluate the product thoroughly, which might be months or years later."
>
> Robert D. Hisrich, *Marketing*

The Old Economy + the New Economy = One Economy

Finally, there are the Old Economy and the New Economy – or are there? Many experts, like successful and respected Jack Welch, the retired CEO of GE, don't believe there are two economies, just one undergoing some radial technological transformations. Writers like Kevin Kelly and Don Tapscott contend that we are in a New Economy – a digital economy different from anything we have ever known before – with new rules for winning and losing. Investors flail wildly, first paying insane premiums for the new dot-com or e-commerce companies, then slamming them to earth when the truth is revealed. Profits do count. Cash does run out.

Even venture capitalists get cold feet occasionally. Internet startups ran through cash at unprecedented rates. The supply of easy money has dried up as wasteful excesses proliferated, and the stock market finally stopped encouraging them. Excitement must be followed by fulfillment or it dissipates rapidly into bitterness. Value must still be established, somehow, for these flagrant ad campaigns and inflated stock values to avoid crashing to earth like flaming rockets. The intersection of the old and new economies is one filled with collisions. The survivors are nimble, fast, powerful, equipped with the best information and fearless – but not foolish! If you want to be a smart marketer in this world, keep reading. The fun is just beginning.

> "Innovation is disruption; constant innovation is perpetual disruption. This seems to be the goal of a well-made network: to sustain perpetual disequilibrium.
>
> Kevin Kelly, *New Rules for the New Economy*

Conclusion

Well, we've covered a lot of ground in this chapter, and touched briefly on each of the Five Smart Things to Know about Marketing. It's clear that certain parts of history tend to repeat themselves, but with interesting and challenging mutations. Each step in speed and reach seems to become greater than the previous one – that's what we call "Progress"! Now it's time to go into more detail on how marketing can capitalize on this "progress".

2 Marketing and Strategy

The five smartest things to know about marketing

- **You must have a plan**

- Get close to the customer

- **Do your homework**

- Remember relationships

- Use the speed and reach of technology

Choosing the direction

As we begin the journey to Smart Things to Know about Marketing, I hope to use this chapter to accomplish several purposes. Imagine we are going on a cruise. The major points of the chapter will deal with "where we are going" and how that is decided. That is the strategic plan. In the process of making this cruise, we must also obtain provisions and arrange the furniture on the decks, so later in the chapter, I will move to these structural and organizational topics. That is part of doing your homework. And few journeys are without obstacles, so I will intersperse stories about different kinds of obstacles – both problems and opportunities – to show where some have gone wrong, and where better choices can be made. Even when you have a good plan, and do your homework, everything will not go smoothly, but don't panic. Just deal with the issues one at a time and concentrate on following your strategy.

> "I see a constant that defines the best (companies). It says that there can be no effective corporate strategy that is not marketing oriented, that does not in the end follow this unyielding prescript: *The purpose of a business is to create and keep a customer.* To do that, you have to do those things that will make people want to do business with you. All other truths on this subject are merely derivative."
>
> Theodore Levitt

Strategy is the framework and foundation

Few parts of a successful strategy are more important than the situation analysis and the decision of what to sell, to whom and how. This is the beginning of any marketing strategy. With sound strategy and the execution to support it, marketing paves the way. Without this strategy, marketing is little more than "smoke and mirrors", which get blown away by the first legitimate competitor.

A common error is to think that the strategy of the business and the marketing strategy are two different things – they aren't. The marketing strategy is arguably the first and most critical part of the business's strategy since it is the part that interacts and communicates directly with customers and prospects. All aspects of marketing must either support or connect with the strategy. Because of this, the strategy must be clearly and concisely stated and broadly communicated to all parts of the company, but especially to all parts of the marketing organization.

> "All advantage is temporary. Accept it. Live with it. Plan your life and strategy around it."
>
> Charles H. Fine, *Clock Speed*

Conversely, the marketing strategy must be carefully integrated into the overall strategy. All of the other parts of the business must understand and be supportive of the marketing strategy. What do I mean by this? The culture and relationships inside the company determine success as surely as the quality of those with customers, suppliers, and other outside constituencies. There is a whole chapter later that addresses these cultural relationships in more depth.

For now, a few simple examples will help illustrate what I mean. If the marketing strategy differentiates itself in the form of a high variety of offerings, then R&D must be prepared to design products with value-added features in a number of tiers or on several different platforms. Manufacturing must plan for flexible production since high variety usually results in forecast errors and volatility of demand for any single model within the assortment. Distribution must be prepared for a variety of models to stock, pick/pack, and ship. Package design must clearly identify and differentiate the various models, both for physical distribution reasons and to clearly communicate the relative consumer/ customer features and benefits versus competing products.

Dynamic strategies and rapid tactics = action

Strategies must be developed in conjunction with the natural introduction cycles of the customers and markets – annual, seasonal, etc. However, revisions of the strategies must be made whenever there is a significant change in customer preferences, competition, or other market conditions. Static strategies are just as bad as none at all, since they become obsolete or out of date as market changes occur.

Strategy leads to the steps required for implementation, often called tactics from the battlefield jargon used to describe business competition as "war". I don't object to tactics, but if you prefer implementation steps or operating plans, or any of several other terms – those are fine too. The key point to remember is that strategy is only valuable in marketing (and in business, war, etc.) if it is followed rapidly with action.

> "Business-as-usual is in a constant state of war with the market, with the Marketing department manning the front lines. Markets once were places where producers and customers met face-to-face and engaged in conversations based on shared interests, Now business-as-usual is engaged in a grinding war of attrition with its markets. No wonder marketing fails."
>
> Rick Levine *et al.*, *The Cluetrain Manifesto*

The speed with which strategy can be converted to action is critical since the competitive world of marketing is a rapidly changing one. Adjusting strategy periodically is important, but adjusting tactics rapidly and often is imperative to survival and success. The challenge for smart marketers is to make the tactical adjustments within the framework of the overall strategy. Otherwise, the confusion and lack of coordination will result in chaos. This chaotic kind of uncoordinated change is a problem that is plaguing many companies whose plans are weak and whose strategic direction is not well defined. Another kind of obstacle encountered can be cultural mismatches. These can stop a strategy in its tracks. Consider this one example.

Toysmart.com and Disney = a clash of cultures

The failure of toysmart.com and its alliance with Disney is a classic case of the parent (Disney) and the upstart (toysmart.com) having big differences in culture-based strategy – in perceptions and measures of success and the path to achieve it. Toysmart was a startup and an innovator, but without much structure or discipline, waiting for consumers to guide its marketing tactics. Disney is an old line, deliberative giant, which was (appropriately) concerned about the intersection of this new startup with its existing cash-cow businesses and valuable brand franchises. The problem is that the collision at this kind of intersection is often fatal to the weaker, smaller, and less well-defined partner.

While toysmart.com argued about the wisdom of Disney forcing them to advertise on Disney media to conserve cash, and whether that limitation was critical to their success or failure, competitors were moving on. What is certain is that toysmart.com's strategy and tactics were not sufficiently well formed and agreed upon at the influential levels of both companies – but especially Disney.

"A company's operational strategy should continually drive it toward zero trade-offs. . . . Zero trade-offs – effectively, not literally – is attainable.

Thomas F. Wallace, *Customer Driven Strategy*

As toysmart.com under-delivered on expectations, it kept adjusting and spending to gain customers. Disney deliberated more and delayed decisions. Who was right? It is hard to say without knowing all of the facts and circumstances at the time these decisions were being made (or not made). Ultimately, the upstart perished.Was it Disney's fault?Was it toysmart.com's fault? Who knows? Probably some parts of both companies were at fault. Culture clashes make for messy marriages, and usually fail.

The result was, of course, disaster. Toysmart closed down in 2000. The lesson – take the time to figure out what you plan to do, and approximately how, *get all of the important decision-makers on board* and *then act fast*. Watch for cultural issues that manifest themselves early and deal with them or they will lead to failure. Then be prepared to adjust plans and actions to competitors and customers behaviors. If you can't do this, perhaps you don't belong in that kind of business! One of the common obstacles in this adaptation and performance area is the complaint that "there will have to be tradeoffs", because we can't do all of those things at once, or equally well. Here is an approach to dealing with that common obstacle.

Zero tradeoffs – marketing's dream come true

What does "zero tradeoffs" mean? It simply means that organizations must stop thinking in terms of either-or on critical determinants of success. Marketing must constantly remind the organization of these "zero tradeoffs" principles:

• Produce zero defects at very low manufacturing cost.

• Ship on-time "all the time" with virtually zero inventories.

• Manufacture a wide mix of items and options in a wide range of order sizes without impacting quality or cost.

• Make some of each item each day (assuming it is needed), as required by customer demand.

• Introduce new products very quickly, very economically, with very high quality.

Will people say you're crazy if you ask for this? Probably! Is it a realistic goal? Yes, absolutely, because if you don't strive for it and a competitor even achieves parts of these levels of performance, you and your company are "dead meat". Some companies are currently approaching this "zero tradeoffs" (ideal) objective thanks to advances in technology, involvement of people, collaboration with suppliers and customers, and the belief that it is possible – and necessary to achieve – somehow! Even if you miss on some of these goals, your performance will be far better than it would have been had you accepted the tradeoff limitations up front.

Marketing and (corporate) strategic planning

There are several schools of thought on this topic. I will refer to them, but take the position that I believe is right for most businesses. Large companies overcomplicate the strategic planning process. They are far too internally focused. This is a process which requires external focus and reflection on the culture of the organization and the capabilities of the business. My position is that if you cannot develop and write a strategic plan or summary on four or five pages, you don't really have one. Maybe that is OK, but it sure is dangerous. It is like playing a poorly organized pickup football game. Nobody really knows exactly what anybody else plans to do, except in the broadest of terms. That kind of sloppy planning when competing against a well-organized opponent will get you beaten every time.

The challenge is to decide on the key elements of the strategy and commit them to writing, simply and concisely enough to be understood by all parts of the organization. A common error is to develop the strategic plan only involving the highest levels of the organization or the corporation. This approach has two major drawbacks: it denies the leaders the valuable input of many other stakeholders in this critical decision; it also is based on the leader's flawed perception of the situations and competencies faced by the organization. All leaders have imperfect understanding of these realities, because their organizations feed them filtered information. No one wants to tell the "boss" *all* the ugly news. Thus decisions they make are similarly flawed. Smart marketing involves strategic planning with the creative input of many people from different levels and functions to arrive at the final strategy.

Here are a few of the critical "homework" questions that must be asked and answered in the strategic planning process and are necessary for the "complete" marketing plan described in the next chapter.

• What business are you in? (Or do you want to be in?)

- Why do you "deserve" to be successful in it?

- What do you want to sell, to whom and how?

- Where/how will you get whatever it is you intend to sell?

- Can you make money at it?

- Is the market you have chosen growing and at what rate?

- Who has the business you want and how will you get it away from them? (And why will you be able to?)

- What will that cost and how long will it take to get the money back (in profits)?

- Where will you get the money you need to start with?

- Can you sustain the cash flow needed to sustain your efforts as the game gets really tough?

- What kind of people – skills and talents – do you need to do this?

- Do you have them now, or must you find and hire them?

If these sound like corporate strategy questions, they are – and that is indicative of how closely linked marketing strategy must be to the corporate strategy. Obviously, tactical execution must be focused within these decision parameters too. Once these are agreed upon and communicated the rest of the organization can be part of the effort to make the strategy successful.

A couple of well-known companies are embarking on new strategic directions, and the linkage between their marketing strategy and their corporate strategic plans are essential pieces of homework for them to do well.

Intel – going where it has not gone

Intel Corporation is a legend of the microcosm era – the dominant industry leader in microprocessors. Intel so dominates its microprocessor market that any upset which seriously threatens that market would threaten the company too. The corporate strategy that Intel pursues going forward will drive its marketing strategy. The questions are, what is that strategy, and how will it work out?

Craig Barrett, Intel CEO and successor to Andy Grove, puts it this way. Intel's microprocessor business is like the creosote bush, a tall desert plant that drips poisonous oil, killing all of the vegetation that tries to grow anywhere around it. Microprocessors so dominate the company that other businesses cannot sprout and grow around it! This is a problem that many companies have, especially industry leaders. Such companies and their marketing strategies are so wedded to and dominated by what they are doing now, that they cannot and do not let new, different ideas emerge. This is especially true if the new idea threatens the core business itself.

"Whoever has the smartest customers wins."

Kevin Kelly

The logical extension of this line of thought is that the leader never comes up with the strategy that knocks them off their lofty perch, because it is unacceptable to do such revolutionary thinking. The leader's job is to "perfect the present", not to "find the future". So, a competitor does it – usually an upstart who has little at stake and can pursue the new idea with passion and purpose.

But let's get back to Intel. Intel is expanding the range of industries from which it can gain these revolutionary ideas: e-commerce, consumer electronics, Internet servers, and wireless phones to name a few. In 1998 Intel introduced a family of chips for networking and communications gear that speeds data traffic through the Internet in the hope of exploiting what was then a $7 billion market growing at 30% faster than PC microprocessors. The challenge was how to market products that threaten to compete with current customers. The answer is "very carefully".

> The leader never comes up with the idea that knocks them off their lofty perch they are too invested in "perfecting the present" to spend valuable resources to "find the future".

In October of 1999, Intel bought DSP Communications, a leading maker of digital wireless phone technology. Then in January 2000, Intel announced a plan to roll out branded information appliances – screen phones, e-mail stations, TV set-top boxes, all sold through telecom companies and Internet service providers. Is this a risky strategy? I think so, but perhaps no more risky than waiting for its core microprocessor business to mature or decline further with nothing to take its place.

This diversification produced results in 2003 with non-architecture products at some 13% of total revenues, but without yet showing a profit (source: Intel website results for 2003).

The marketing point for you smart marketers is that there are whole new groups of customers that Intel will need to reach and convince. There are also entirely new groups of competitors in areas with which Intel management may not be familiar. But to repeat Steve Goubeaux's great line, *"If you don't go where 'you don't go', you won't know what you don't know!"* But if you do (go there), be prepared for some unexpected and potentially painful lessons. That is when it is important to fall back on marketing basics.

Microsoft – betting the company?

Microsoft, the vaunted software company, celebrated its problems from an unfavorable anti-trust judgment in its own unique way. It announced an initiative that would radically change the business

> Q: What keeps companies from entering markets whenever and however they wish?
>
> A: There are barriers to entry that make it difficult or impossible for companies to enter markets at will. A list of the major types of these strategic barriers is shown below.
>
> **Barriers to entry**
>
> - Economies of scale – the entrenched competitors are so much bigger, stronger and more dominant that they can and do squash new entrants.
>
> - Product differentiation – the unique or proprietary aspects of the products make it difficult for competing products to gain space in the market.
>
> - Capital requirements – the investment required for entry is very large or built up over many years and only large and very well funded competitors can even aspire to enter.
>
> - Switching costs – customers have a significant investment of some form in using the current suppliers' products or services so that changing would be difficult or expensive.
>
> - Access to distribution channels – the new entrant cannot access the distribution because of limitations such as franchised areas, qualifications that are hard to meet, etc.
>
> - Cost disadvantages independent of scale – if other costs such as facility locations, technology, logistics, etc., are prohibitively high.
>
> - Government policy – limitations on sales to certain markets, countries, or in types of technology that threaten national security, the environment, etc.
>
> Michael E. Porter, *Competitive Strategy*

model of the company – Microsoft.NET. In doing so, it showed a willingness to *"Go where it has not gone before"* in a big way. Executives admitted that the strategy was a "work-in-progress" and that they "don't know precisely whether we'll get paid for everything". This new step is based on Microsoft leaders' Bill Gates and Steve Ballmer's beliefs that the web truly has changed everything. So the new strategy is to use the web as the leverage point, building on the potential of XML (Extensible Markup Language) being "the next big thing" and Microsoft being out in front in its use and application. This is a much more open-architecture based move than Microsoft is known for. Is it a wise move? Time will tell. At least they are not sitting there fat, dumb, and happy, resting on their laurels and cash hoard from the 1990s until it is exhausted and some competitor like Sun Microsystems has eaten their lunch.

Customer acquisition and retention – strategic issues

If the purpose of a business is to create and keep a customer, then the question is what obstacles do marketers face in helping their companies do this. Customer acquisition is the process of identifying and calling on the prospective customer until a sale is made. While this is primarily the job of sales, it is marketing's responsibility to identify the prospect and prepare the tools sales will use to go after those prospects. Unless this is an entirely new market or product, someone already has that business and won't want to give it up. Entrenched competitors will erect barriers to keep new entrants from taking their business. These barriers represent two sides of the same issue. For the new entrant, the barriers are to keep them from acquiring the customer. From the incumbent supplier's position, the barriers are to help them retain the customer. Let's examine these areas and what influences them further.

Barriers to market entry (or exit)

When we talk about entering markets and getting business from competitors, or keeping them from getting it from us, we are talking about overcoming barriers to entry. All entrenched competitors will attempt to erect barriers to entry, which make it difficult or impossible for new market entrants to steal their business. The barriers may be based on many factors: brands, relationships with customers, capital investment, advertising and promotional funding, product variety, price/programs, and many others. New entrants must consider each factor, just as entrenched market share leaders consider each.

"If we weren't in this market now, would we get into it?"

(And if the answer is "no", how can we get out of it?)

New aspiring suppliers must find reasons for customers to change suppliers. These reasons can deal with any or many of the factors mentioned above. Entering a totally new market, while a far less common situation, eliminates some of these issues, but there is still the challenge of competing for the available funds of the purchaser in the face of many other alternative purchases.

If strategy dictates abandoning/exiting a market, there may also be barriers to this action. These exit barriers are usually in the form of economic penalties that can take many forms. Customers may insist that undesirable products be continued if desirable ones are still to be purchased. Leftover inventory – both finished products and materials/components – can be a difficult economic barrier to exiting a market or segment.

An even greater exit barrier is often fixed assets – plants, equipment, tooling, etc. – which is carried on the books of the company as a highly valued asset. Exiting the market might require selling or otherwise disposing of these assets at a considerable financial loss, and the resulting unfavorable impact on the income statement. Some countries (particularly Japanese and European countries) have laws that severely limit the closing of established factories and offices, and the termination of these employees. The financial penalties presented by these laws can be formidable barriers to exiting a market in these countries.

Switching costs and customer loyalty

An obstacle to market entry can be the cost to customers – or suppliers – of switching. If the customer has a large investment in either inventory or commitment to a given supplier's products, displacing these products can be costly. Retailers may not want to switch because of disruption to their store layouts. Industrial distributors may have developed a loyal following of customers based on a given supplier's products, and switching suppliers might require them to re-educate and resell their customers.

Then there is the issue of disposing of the inventory even if switching suppliers is planned. In retail settings, it is not unusual for the retailer to require the new supplier to buy back the competitor's inventory (and then dispose of it at a loss). The grocery trade usually requires payment of slotting allowances – cash payments in return for spots on the retail shelf. This can be a large barrier to entry and switching cost for a prospective supplier. A smart marketer realizes that these costs must be factored into the profitability of a product and market. It is not unusual for the switching costs to wipe out the entire first year's profit from a new market entry.

> *"...ultimately, your customer will determine whether you live or die."*
>
> James Daly,
> Editor-in-Chief,
> *Business 2.0*

Even when the economic issues have been addressed, there is the psychological issue of change, and risk versus reward weigh on the mind of the buyer. Buyers are fundamentally insecure. Change is a risk. Nothing is a worse error than for them to switch from a proven supplier to a new one and to have the transition go poorly. Only when the new supplier provides a significantly greater value, will most buyers be willing to change. For smaller incentives, the risk and disruption is not worth the reward.

Occasionally a buyer will encounter supplier problems and invite a new supplier to enter the market or become a supplier. This is the ideal situation, and one that calls for flawless execution. Done properly, such an entrée is the least painful, potentially most profitable way to grow against entrenched competition. Smart marketers treasure such opportunities and spend great efforts and resources to make sure the transition is handled flawlessly.

Customers have many choices available to them. Marketing's job is to make sure it understands the full range of these choices and properly positions its offerings as favorably as possible. It has often been proven that the most profitable avenue for growth is to grow with existing customers. That is true, unless the market is stagnant and you hold a dominant share of existing customers. Then there may not be enough growth potential available, and looking to new customers and markets may be the only option. Once chosen, the opportunities must be managed superbly – especially in its early stages – to yield the best possible results. Whether you choose customer retention or customer acquisition – once you commit to it, then speed, persistent commitment, and quality of execution become the critical success factors. Another of the obstacles encountered in finding business is that the current supplier is what I call a "gorilla". This is a large, powerful, competent and financially strong competitor, who has the business you think you'd like to get. If that is the case, there are two rules you must remember:

- If the "gorilla" is sleeping, don't wake him up.

- If you wake him up, don't make him angry!

> "The time between new ideas and their implementation moves toward zero. Competitive advantage comes not from making things but from defining choices."
>
> John Browning and Spencer Reiss,
> "For the New Economy, the End of the Beginning"

Think twice before taking on a "gorilla"

One of the natural tendencies when coming up with a marketing idea and plan is to look at the large market segments where there are large opportunities. That is not a bad idea, but there is a trap because these are market segments occupied by "gorillas". These gorillas can squash small annoying upstarts before they can even get started. Netscape was almost crushed by Microsoft until America Online came to its rescue. Wal*Mart has crushed most of the smaller regional discount store chains. Avoid full frontal assaults on gorillas.

An example of a company flirting with this problem is Playtex. Playtex makes and sells feminine hygiene products – specifically tampons. And it is stealing business from the number one brand, Tampax, which is owned by Procter & Gamble. As it does so – and it is now the number two brand in the US – it is dangerously close to annoying that "big gorilla"! Although Playtex is trying to diversify into baby products, and use niche marketing in its tampon business, it is perilously close to being squashed by the P&G gorilla.

What do you do if a gorilla occupies the market space you wish to enter? Don't wake it up – or make it mad! Change the spelling of the word to "guerilla" and become a swift, clever, and stealthy niche competitor. Guerilla competitors did great damage to Rubbermaid, who was once the dominant industry leader in plastic housewares. No single competitor was all that large or troublesome, but in the

"With the freedom to choose come the consequences."

Max DePree

"You can buy people's time; you can buy their physical presence at a give place; you can even buy a measured number of their muscular motions per hour. But you cannot buy enthusiasm . . . you cannot buy loyalty . . . you cannot buy the devotion of their hearts. You must earn these."

Revd Martin Luther King, Jr

aggregate, small, nimble guerilla competitors can unseat a "gorilla". But do it carefully, and hide when you aren't attacking.

Organization

The marketing organization is changing constantly as the competitive landscape changes. Both functions and titles that were commonplace a decade ago are being replaced with new and unheard of titles. (What was a "web-master" as of 1990?)

The typical marketing organization develops as it grows and usually becomes either a functional hierarchy or a cross-functional business-team style of organization. There is inevitably the leader, whose title is usually VP or General Manager, although some companies have recently even designated people with "President" titles in marketing. Manager and Director titles usually go with specialties based on specific disciplines such as product management, brand management, market research, advertising and promotion, merchandising, category management, and marketing services – a term which might cover a wide range of administrative support services such as forecasting, planning, documentation, etc.

> "Never doubt that a small group of thoughtful, committed people can change the world: indeed, it's the only thing that ever has."
>
> Margaret Mead

The challenge of marketing departments of the future is to avoid each of these titled functions becoming "silos", power bases, or becoming "limiters" instead of "explanatory enablers". Teamwork must be built around the needs of the customer and the peculiarities of the product or market segments chosen. This teamwork requires that each of the functional specialists understand the targeted customers, products and markets and applies their expertise to the best advantage.

This is why having documented a clear, concise, and well-communicated strategy and execution plan is so critical. The roles of the various members to the organization must be understood inside and outside the organization, and that is probably the best argument for titles (other than that people like to have something that describes their job/role). I personally prefer cross-functional teams focused on either customer or product segments. Functional organizational hierarchies usually breed bureaucracy and politics, which lead to boss-pleasing instead of customer service.

> "Integrated marketing and communications is key to a successful campaign. It is amazing how companies still maintain silo marketing from product to product and communications to communications."
>
> Gary Medalis, VP Advertising & Communications, Manco, Inc., a division of Henkel, KGaA

An approach that has developed in recent years has been to institutionalize these cross-functional teams as "Customer Development Teams" which include sales and use the customer as their primary focal point. Another related approach, which is more product-centered, is that of a category management. This approach takes on all of the space in a given customer setting, and attempts to meet the needs of a customer by maximizing the productivity of the resources allocated to that "space".

At this point, you may be thinking, "you're only talking about retail". Wrong! I am talking about any kind of customer. An industrial distributor or a factory tool crib is also concerned about having the best assortment of products for a given amount of resources allocated (space, money, etc.). The consequences of bad category management in an industrial setting can sometimes be far more serious than in retail settings. Large production interruptions due to inadequate supply of materials or maintenance items can be even more costly than lost profits on missed retail sales.

Above all, remember that people tend to act like what we call them, so think carefully about titles and make sure the people know what they are supposed to do if the title is not clear. Also remember that hierarchical organizations filter information as it moves up and down, so flatten the organization and make it cross-functional as much as possible. But above all – never forget the two primary rules:

- "The purpose of a business is to create and keep a customer." (Ted Levitt)

- "Marketing is having what will sell." (Roger Blackwell)

Then, once these two rules are met, the challenge is to keep listening to the customer, then communicate effectively with the customer and with your internal organization. The structure of the organization is important because people have a tendency to try to please their boss (instead of the customer). The challenge for the "boss" is to make sure the people in his/her organization know that the best way to please him/her is by doing a good job of serving and delighting the customer.

The other aspect of hierarchical organization structures is that they make people feel limited to what they are "supposed to do" instead of doing as much as they are capable of doing. Status is associated with rank on the org chart – this is not surprising considering that hierarchical organizations originated with the military where rank and authority did equate to position in the hierarchy.

A better mental model – one that works well in the case of marketing – is one I described in my earlier book *The Shape Shifters* (Wiley, 1997): the theatrical repertory company. In this organizational model, there is a director who "directs" the entire performance, but the performers take larger or smaller roles based on the needs of the performance. In musicals, singers are the prominent performers. In

"Finding a keeper" (for e-business companies)

Six rules for finding a marketing executive worth having and keeping:

- Look for strong marketing experience at a good traditional company.

- Look for e-business marketing experience in less seasoned candidates.

- Hire the candidate who proves an ability to clearly communicate the value of your company's products, can identify with your customer base and can explain your mission.

- Hire the candidate who has respect for product developers and other colleagues in technical positions.

- Be on the lookout for high energy and a strong sense of commitment

- Look for a candidate with experience in building cohesive and creative teams.

- When in doubt, hire quality and pay for it – this is no place to save a few bucks!

Toni Logan, "Marketing VP=VIP"

dramas, singers take a lesser role, and dramatic actors come to the forefront. Neither feels elevated nor diminished when the particular show makes their roles larger or smaller. Their talents are known, recognized and used to make the entire performance successful. No one is more or less important except in the context of the job that needs to be done – in this case, taking care of the customer.

Budgets and finances

Marketing expenditures may vary widely by industry type and company size. As industry boundaries blur, these neat spending guidelines of the past are like road markers on the shifting sands of a desert. This is why continuously updated financial metrics and score sheets are necessary. These measures come in many forms and unfortunately are usually recorded after the deeds that caused them have been done. It is hard to manage by looking only at the past – like driving a car by watching the rearview mirror – far more of what you see will be your mistakes, rather than information about what to do next.

Financial planning and management

A business and the marketing organization within that business must make financial plans. These plans describe the resources needed to successfully achieve the results intended in marketing and strategic plans. The financial plans must also show the returns to be earned from these successes; otherwise, investors will never hand over any of their money to fund the efforts. A common error is to make these plans either too optimistic or too pessimistic.

I know we're making a profit, but are we getting a return greater than our cost of capital?

In the former case, you construct plans based on all the things you want to happen, and factor in too little in allowances for things that may go wrong. Things will go wrong! An over-optimistic plan may gain funding more easily, especially if investors are unfamiliar with the territory of the business. But, after the failure of such a plan (or more than one failure) funding will become scarce very quickly – as will your promotion potential.

The pessimistic plan considers too many of the potential problems and never gets off the ground. Business is risky and markets are volatile and uncertain. Factor all of that into a plan and no one will invest in it. This means finding a balance between optimism and pessimism. A good way to achieve this is to quantify the best, worst, and most likely case plans and list the assumptions used so you can evaluate if those are coming to pass. Then set aside a contingency fund for adversity, perhaps listing the most likely kinds of problems that it will cover, but not allocating it to them specifically. This kind of a process is pragmatic and understandable, but most of all it is credible to investors and provides a tracking tool to managers.

Strategic investments vs. expenses

A common error is to confuse the categorization of various marketing expenditures. Spending is not all equally important or valuable. Expenditures on brand building, advertising, and product launches, if done prudently, fall in the category of strategic investments on which you should expect a long-term return, but perhaps not a very good short-term return. Be careful, however, because this can be carried to extremes, as with Jeff Bezos and amazon.com. From amazon's foundation in 1994 to its first year of profits took nearly a decade. There is a point at which revenue must exceed expenses, and this point cannot be deferred forever.

Does senior management fully realize the dangers posed by new, unconventional rivals?

On the other hand there are expenses which are just that. Fancy offices, expensive company cars, first-class travel, and large administrative staffs are all forms of expenses that are not strategic – they are wasteful. Wring these out of your financial plan. Investors want their money used to pay for your product launches, brand building, and advertising, not your company car or country club membership. Sales travel can be a good strategic investment, although many trade shows are boondoggles on which companies waste money and time, sending far too many people for far too long a time.

Build the financial plan as if the money were your own! It may be – now or later – but spend it that way all the time. This will make sure the blend of optimism and pessimism is balanced. Find a good CFO and/or controller to help with evenhanded management of the financial resources. This person can be worth his/her weight in gold!

Pricing and competition

Pricing is all about the strategy you have created, the value of your offering, and, above all, what the market will bear for a product – and not what it costs to make the product or deliver the service. But what it costs will make a big difference when you consider if you can make money in that business. The answer to this question depends on competitive pressures.

I can't begin to relate the number of times I have seen companies either underestimate or overestimate the competition. Both are problems. The former is the greater problem in that it can be terminal. Why do they do this? Laziness usually is a primary cause, followed by apathy or ignorance. There is a lot of information about competitors available to someone ambitious and creative enough to find it. If it isn't you and your company, it will probably be your competitors who find it about you. If that happens, "Sayonara, baby"!

Are we and our competitors both generating positive EVAs? (Economic Value Added)

Get out there and dig. Ask customers and their suppliers; get competitive quotes from their suppliers, interview their former employees; surf the web for whatever is out there; go visit the towns where their plants are located and hang out in the coffee shops or bars and keep your eyes and ears open. Inquire by phone or mail/email with the state and local development organizations about opportunities to locate a plant there. They will bury you with information, and some of it will be about your competitor's environment, and maybe even their job titles and wage scales.

Buy competitors' products and tear them apart. Weigh the parts and have your engineers and procurement organizations estimate what those parts might cost. Have your operations people study how the competitive products are made. Your entire organization will learn a lot from this exercise.

Always provide a means for the sales force to share any competitor's pricing information. Buyers will try to use vague pricing threats as negotiating tools. Your organization must know all it can about the real market pricing, or it will be at a disadvantage. Teach the sales people to work trade shows, to ask naïve questions about competitors and then listen hard for any answers they get. Read public pronouncements carefully and look for *what they don't say*. Companies tend to brag about their achievements, but the absence of a mention usually means that there may be a problem, or at least that there is nothing to brag about.

Mix/margin analyses

Some people will argue that I am now venturing into tactical or operational areas with this topic, but I believe that this is one of the most useful *strategic* tools any marketing person can use. I am not sure why so many companies still ignore it or use it very little. A mix and margin analysis is usually easily assembled from data already available within your financial systems. This is too large a multi-column format to show here. It also needs to be tailored to your specific products and needs. Because of that I am listing what it contains below, with the qualification that you should tailor it to your situation. Try doing one and them making adjustments as you see what it does for you.

- *Products*
  Down the left side: major products (or product lines) with subtotals by category.

- *Performance information*
  Across the top, headings in three major groupings: Actual, Budget, and Variance.

- *Frequency*
  Separate reports should be run as often as fits the needs of the

business, but no less than monthly – for the prior month and year-to-date. A comparison to the prior year is optional.

Mix and margin analysis

Column headings: actual data – for month and for year-to-date

- Unit sales

- Dollar sales

- Average sell-price/unit; (if this is relevant for your business)

- Volume mix – dollar sales as % of total sales, either within a category and/or of the overall total, depending on how the mix of sales is reported in the industry, and considered strategically

- Gross margin dollars

- Gross margin %

- Profit mix – gross margin dollars as % of total gross margin dollars (same comment as above)

Budget

- Unit sales

- Dollar sales

- Average sell-price/unit;

- Volume mix – dollar sales as % of total sales, either within a category or of the overall total, depending on how the mix of sales is reported in the industry, and considered strategically

- Gross margin dollars

- Gross margin %

- Profit mix – gross margin dollars as % of total gross margin dollars (same comment as above)

Variances

- Sales dollar variance

- Gross margin dollar variance

- Gross margin points variance

- Comparison of the budgeted mix to the actual mix for both sales mix and profit mix

"If a company's first priority is the bottom line then its bottom line probably won't be as good as it should be."

Thomas F. Wallace

Don't limit the use of this tool. Think of it as showing how the "pie" of sales and profits is divided based on actual results compared to how you thought (or hoped) it would be divided when you made your plans – or compared to the same time frame last year, last quarter, last month, etc.

Do these analyses for product lines and/or individual products, or even for a customer/product or market group or a geographic market segment – or whatever you choose. Simply compile data in the format described below and study what it tells you. This is different from the traditional budget analyses, which just tell you whether you made your top and bottom line and by how much. This helps you see why and where you did (or didn't!).

This is a powerful tool for managing your marketing mix, profitability, and even strategic market position. Try it. Learn to use it and you'll see.

Financial perspectives from the customer's viewpoint

A common consumer/industrial product marketing error is to calculate to three decimal points the pricing and profitability of a product or product line you plan to introduce, and to ignore the same analysis from your customer's viewpoint. When you conceive the product, you should have set targets for cost and price. The cost is largely within your control. The price isn't.

A smart marketer will anticipate the pricing and margin situation of his/her customer and know in advance where issues will arise. Create a line of products or services which command prices that permit acceptable levels of profit for both the customer and the supplier and you will soon be writing these books instead of reading them. Ignore these critical factors and you will be reading self-help books on how to find a new job.

The easiest way to generate profit in the short-term is to slowly liquidate the company. Is that what we want to do?

Just add columns to the mix and margin analysis described earlier to cover your customer's situation, and the data will be invaluable to both marketing and to sales. Usually sales takes the brunt of a customer's complaints if you don't do this – and you may lose the volume because of this kind of omission. A little homework will go a long way. Do it!

Conclusion

Now that you have a strategy, it is time to make a plan of action. Perhaps you have considered what kind of action must be taken, but don't "leap before you look". Homework needs to be done. For a little useful side reading on the "warlike" aspects of competitive strategy, read *The Art of War* by Sun Tzu. It is short and to the point, and many competitors will have read it too. My favorite rule has always been, when you don't know what to do – *attack*: this will put the competition on the defensive and may make them blink. When they blink, you strike again. Getting ready to be an attacker is the smartest marketing advice this book can give you. Now let's move on to some specifics about creating a marketing plan upon which to base these attacks.

3 Defining Marketing and Creating the Marketing Plan

The five smartest things to know about marketing

- **You must have a plan**

- Get close to the customer

- Do your homework

- Remember relationships

- Use the speed and reach of technology

Too many definitions

The technical definitions of marketing are so numerous that I could use the first half of the book to list them all, but it would just confuse you – so I won't. Instead I'll use a couple of very simple ones and spend the rest of the space to explain more about marketing, so smart readers can develop their own definitions.

As I cited in the introduction, my old friend Roger Blackwell gave me the best and simplest definition of marketing years ago when he described the difference between marketing and sales. His response was simply *"Sales is selling what you have and marketing is having what will sell."* What a wonderfully simple yet elegant way to put it.

The American Marketing Association definition of marketing is succinct too: *"Marketing is the performance of the business to consumer or user."* In this definition, marketing starts with the creation of goods and/or services and ends when the end user consumer has benefited from those goods and/or services.

> "Marketing is the process by which decisions are made in a totally interrelated changing business environment on all the activities that facilitate exchange in order that a targeted group of customers are satisfied and the defined objectives accomplished."
>
> Robert D. Hisrich, *Marketing*

Marketing – one definition

Marketing is the practice of understanding the needs and wants of customers, discovering or creating products/services that meet those customers' needs and wants, and then communicating this internally to the organization which must create and deliver the products/services and externally to the customers for whom they are intended, so they will desire them and buy them.

What marketing is NOT

Marketing is not sales. Sales is different in that it involves the presentation of the outcomes of marketing's efforts. This does not mean that marketing never sells anything – it does. But it primarily sells concepts and plans, more than specific products. Marketing is not

R&D or product development either. These are the idea-grounds and the implementers of what will meet the customer needs and wants which were discovered and communicated by marketing. Finally, marketing is not logistics. Logistics is the deployment of people and resources to assure that the materials needed are in the right place and the right time, with the necessary information to assure fulfillment of the customer's orders.

Marketing is truly a series of different, but interrelated functions each of which must be carefully and closely integrated with the others if the final outcome – *having what you can sell* – is to be achieved.

> "Without some element of governance from the top, bottom-up control will freeze when options are many. Without some element of leadership, the many at the bottom will be paralyzed with choices."
>
> Kevin Kelly

Strategy is where marketing starts

The first smart thing to know about marketing was the topic of the prior chapter – that strategy and marketing are inextricably linked. A business must start with a strategy. That strategy is usually built on answers to a few simple questions (only the questions are simple – the answers usually aren't!). When it comes time to translate that strategy to marketing, here's the key question: *What do we want to sell, to whom, where, and how?*

Once that has been asked, and answered, the real work of marketing can begin. When I talk about "products" I also mean services or combinations of a product and a service. I will revisit this topic of strategy repeatedly because, in the real world, the question will need to be asked repeatedly as you adapt time and again to changes in conditions, situations, information, and constraints. Often there is a core idea, perhaps a proprietary technology, or a crying need for something – a product or a service. Once this idea exists, marketing can run with it. The Palm Pilot, the Polaroid instant camera, and digital cellular phones are examples of solutions to consumer needs and wants based on specific technologies.

> "With few exceptions, nature reacts in real time."
>
> Kevin Kelly

The creation of FedEx was a case of fulfilling a need the customers didn't know they had, because they didn't realize it was possible to "absolutely positively" get packages delivered anywhere in the US overnight. In fact, FedEx founder Fred Smith first exposed his idea in a college thesis and almost failed the course because the professor thought it was such a dumb idea. Imagine, taking everything to Memphis, Tennessee and then redistributing it back to the entire US overnight. How ridiculous – *not!* Smith proved the concept worked and now UPS and others have improved on it.

Answer the "what questions"

Deciding what will sell is not obvious. There are many occasions when it should be simple for marketing to know what will sell. There are records of what has sold in the past and market research information about what customers and consumers think – or at least what they said they thought (careful, these two things are not always the same!). The problem is that everything marketing people know is about the past or based on conjecture on the part of others, and everything that will happen occurs is in the future, which is uncertain. These make the "what" decision much tougher than it appears on the surface.

There are a couple of other things that a smart marketer needs to know about answering the "what to sell" question. The first is that market boundaries are more blurred than ever. No longer can you find nice neat pieces of markets to target. Think about telephones. It

"The new game of strategy is not playing within a boundary, but playing with the boundary – how to change the boundary. . . . When anyone plays with the boundaries, there is no longer a clearly defined or predetermined turf."

C. K. Prahalad, co-author, *Competing for the Future*

used to be a pretty straightforward market. There was an instrument that sat on your desk plugged into the wall and had either a dial or pushbuttons on it. Pick it up, hear a dial tone, and start dialing or pushing buttons.

Now the question of where the boundaries of the phone market are – if there are any – is very complex. Cordless phones, cell phones, two-way pagers, satellite phones, PDAs with built-in satellite links, computers with infrared and RF ports, two-way radios, and Internet telephony are only some of the parts of what was the telephone market – in addition to the old wired phones which still exist. So, if you want to sell the phone market, the next questions are which segment of it, how broadly, etc. Define your market carefully and stay flexible as conditions change. It may need to be redefined.

"Value is shifting from companies that provide products to companies that can provide high customization at low cost (Dell) or who are solutions providers (IBM)."

Dr Philip Kotler

Answering the "what to sell question" is an iterative process. Answer it, then test the market and adjust. Then do it again and again. Answering this question is important because it determines where you will focus resources. The smart marketer knows that focus is an important concept. Both human and financial resources are limited, so directing those valuable resources at anything but the center of the market target might mean wasting them, or at least not getting the best results. Bottom line: make sure you think carefully about *what* to sell, and be ready to adjust as more information becomes available. Also, make sure your *company's strategy* is clear on this issue or "smart" is not one of the words that will be used to describe your efforts.

Next decide "to whom and where"

If you can answer the "what questions", then come the "to whom, where", and a little later, the "how" questions. Marketing's job is understanding what goes on in the mind of customers and consumers and then translating that into products and services priced to sell and delivered to satisfy – no, better yet – to excite and delight the consumer. After all, you want them to come back and buy from you again! Deciding "to whom" to sell a product is perhaps marketing's most critical job. (Assuming that your company has already decided the "what".) Pick the *target market* well (that's what we call the "whom"), and you have a chance to succeed. Pick it poorly and you will almost certainly fail.

"One of the major issues marketers face is the increasing reliance of consumers and prospects on perceptions rather than facts when making purchasing decisions."

Don E. Schultz et al., *The New Marketing Paradigm*

Later, I will go into more detail about target markets and customers/consumers. For now, let's just get the terminology straight. Customers are the people who buy the product or service from you. They pay your company for whatever they buy. Consumers may or may not be your direct customers. If you sell to a retailer or distributor, the end-consumer is the end-user. It might be a consumer who buys at the retail store, or it might be the company who buys from the distributor. The same goes for services.

The "where" is sort of a dependent question. "Where" can mean the geographic location of the chosen target market customers. It can also mean the scope of the geography you choose to target. Deciding "where" is important because it is also about focus. In fact, much of marketing is a matter of focus. Focus means deciding where you are going to spend resources to get results, and then measuring how you did, adjusting and trying again until you get it right – or run out of resources – at which point you might need to update your résumé.

The marketing plan

The *marketing plan* is the name we use for the tool that is most commonly used to describe how these different interrelated functions are to be integrated. The marketing plan takes many forms but the most common is a written document, which outlines the key elements that must be considered and then implemented. There are lots of formats for marketing plans. Some come in textbooks and software packages, and others have evolved over a period of years at leading companies.

Do we have a plan and do we agree on what it is?

I won't get hung up on the format. That's the easier part, and many companies already have one they want to use. The harder part is what goes in the marketing plan and how/why those pieces work together to come up with "what you can sell, to whom, where and how". One point is very important – the marketing plan does need to be *written*, and it must be done clearly and concisely. If it isn't, it cannot be easily communicated, and it will be of no use to many of the key people who must understand it, but were not involved in its development.

A good marketing plan begins with *strategy*, and strategy begins with a careful *assessment of the current situation* in your chosen market or market segment. That's a big sentence. "Careful assessment" means *really thinking* about what's going on the current situation. Too many people deceive themselves about how strong or weak their company is or how good or bad the competitors are. The result is a plan that is destined to fail because it is built on erroneous assumptions.

Have we communicated the plan to all the people who need to know about it? And, have we listened to their reactions?

A *clear understanding* of the current *reality* is critical at the outset. Sometimes that means getting outside help to form objective conclusions. Companies usually overreact or underreact to competition. If competition is doing well, it is easy to overestimate how good it is. If competition is doing poorly, it is even easier to underestimate them.

Who, what, where, how . . . ?

The "chosen market or market segment" is a challenging set of words because it requires that conscious choices be made? *Defining the target market/segment* is often the hardest and most critical thing to do in a marketing plan. It is also a critical starting place.

> "The leaders in real time management will constantly monitor even the most minute changes."
>
> Regis McKenna, *Real Time*

Once careful assessment (thought) has been given to the current situation, the choice of which markets to serve may become more evident. While it sounds obvious, it is desirable to serve markets that are more readily accessible and in which strong competition is absent. Of course those are hard to find! Some real innovation may be required! Taking on well-entrenched competitors in slow-growing markets is not very much fun – and it is usually less profitable.

The most fun place to go after sales growth is in a growing, profitable market. Obvious statement? Sure. But look around at how many companies slog along in markets growing at 1–2% or even declining due to deflationary pricing, and try to generate sales growth at double-digit rates. Even to the not-so-smart marketer, this must seem silly.

To grow in mature, slow-growth markets, you simply have to take share from competitors who are trying to do the same thing to you. Or, if you are really original and take the advice of gurus like Gary Hamel and C. K. Prahalad, you need to exercise some "industry foresight". Hamel admonishes you to become revolutionaries, and rule-breakers, but this is nigh impossible while peacefully coexisting within the walls of industry incumbents.

To grow faster than a mature market, long term, you have to re-define the market, expand the market, and generally start a revolution. When you do that profit growth can (doesn't necessarily) come along – and it's your job as an aspiring smart marketer to be sure that it does. Everyone from your president to the union rep,

How to survive the five stages of the revolution

- *Experimentation*: Be persistent, flexible, and very willing to experiment. (But, manage your losses, and don't fall in love with your own ideas unless lots of customers do!)

- *Capitalization*: Have vision, connections, skillful salesmanship, and a source for good advice. (Cash is like oxygen. Without it you die. Manage it accordingly.)

- *Management*: Cultivate experience, teamwork, motivation, and an obsession with detail. (But don't let postponed perfection get in the way of planned progress.)

- *Hyper-competition*: Have deep pockets. Be paranoid, responsive and market like hell. (And when you finish that "leap a couple of tall buildings in a single bound" just to stay in training – that will be what it takes.)

- *Consolidation*: Become a dealmaker, negotiator, and public relations flak – and hire good lawyers. (If you have a choice don't be one of the "consolidatees", try to be one of the "consolidators" – even if you have to start small! The management in them is less likely to get downsized out onto the street.)

David Raymond and Hal Varian in Forbes ASAP
(and with my parenthetical comments!)

from the engineers to the janitor should like that. With more profit, there is simply more wealth to spread around.

To smart marketers profit is certainly not a dirty word! It is a wonderful word, because it also guarantees that you will have a chance to compete another day. Profit comes most easily when you have proprietary products in areas that are growing rapidly and have not yet been overpopulated with competitors. For the majority of companies, these kinds of opportunities are few and far between – but that is no reason to stop looking for them.

What are we going to sell to whom, and how? And can we make money at it?

Once the marketing plan has outlined what markets/segments to serve, etc., then it is time to move on to a couple of other important decision areas. Exactly what combinations of products and/or services will you sell to these chosen markets, at what kind of pricing, profit margins, and in what kind of product line structures. These are critical decisions because the choices made here determine how direct the competition will be and how profitable success will turn out to be.

There are very few product or service categories which consist of a single offering. Multiple offerings in a category help thwart commoditization. Multiple offerings help provide added opportunities for differentiation and with differentiation comes increased profitability. Many companies are also successfully bundling products and services at far better profitability than selling products alone. The potential for market growth, penetration, and profitability lies in finding the right variations to match what the end-user consumers will prefer.

This leads to the next part of the marketing plan, which is the market opportunity analysis and market research. It is absolutely surprising how often people attempt to enter markets or make plans

Q: Where can the significant growth come from?

A: Significant growth can only come from four places.

- Target markets that are growing faster than the norm

- Find new products (or services) to sell into established markets

- Find new markets (or geography) to sell established products

- Innovate and introduce products (or services) that expand the market

for growth in sales without even fully understanding w
opportunities lie, who has the volume now, how entren
competitors are with desired customers, and so forth. It
amazing how little some people know when they venture into a
market – and blunders are common in these circumstances. *"Ignorance is not bliss"* – at least not in marketing."

But do not despair, because there are several excellent tools that can
help with market opportunity analysis and identification of competitive situations. I'll cover those in more detail later. Well-planned and
professionally executed market research can provide useful information about how to go to market and gain competitive advantage
against the current incumbents – *but you have to move fast* – because
someone else is probably targeting the same market as you are, especially if it is an attractive one.

> "There is no such thing as a commodity. All goods and services can be differentiated and usually are."
>
> Theodore Levitt, *The Marketing Imagination*

What the complete marketing plan must contain – a checklist

☐ Market definition and target segment(s) and customer(s) with size and growth rates.

☐ Current and projected situation analysis

  ☐ Market opportunity analysis

  ☐ Competitive analysis

  ☐ Market research (required to verify)

☐ Product/service definition(s)

  ☐ Features and specifications

  ☐ Product line structure

☐ Strategies ("what" statements)

☐ Implementation steps ("how" statements)

> "The competitive environment will no longer tolerate slow response or delayed decision making."
>
> Regis McKenna, *Real Time*

☐ Tactics or operational action plans

☐ Sales strategies

☐ Communications plan

☐ Advertising and promotion plans

☐ Packaging, collateral materials and support

☐ Launch plans, timing, and resources

☐ Milestones, measures, and feedback

☐ Product/service acquisition, delivery, and logistics*

☐ Sourcing

☐ Production

☐ Distribution

☐ Order fulfillment

☐ After the sale customer service

☐ Economic analysis

☐ Feasibility and viability

☐ Mix and margin

☐ Budgets – expense and capital

☐ Return on investment

*Note: May be furnished from outside marketing organization

Get help from partners – outside and inside

The marketing plan must include a clear definition of the opportunity and what market research is needed to confirm those opportunities.

These two areas combined with the situation analysis and strategy lead to the product development section of the plan. Here's where marketing usually gets in a hassle with R&D or Product Engineering. The common "wish" (request) is for more features, better specifications, higher quality, and faster delivery all at a lower price. But it doesn't hurt to ask. Frame your requests in terms of what the customers would wish for, so the inside partners can add insight into "how to do that". If you are smart, and have made these other functions *partners* instead of outsiders, you might even get some of those wishes fulfilled!

Marketing must work closely with R&D to assure that the product or service upon which this marketing plan is built is both *feasible* (it can be made or delivered) and *viable* (it can be made or delivered at a cost that allows it to be sold at a profit). Once these requirements have been met (which is not an easy task by any means), then it is time to move on to two more critical areas of the marketing plan. But, before leaving this area, there is a "nit" that requires mentioning because it is too often taken for granted.

That "nit" is the packaging of the product. Packaging is an advertising, merchandising, and communications element as well as an important physical distribution element. Industrial products packaging may be a critical element in the manufacturing process or the materials movement, distribution, or storage processes. In consumer products, the package may be all that the consumer sees before buying the product. Is it important? Do I really even need to ask that? Because decisions made in the design stage of products often define or limit the packaging, product engineering must work closely with R&D to assure that the product and its package are well integrated and that both are considered carefully as the marketing plan is developed and completed. In some cases the package costs as much as the product – but that may be just fine if that is what you intended.

"Expertise now resides in fanatical customers. The world's best experts on your product or service don't work for your company. They are your customers."

Kevin Kelly, New Rules for the New Economy

What can we do that the customer would love to have, that no one has done before?

Marketing and sales tactics

I don't want to take on this subject too early in the book, but it is a key part of the marketing plan. There are some tactics that must be mentioned here so they will be planted in your mind as we go through a lot of other material. While strategies are the "Whats" of the company's plans, tactics are the "Hows". In marketing there are many tactics that can produce predictable strategic results (at least as much as anything is predictable in these turbulent times). Each of these tactics has some very strategic elements – like the resources required to support them. Here is a partial list of some common marketing tactics.

> "Wars may be fought with weapons, but they are won by men."
>
> General George S. Patton

1 *Market attack:* To aggressively go after a major position in a given market by deploying substantial resources with a product or service offering that is at parity (or better) with entrenched competition. Usually used by large industry leaders.

2. *Price signaling:* To make price adjustments in such a prominent and obvious way as to encourage other participants in the market to follow those moves. Used by industry leaders or members of an oligopoly. (Major airlines ticket prices)

3 *Retaliation:* To attack a competitor in a lucrative market segment as a direct result of that competitor coming after one of your important segments. Can be used by any type or size of company, with varying success. (Microsoft going after Sun's Java programs)

4 Guerilla *attack:* To go after an important piece of business either with a clandestine and/or varied attack (in location, strategy, pricing, etc.) in hopes of undermining a much larger competitor in a particular market niche. (Apple Computer rebuilding market share vs. Dell, Compaq, HP, IBM, *et al.*)

5 *Blitz:* An attack on a given segment of a market with excessive

resources, product offerings, distribution, promotion, etc. (Any number of dot-com companies – like *monster.com* to name one – spending advertising money freely elbowing for position in an overcrowded market)

6 *End run:* Instead of a frontal assault on the market position of an entrenched competitor, altering some of the specifications, features, services or programs and going after an exposed flank. Perhaps attacking a weaker product, a vulnerable customer position, or remote piece of geography and then working in to the larger pieces of the business. (Steel mini-mills vs. Integrated/large steel mills) There are many other types of marketing tactics and a distinct overlap with sales tactics, but these few give a flavor of the "war-like" metaphors used to describe them. Just be sure your war is against competitors and not customers!

Critical resources – time and money

The two resources that are always scarce are time and money. And yet, few marketing plans can be successful without adequate amounts of both. Here is where the reach and speed of the Internet has changed the ball game dramatically. Information and knowledge can be spread around the globe in a matter of seconds. Technology and know-how can move among continents in a matter of days. Product lifecycles have gone from years to months and in some cases to weeks, days or even hours (i.e. some web sites change their content several times a day!).

Obviously the time element in marketing plans has taken on a whole new importance. The other area that is been changed by the explosion in e-commerce and dot-com companies is that of available financial resources. Thanks to the venture capitalists of Silicon Valley and the investment bankers on Wall Street, more capital seems to be available now than ever before. The hugely successful IPOs (Initial

"Learn as much as possible about the sources of your competitors' profitability."

- "It could be great supplier relationships or global sourcing instead of just domestic sourcing."

- "It could be a more efficient and customer friendly supply chain or simply better people working smarter."

- "It could be line extensions where the basic product is not very profitable (cake mix) but where the line extension is very profitable (frosting)."

- "It also could be a distribution channel where you do not compete – Internet, commercial customers vs. retail customers, etc."

W. W. "Wally" Abbott

Public Offerings) of the dot-com companies provided an abundant new source of capital. Strategic investors in the form of large successful technology companies like Microsoft, Intel, Cisco, etc., have introduced yet another large source of capital. Conventional (read that as old-fashioned, hard-asset based) companies incur a much higher cost of capital (or have set internal investment hurdle rates higher) than these new start-ups and can easily find themselves at a distinct disadvantage in new product marketing.

Do we have deep enough pockets to hang in with the competition?

Money can't buy time in the broad sense, but an abundance of funding can help by providing massive amounts of people and technology resources when the need occurs. Microsoft's rapid recovery from an Internet also-ran circa 1995–1996 to a major competitive factor just a year or two later, is just one example where massive resources "bought time". This kind of "catch-up" rally is not always possible, demands huge resources, and is not wise to build a plan around.

What can we do that will mislead the competition and throw them off balance?

Another aspect of the marketing plan that is often given too little consideration is the need for adjustments after the initial plan is made. The smart marketer realizes that the marketing plan must be a living document, constantly being tested and adjusted to the changing competitive environment. The probability of some bright young upstart coming after business with a fresh new approach is an increasingly common occurrence. Both the upstart and the incumbent must be prepared for "reactions".

Upstarts sometimes get stopped cold

For a recent example, the Harvard Business School conducts an annual business plan competition for the graduates of its MBA program. In the 2000 competition, a 27-year-old student, Tawfik Hammound was the runner-up and he presented a plan for a company to be called "eBricks.com". This business would revolutionize the staid $250 billion market for building materials by creating an online marketplace where contractors could organize their buying, check prices against big suppliers, and, with a click of a mouse, buy every thing they needed, faster, cheaper, etc. – or so he thought. Within a few months, eBricks.com had seed funding of over $3 million, then merged with Blueline Online, a Silicon Valley construction planning service, called, for a time, Cephren Inc, now merged with Citada.com.

If we do that, will we wake up some sleeping giant (who will make our life miserable)?

The new marketing effort woke up the competition – "awakened the sleeping giants" – to use a cliché. The "sleeping giants", including established building supply distributors like $1 billion lumberyard chain Wickes Inc., greeted and hindered the new entrant with well-funded, well-branded, and customer loyalty-established competition in the form of its own web sites and buying systems. In business as in nature, nothing happens in a vacuum. Like the laws of physics, *for every action, there is an equal and opposite reaction*. Smart marketers understand this and prepare an appropriate new action to blunt the competitive reaction! Then it happens all over again, until at least temporarily, a victor emerges.

> "Venture capitalists say one symptom of too much money is sloppy thinking – 'Build it and they will come' – when the idea really is 'Spend it and hope they come'."
>
> Carol Pickering, citing Tim Draper in *Business 2.0*

Level the playing field of technology

There is an inescapable fact of the 21st century: technology can be a powerful advantage or a deadly disadvantage – but any business must have a minimum level of relevant technology to even participate in the competition. By this I don't just mean Internet-based technology or product and process technology, but all forms of technology that are relevant to your business.

When in doubt we should attack, because the attacker has an advantage – s/he knows what the next move is going to be – it's his/hers! The best defense is a good offense.

No company in the late 20th century could imagine operating without a good, functional telephone system. In the early 21st century a comprehensive web-based information and communications technology base will be imperative. In marketing, the simple ability to manage information about customers, products, promotions, markets, etc., is a critical success factor. If you want to be a smart marketing professional in this new millennium, learn all you can about how to gain, manipulate, and manage information. If your competitors gain this edge before you do, you will always be *a day late and a dollar short*".

If you gain the advantage of more, faster information flow, your decisions will be based on better knowledge. Then it is up to you to use a lot of Smart Things to Know about Marketing to your advantage.

Don't just tell them, sell them!

The marketing plan must now move to the communication and persuasion phase. A smart marketer understands that advertising, promotion, public relations (and investor relations) are all-important pieces of this phase of the marketing plan. S/he must carefully and quickly analyze, decide, and then lay out how to tell both consumers and investors about the great new product and/or service being offered – and why it's "great". The marketing communications must also convince them that "it" is distinctively different and/or better than competitive offerings. If this is done well, the marketing plan can move to a new stage successfully. If this is not done, or is done poorly, then as the popular game Monopoly® says, *"Stop, go back to*

The most valuable list I ever found!

- The purpose of a business is to create and keep a customer.

- To do that you have to produce and deliver goods and services that people want and value at prices and under conditions that are reasonably attractive relative to those offered by others to a proportion of customers large enough to make those prices and conditions possible.

- To continue to do that, the enterprise must produce revenues in excess of costs in sufficient quantity and with sufficient regularity to attract and hold investors and at least keep abreast and sometimes ahead of competitors.

- No enterprise, no matter how small, can do any of this by mere instinct or accident. It has to clarify its purpose, strategies, and plans and the larger the enterprise, the more important that these be written, clearly communicated and frequently updated by management.

- In all cases there must be an appropriate system of measures, rewards, and controls to assure that what is intended gets done and when that doesn't happen, that corrective action is taken.

Theodore Levitt

Start and do not collect $200." There will be lots more on this important topic in later chapters.

Selling what you have!

The next stage of the marketing plan is "where the rubber meets the road". This is the part where sales and marketing work together on the positioning of the product against competition and on the necessary collateral and presentation means to communicate that positioning. Target customers within the market/segment are identified and specific sales approaches are outlined in the marketing plan. Now it is time to go sell the product! But wait a minute! The marketing plan has pricing plans and promotional funding in it, but will they work? And will they be competitive? And what does the salesperson do if the competitive environment has changed from when the marketing plan was made?

Did anyone remember to ask for the order?

Even a smart marketer can't eliminate uncertain factors such as this, nor can they be totally covered in a marketing plan, but they must be considered. Several things are certain. Communications tools are different, faster, and more powerful than at any time in civilized society, and those who use communications wisely gain a distinct advantage. Competition is broader, deeper, more globally distributed, faster, and more intense than any time in business history. Competitors will not sit by idly while you come in and take their business. Their response will be (at least) an improvement in pricing or programs. They may use leverage based on their other volume with the customer to squeeze your new offering out of the customer's buying

"There is no such thing as 'soft sell' and 'hard sell'. There is only 'smart sell' and 'stupid sell'."

Charles Brower, *Sales and Marketing*

plans. They may even attack your existing products at other customers, in an attempt to take business away from you, even as you're trying to take it away from them.

A smart marketing plan thinks about issues like this well in advance and builds in some contingency funding for pricing and program flexibility. Make sure yours does!

Conclusion

In this chapter, I have touched on the major ingredients of the marketing plan and its use. There are many marketing factors that I have not included specifically in this discussion of the marketing plan. This doesn't mean they're unimportant – it just means that they involve a broader range of strategy, marketing information and know-how than the particulars of the marketing plan itself. Some examples of these are product launches, advertising, market segmentation, brand and category management; marketing and competitive information; and logistics and distribution. These and many others will get their "air time" in later sections of *Smart Things to Know about Marketing*.

The Fundamentals

4 The Basics of Marketing

The five smartest things to know about marketing

- You must have a plan

- Get close to the customer

- **Do your homework**

- Remember relationships

- Use the speed and reach of technology

The elements of marketing

If this is going to be a "smart" book, and you are going to be a "smart" reader, you need to know something about the basic elements of marketing and how they are interrelated. In order to keep the reading time shorter, I will describe each topic briefly and provide a few anecdotes to help clarify the application of the basics. I call knowing about these principles and practices "doing your homework". Skipping steps is dangerous. Not knowing about steps that were skipped is even more dangerous. Since I can't possibly cover all of these basics in depth in this one book, when you find one where you need more information, do more homework. The Internet is a wonderful tool for that.

> "One of the most important things that needs to be covered is integration. How do you get all of these elements working together so that synergies and consistencies result? There needs to be a strong statement regarding how to make all of the elements of marketing work together. Again, it's typical of textbooks to treat these all independently. A bad idea."
>
> Sarah Gardial is Director of the MBA Program and Associate Professor of Marketing at the University of Tennessee–Knoxville

Positioning and strategy

In 1981, Al Ries and Jack Trout wrote one of the most interesting marketing books I ever read: *Positioning – The Battle for Your Mind*. Although the examples are dated, and history has exposed a few errors in their predictions, the principles are as true today as the day they wrote it. You would be smart to buy it and read it, and/or its successor book, *The New Positioning – The Latest on the World's #1 Business Strategy*. I don't think it is as good as the original, but it is much more up to date.

The smart thing to do is to integrate your strategy and positioning into a powerful message to the desired target consumers/end-users. Remember that the purpose of positioning is not necessarily to create something new or different, but to manipulate what's already in the minds of prospects so that it connects to your product, service, or marketing message.

The closing chapter of *Positioning* provides a good checklist for what

"Positioning starts with a product. . . . *But positioning is not what you do to a product.* (My emphasis added) Positioning is what you do with the mind of the prospect. That is, you position the product in the mind of the prospect. Anyone can use positioning strategy to get ahead in the game of life. And look at it this way: If you don't understand and use the principles, your competitors undoubtedly will."

Al Ries and Jack Trout

to do if you want to use positioning as a competitive weapon – and you should! I have paraphrased and added to the list from the book so you can be smarter, faster!

- You must understand the role of words. The meanings are not in the words, they are in the people using and hearing the words.

- You must know how words affect and influence people. Words are triggers, which connect with meanings buried in the mind.

- You must be careful of change. The more things change, the more they stay the same – mostly. The challenge is to see what has changed.

- You will need courage and persistence to succeed. Don't rely on luck and timing – they can help but are not dependable.

- You will need to be objective. Don't fall in love with your own ideas. Bounce them off a truth-teller you can trust.

- You will need to learn subtlety. As all of the market segments get more and more crowded, finding the niche, the right spot or the overlooked opportunity is tough.

- You must be willing to make sacrifices. To get something, you must give up something else, or you risk trying to be all things to all people and end up being nothing to anyone.

- You must have patience – but not too much. Just as a running back in American football must wait for the hole in the line to open, so must you. Then you better hit it fast or it will close and/or be filled with other people.

- You must take a global outlook. The world is a big place full of opportunities. Don't limit your options foolishly.

- What you do not have to do: You don't need a reputation as a marketing genius – in fact this could be a disadvantage. Leaders and geniuses make mistakes of thinking they know how to do something because they did a different thing successfully. The revolutionaries are winning the new battles.

Product planning

A wise man once told me that *"failing to plan is planning to fail"*. Yet, how many companies have no formal product plan? These companies have only a rough idea of where they are going with new products. They await the collision of a new idea and a market need, or react to a competitor's new product thrust like a medieval jouster. Even those who claim to have a product plan usually fail to simplify it so it can be broadly communicated and used by the very people who must innovate, design, develop, launch, and produce the new products.

Product line matrix

There are simple ways to communicate product planning information that are more easily prepared and understood than long-winded narratives so often found in product (or strategic) plans. The smartest one I have found is the matrix. Everyone knows how to read a matrix. The daily TV listing is one of the most common matrices encountered. The weather summaries for various cities is another. Apply this tool to product planning and you will be a smart marketer.

Create a product line structure to get started. Are there tiers of products at differing feature and price levels? If so, list them vertically and then, on the horizontal part of the matrix, show the timetable of development, introduction, launch, etc. If there are not product tiers, then the vertical axis of the matrix can be used to show different market segments to be served by the product.

The matrix format allows insertion of competitive products down the side just below and/or interspersed with your products. Another good use of the matrix is to show columns across the top with costs, selling prices, margins, and that means not just prices and margins to your intermediate customer (such as a retailer or distributor) but also

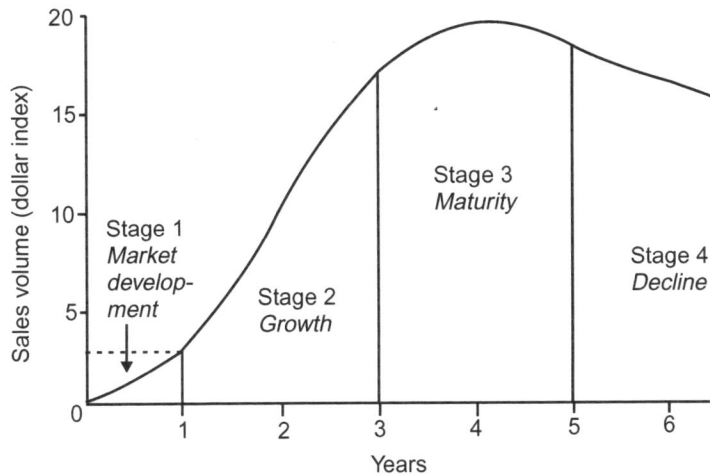

Figure 4.1   The product lifecycle

The product lifecycle

Stage 1 – *Market development:* When a new product is first brought to market with proven demand but before it has been fully developed. Growth is slow; sales are low.

Stage 2 – *Market growth:* Demand begins to accelerate and market size expands rapidly – also called the "takeoff stage".

Stage 3 – *Market maturity:* Demand levels off and grows only at replacement or intrinsic market growth rates.

Stage 4 – *Market decline:* Loss of consumer appeal, sales drift downward more and more.

Theodore Levitt

prices and margins to the end-user. Doing it this way requires you to consider the downstream pricing pressures and reduces self-serving denial about the price competitiveness of planned new products.

Remember, this information must be done over and over, and constantly updated for new competitive pricing trends. Think about how this was happening at PalmPilot after the late 1999/early 2000 introduction of Handspring's Visor which offered all of the PalmPilot's functionality, and better expandability at substantially lower prices. You can bet that PalmPilot readjusted its pricing and product planning matrix fast (if it had one)! It's still making adjustments, too.

Product line/business portfolios

A couple of decades ago, Bruce Henderson and the Boston Consulting Group devised a graphical means of looking at groups of products or entire businesses using a two-by-two matrix. This technique exploded across the business landscape in such a variety of ways that it is inconceivable that any consulting firm (or book on marketing) could avoid mentioning or using it. In its simplest form, here it is. The basic premise is that the most attractive segments of markets are those with high growth and in which you have high relative market share.

Who will do what by when...and did you do what you said you'd do?

The nomenclature indicates the profitability of the quadrants, and later use of this tool allowed better visualization by placing circles in the diagram whose size was proportional to the assets or revenues of businesses or product lines. A star was to be nurtured, supported and carefully protected. A cash cow was to be "harvested" for its milk – cash – to be invested in more attractive businesses. The dog was to be divested, as an unattractive business to be in. The ??? was to be moved, if possible to another quadrant in which its profitability and fate would be more clearly evident.

Obviously there is much more to this analysis than I can cover here, but this is the essence of it. Many businesses and/or product portfolios contain might individual pieces that fit this kind of visual categorization. If such graphical representation is useful, use it. More

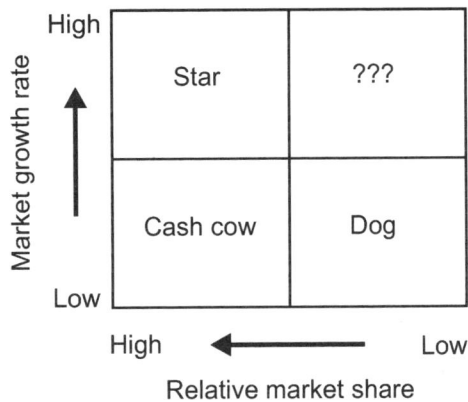

Figure 4.2   The Boston Consulting Group growth/share matrix

uses emerged for this kind of four-square or two-by-two matrix displaying any number of characteristics on its two axes and defining the quadrants as more or less desirable based on those attributes.

Project management

All new product plans result in some kind of project, leading to the creation of the new product. This is why smart marketing people must understand the basics of project management. Project management in its simplest definition is the management, allocation, and control of resources – people, money, and time – to complete some specific set of goals and objectives within a defined time schedule.

Thus, the key things to know about project management have to do with answers to the questions: Who will do what, by when, how and/or how much, and did they do what they said they'd do? Learn to ask those questions over and over, during the inevitable, endless meetings, and write down the answers – then track progress. There are many inexpensive PC-based project management programs. Microsoft Project Manager is just one popular one.

> Who will take responsibility for this getting done?

An important aspect of project plans is that they all have something called a "critical path". The critical path is the accumulated time of the most time-consuming series of events that must happen in sequence to achieve the goals of the project. In the mid-20th century, whole disciplines evolved to track these critical paths on military or aerospace projects. The two most common such disciplines are PERT (Program Evaluation and Review Technique) and CPM (Critical Path Management or Method). If you hear these terms, don't be surprised. While they arose from bureaucratic defense industry roots, they contain useful ideas.

Nothing can get finished faster than the critical sequence of jobs that must be done one after another. For example, during my time with

Rubbermaid, the design of plastic products had to be followed by design and construction of molds to make the product. Then sampling the molds, correction of errors found, refinement of production parameters (mold temperature, molding pressures, etc.), was followed by pilot production runs, and finally full production. There was no way to "telescope" this schedule and do these things concurrently, so they usually were part of the critical path on any new molded product project. When attempts were made to skip critical path steps, the result was usually a lot of bad parts to be scrapped but no earlier dates for good ones.

> "The pattern of the second (or third or fourth) market entrant's prevailing over the early trailblazers shows up throughout the entire history of technological and economic change. No, they were not first. They were better. And except in rare cases, best beats first, even if it takes a long time."
>
> Jim Collins

Once you know the basic principles of project management, you are equipped to be a smart participant in these important meetings. Remember that time is the one truly perishable resource. Once gone, it cannot be regained. Money can sometimes "buy time", through the use of overtime production on key critical path jobs, air freighting of materials, electronic transfer of information, etc., but only to a certain extent. Sometime the laws of physics intervene. Material can only be reshaped or machined at some limiting rate. Even airplanes can only go so fast in delivery of materials, and ground transportation time is still involved. Coordinating the efforts of many organizations (people) in a large complex project is a difficult task. Just ask anyone ever involved in one. If key people are not responsive with promised actions and needed information on a timely basis, lost time may never be regained. In today's cyber-speed world, the competitive difference from such delays can be huge!

Products vs. services

Although I qualified my terminology earlier when I said I'd use "product" to describe both products and services and combinations thereof, there is a difference worth discussing. Product planning for a service provider has a dimension that is becoming increasingly critical. People – the availability and training of them – are one of the limiting factors for many service providers. This limitation will get worse in the next decade as most developed countries go through the "baby bust", a trough in the number of people in demographic categories that makeup the prime sources of professional and technical workers – ages 25–44.

> What is the critical path item that limits our speed to market?

Even if the needed people can be found, they must be trained and retained. Training people, while not easy, is usually within your control. Then the people must be equipped with the proper technology to help them do their job and be productive. Losing those people after the investment in training, especially to a competitor, is a crippling blow. The critical path challenge on service product offerings may not be getting the offering in the market, but scaling up to handle the demand if the offering is successful. The smart thing to do is to think this area through carefully in advance, and have some contingency plans already in mind.

> "We might fall behind at first. But we will learn from our own mistakes and the mistakes of others. We don't have to be first so long as in the end we figure out how to be best."
>
> Cyril Yansouni, General Manager, Hewlett-Packard
> Personal Computer Group, circa early 1980s

Market opportunity analysis

This term may mean different things to different people, but let's not complicate things. Let's take it at face value. What is the opportunity – in the markets you have chosen to target or conversely, for the products you have chosen to sell? If we start with the assumption that value is the metric upon which customers base their purchase decisions, and that value is a constantly shifting thing, then value perceptions become the basis for market opportunity analysis (MOA). In their book *Know Your Customer*, Robert Woodruff and Sarah Gardial tackle both the pivotal issues: customer value determination and market opportunity analysis.

As they say early in the book,

> Value is as your customers perceive it, and so every organization must find ways to draw out from customers how they see value – now and in the future. For this reason, 'identify the value' is where planning a customer value delivery strategy must begin... by the time you begin a customer value determination process, you must already know which current or potential customers are strategically important....Identifying these customers is one activity in a market opportunity analysis...

> "You have to kiss a few frogs if you hope to find a prince."
>
> Bill Kahl, Executive VP Corporate Development, Manco Inc.

While Woodruff and Gardial take a thorough and orderly route of building an MOA based on customer value determination; there is another route that smart marketers are forced to consider. I call it the simplistic, "quick and dirty" one. Any time you are caught in a situation where a market must be analyzed, opportunities assessed, and decisions made, this is a starting place. It will provide considerable quantitative but little or no qualitative information. Who has what existing business now? I call it a "who sells – who buys" matrix. Yes, another matrix.

Who sells what, where?

Create a matrix either on paper, on a whiteboard or an easel or better yet, in a computer hooked to a projector. Learn to use Microsoft Excel – it will be a valuable tool. Get all the parties involved – sales, marketing, general management, customer service, and even the controller and CIO (that's the Chief Information Officer – used to be head of MIS). Then start by listing your own company and the top 5–10 competitors (more or less depending on how concentrated your industry might be) down the left side of the matrix. Across the top, list the top 20 customers who buy from your company and its competitors. Use two rows, and two columns for each competitor and customer name – I'll explain why later. At the bottom of the competitor list, and at the far right side of the customer list, put an entry named "Other" and then put "Totals" for all of the columns and rows, and a "Grand Total" at the bottom right corner.

Now fill in the sales of each competitor to each customer in dollars, euros, yen, or whatever currency you work with. Do your own first – you should know them. Then fill in the others with your best collective information or estimates. Also, use industry statistics, government data, etc., to fill in the total market size at the bottom right corner. Use published data to fill in sales for customers and purchases from competitors. Surely some of them are public companies and must publish sales to largest customers by market segment in the back of their annual reports. Don't forget to reduce customers' purchases by their gross profit margin if you derive or estimate them from sales figures in their annual reports.

An easy exercise – right? *Not!* I'll bet that sets the room abuzz for an hour or more. Agreements are hard to reach for many of the cells of the matrix. And by the way, set up the matrix to compute the "other" numbers by adding row or column data and subtracting from the Totals. *If you want to go after business in a market, you have to know*

The matrix – who sells – who buys?

Customers	A	B	C	D	Other	Competitors' total
Competitors						
You	$$%	$$%	$$%	$$%	$$%	$$
	%	%	%	%	%	100%
1	$$%					
	%					
2	$$%					
	%					
3	$$%					
	%					
4	$$%					
	%					
Other	$$ %					
	%					
Customers' total	$$ 100					Grand total

who has it and how much they have. If you want big increases, you better target customer–competitor intersections with large numbers (big "market opportunities"). While you are doing this, imagine the same kind of exercise is going on at competitors. Those companies will be targeting your big numbers.

Who has the business we want and what will it take to get it away from them?

You can do this matrix for product families or an entire industry. You can do geographical ones by region if you sell limited market areas. You may also want one for product categories – listing customers on one axis and product types on the other – then do it again with competitors on one axis and products on the other. The reason for allowing two lines per named customer, competitors, etc., is that on the second line you compute the percentage that value is of the totals. This will give you a quick feel for how concentrated the industry is. Those concentrated kind of industries are often harder to "crack" without some revolutionary marketing approach or product breakthrough.

> "If A = B & B = C, then A = C"
>
> "In a B2B environment, spend a little time getting to know your customers' customers. If your customer has hitched his wagon to a large, low margin company that has poor long-term prospects, then so have you. This is bad geometry!"
>
> Steve Goubeaux

What else could be sold?

After thoroughly considering who has the business now, where that business is located, how large it is, etc., there is another kind of opportunity analysis to be done. Many industries consider themselves mature, low growth (<3% per year) and wonder where new growth will come from. These companies may not say it, but may be in deep denial. Making and then missing plans predicting 10% growth is a common practice of soon-to-be-extinct companies in slow-growth industries. What the management of these companies must do is broaden its definition of the target markets until its share is under 10% – then look for opportunities. For example, Jack Welch, the highly successful ex-CEO of General Electric, led a group of executives who have excelled at finding service businesses buried among old-line hard goods industries.

> "…sellers said, 'We have to provide service', but they tended to define service by looking into the mirror rather than out the window. They thought they were looking out the window at the customer, but it was actually a mirror – a reflection of their own product-oriented biases rather than a reflection of their customer's situations."
>
> Theodore Levitt

Bundling the repair, maintenance, upgrades, and continued relationship of services based upon the sales of products is a wonderful way to what Seth Godin calls "creating a subscription" as a continuing stream of permission to stay in touch and do business. Looking at related industries is often the first step to finding new and more attractive markets for growth. Then find ways to extend permission into subscription to sustain the revenue stream.

Market opportunity hierarchy

Returning to Woodruff and Gardial's work, there is another concept that is important to smart marketers. That is the concept of customer value hierarchies. We all think in terms of *attributes* of products. The car has airbags and anti-lock brakes, which describe the product and the "hardware". Attributes are at the bottom level of the hierarchy. We really choose those attributes because we want to enjoy the *consequences* of them – personal safety in a collision and better control/stopping under adverse driving conditions. Consequences are the mid-level of the hierarchy. Ultimately, we chose those attributes because we recognized the consequences would lead to meeting *higher-order needs or desired end-states* – a safer, more secure environment for ourselves and our loved ones who ride with us. These higher-order needs or desired end-states located at the top of the hierarchy are what we are really willing to pay for, and these are a much more stable target to aim for. Understanding this hierarchy is important – using it to guide marketing decisions is smart!

What do we really need to know, and from whom?

Market research

Well-designed and professionally executed market research is the smart marketer's best friend. Design it poorly or execute it in an amateur or imprecise manner, and it is the marketer's worst nightmare. It is easy to imagine what research is desired. It is hard to design and execute the actual research so the results are not biased or misleading. The Smart Thing to Know here is to get professional market research help on all but the most mundane research needs, and then learn from it. This doesn't mean that quick, simple surveys can't be done without professional help, but *be careful*. There is a tremendous tendency to attribute authoritative accuracy to simple research efforts that were done to get crude directional information only.

Conjoint analysis

Conjoint analysis is name given to the application of an analytical technique called "design of experiments" to obtaining insights into individual customer preferences. An important result is that the output is the *quantified* preference of an individual for a set of attributes of an product/service, etc. This set of individual preferences can then be used to simulate a market. For example, given a product with certain attributes, how many individuals within a test set will choose that product, when considering that other products with other attributes are also available. Because the result is an individual preference of choice, many consider it to be a direct measure of value to an individual over a given attribute set. The use of choices of many individuals through simulation can lead to establishing a value for a market.

Having said all that, be careful – consumers and markets behave in the most illogical way at times. Analyze them thoroughly, then apply some common sense and talk with customers – it's safer that way!

Some forms of market research

I'd like to go into all of the forms of market research here, but that would be a book in itself. I'll mention just a few of the common ones, and comment on them briefly.

Surveys

Telephone surveys are very popular. They are often called "polls". They are quick, easy, fairly inexpensive, and potentially reliable – *if* the sample size polled is large enough and *if* the sample respondents properly represent the target market or audience, and *if* the pollster has constructed questions that qualify respondents before asking for information, and *if* the questions are designed so as to not bias or lead the responses, and *if* the analysis considers statistical reliability and error rates, and *if*…Well, you get the idea. For each type of research I discuss, these "and *if*s" will apply – remember them!

> "The online customer, for some reason is thought to be a separate beast from the person who strolls into their local mall or hardware store with a shopping list in hand and a wallet in their pocket. And it's a mistake that could prove severely damaging to some e-commerce companies."
>
> James Daly

The Internet is a medium whose speed matches the fast pace of today's marketing world. Getting answers fast can be a great advantage – if they are reliable answers. Some experts claim that there is no alternative to doing good research. Others claim that by the time organized research is done, a competitor will beat you to market. My advice for smart marketers is to do research, do it as fast as you can, but be sure it is done reliably. Wrong answers from flawed research usually lead to disasters because companies invest in supporting them. On the other hand, some information is better than none – and better than just applying gut feel, instinct, and prior experience. Bottom line: find fast ways to do good research. Contact the web experts at places like Harris Interactive, Greenfield Online, Knowledge Networks, Gallup, The Roper Center, Neilsen, or NFO worldwide, and ask for their help.

Focus groups

This is a great way to get qualitative feedback on a product. Small and personal, these sessions are conducted by a skilled moderator, and are observable through a one-way window, can even be video or audio taped to review later, and can be done fairly rapidly. But if the moderator is not skilled or if there is a dominant member of the group who overwhelms the others with his/her opinion, then results can be distorted. The keys are defining the questions/issues, finding a good moderator and interviewing/choosing the right mix of participants. Do those well and focus groups will provide many useful qualitative insights – but no quantitative information – too small a group.

Intercepts

These may be done at a shopping mall, at some kind of event, in public places like parks, or anywhere that the traffic contains a large number of people who are representative of the target market. Preferably you want a private place to take the respondents if they must look at products, but sometimes, the intercept can be done at a stand or a booth, right in the middle of the "action". These work well when there are choices of a similar nature, so the respondent is choosing among several, similarly priced alternatives of familiar products. As a general rule, no kind of market research is very good for predicting the success of radically innovative products. Consumers are just not very good at relating how they think about things they never knew were possible before.

Questionnaires

These could have been included in surveys, but customer satisfaction forms are so prevalent, I would rather talk about them separately. This is a cheap way to gather information. Like all things, you get what you pay for. Unless the respondent has a specific situation that drives their reply to one of the extremes, and writes comments that explains further, these are mostly corporate feel-good tools. Even

Focus groups – a powerful tool if properly used

Four basic elements of focus groups:

- The purpose is research – answers to questions about how customers view your product/service, etc.
- The focus is on one subject – more subjects equal less reliable results.
- The format is a group discussion – but with a definite purpose and a direction.
- The group must be kept small (6–10 people and a facilitator) or it will be unruly and unproductive. Split larger groups into smaller ones if necessary.

Informal focus groups can be organized at the spur of the moment, but care must be exercised. Planning is still necessary, as is an experienced facilitator and a good, representative set of participants addressing insightful questions. Otherwise, what can be a useful tool could become a dangerously misleading one!

The critical steps to doing it right are:

- *Question development*: Do your up-front work here and develop good, focused, non-biasing questions. Good questions make the analysis easier and the conclusions more reliable.
- *Participant recruitment*: Find the right mixture and kind of participants and make sure they will attend. Focus groups are small to begin with, but missing a few attendees can render them much less effective. (There is nothing like cash to enhance attendance!)
- *Facilities*: Many rooms are suitable, but if management wants to observe, then a specific focus group room with a one-way mirror and sound control is needed. This is usually a valuable addition to the process.
- *Moderation–facilitation*: Decide on how you would like the discussion to proceed. Is it to be unstructured, or is there a direction desired. Are answers preferred to be specific or open-ended? A good moderator/facilitator is imperative to make this work.
- *Analysis and reporting*: Many people prefer that the group be video taped, since this gives both verbal and non-verbal responses. Copies of any written material, easel work, etc., must be included. If this is a confidential or private type of project, then protect the transcripts and work products carefully – it is easy to give away your next new product success if these fall into the wrong hands!

Martha Jo Dendinger, CPM in *Meetings & Conventions*

customers who mark "very satisfied" on these forms have been proven to be disloyal and easily stolen away by competitors. At most, these forms can give snapshots in time that can be compared to see whether a situation is getting better or worse. At best, they will reveal serious problems. Otherwise, they mostly help management practice denial and pat itself on the back. Be careful of them.

> "Don't simply blast customers with bland marketing blurbs. Get inside their heads. Find out what's right – and, more importantly, what's wrong – with your products and services."
>
> James Daly

In-depth interviews

Done well, these are among the most powerful (and most expensive) forms of market research. This approach can be used along with other methods and result in significant information upon which decisions can be based. Woodruff and Gardial's book *Know Your Customer* has excellent sections about measuring customer satisfaction, analyzing the results, and arriving at assessments of customer value perspectives.

Internet research

This one could be called potentially powerful and probably perilous – unless you can somehow qualify *whom the respondents really are*. The attractiveness of the Internet as a medium for research is unquestionable. Its global reach and potentially rapid responsiveness and speed can make it a truly wonderful tool. But first the users must find some way to assure that the respondents are who they are thought to be – and that is hard to do. Passwords and identification codes are probably the best approach, but even those are not always secure or certain.

Hopefully as more people attempt to reach and query the diverse users of the online world, this area will get better and better, because the speed of decision-making requires that the speed of market research techniques increase dramatically. One of the most promising market research services in the Internet field is the way National Family Opinion (NFO) reports, via a pre-qualified 2000–4000 household database, on family grocery-buying habits. This is a mixture of old and new economy companies and technologies at their best.

Q: When does Internet research work, or not work?

A: Here is a short guide to some common situations:

Yes, use the Internet –

- When a niche is targeted and you can address that targeted niche – you can send thousands of emails cheaply and quickly to a list of far away people who fit a particular niche.

- When the survey is huge – sending 10,000 emails doesn't cost much more than sending 1000.

- When speed is critical – Internet surveys get there fast, and usually get answered faster too.

- When your confidence in the identity of the respondents is high.

No, do not use the Internet –

- When absolute certainty is needed – there could be discrepancies between the web population's characteristics and those of the general public.

- When it's a focus group – on-line focus groups do not show non-verbal responses or provoke brainstorming

- When it's a small-scale survey – web surveys have fairly high initial costs regardless of size, so they can be expensive for small surveys.

- When you have no means to verify or quantify the identity and reliability of the respondents.

Responses, biases, and interpretation

Because biases can be introduced innocently, be wary of where research is done, how it is done, and who interprets the results. Ask whatever you want, and if the question is not phrased properly, the answer will be worthless, and often predictable. *People don't believe what they see – they see what they (already) believe.* The same is true for questions that steer the answers to familiar (and desired) territory. Politically motivated polls can be and often are done this way.

Depending on how the question is phrased and posed to the respondent, the answer can vary widely. Be sure you know what you are doing in this area. The smart thing to do is get help. It is not all that expensive and is worth its weight in gold when it comes to getting reliable answers to important questions.

Do we believe what we see – or do we see what we believe?

Widely marketed products must be tested in varying geographical and cultural areas. Research done in Dallas will differ from that in Boston. Los Angeles will yield widely different results than London. Large cities vs. small towns, rural or metropolitan, rich or poor, developed or less developed, ethnically concentrated or not – all of these can alter market research dramatically. Define the target market/audience clearly and then find places to do research that are representative of that market or audience. Otherwise, save your time and money, have a couple beers and just guess. Your chances will be just as good and the costs a lot lower.

A personal survey – Internet style

One of the most compelling stories of "market research" involves the

What they say they want vs. what they need

"When your instincts tell you that the customer is wrong, find a professional, patient way to confirm that and then help them get what they need. Recently, in designing a product our customer was positive that it could not afford one of the features we suggested.

After a few conversations we sent a prototype and asked them to give it a try. The customer called back and said the people loved the feature! The trick is not to 'take them on' or argue with customers, but rather to let the customers 'try it on' and see the value of what they need."

Steve Goubeaux

launch of Lincoln-Mercury's new Lincoln LS auto in 1999. Jim Rogers, the 49-year-old former consultant who was head of marketing at the time dropped in on a chat room at Edmunds.com, a leading automotive information site. After months of reading comments, he chimed in revealing himself as a member of Lincoln management.

Not only was he inundated with questions about the car, but he also was the recipient of numerous comments and some complaints. After scrolling through over 5000 posted comments on the car his division was marketing, Rogers encouraged other employees to monitor such chat rooms. In his comments Rogers reveals his feelings about this new, Internet-enabled form of market research, and consumer contact. "The difference is in the detail", says Rogers. "With this, I get people who just bought a Lincoln LS writing paragraphs on what they like, what they didn't like and what they thought of the dealer. There's no other way to get that kind of information."

I'm not sure that final statement is true – perhaps he meant "no other way to get that kind of information *this easily*". Statistically, this can be a dangerous basis for forming quantitative conclusions, but qualitatively there is a lot of information value here. The anonymity of the Internet may make for greater honesty of feedback. This can be offset by the risk that those responding are not real buyers, and are just posing as buyers for a variety of reasons. Overall, this exposes another new dimension that the Internet brings to marketing information.

Zara – fast turns yield fast info

Zara is a Spanish retailer, headquartered in the port city of La Coruña. Zara's parent company, Inditex, has built a fashion chain of 647 stores in 48 countries. What makes Zara special is the speed with which it turns its merchandise and styles. Twice a week clothes are delivered to its shop, and consumers react by flocking in to see what's new. Competing with stores like Gap, who built its advantage on rapid logistics, Zara is raising the speed bar another notch.

Using tight control of design and production, Zara can take a trend from catwalk to sidewalk in as little as two weeks. The faster trends make it into the stores, the faster the readout on how consumers like them – and buy them – or not! This rapid information feedback loop allows replacement of poor sellers with new styles very quickly. Whether this speed can be rolled out across oceans is still to be seen, but meanwhile, fast response leads to fast feedback, which leads to even faster response. And one thing that is proven over and over is that the sooner you know how consumers like something, the better off you are. The other important point is that the best market research is based on customers voting with money.

Heinz – "guts is cheaper than testing!"

"Guts is cheaper than testing!" is the line on a sign over the conference table in William R. Johnson's office. Johnson is president and CEO of the Heinz Co., a huge US-based food company. Johnson says the sign reminds him that, at times, he must "stick his neck out" and make decisions before all of the requisite information is available to him. This is usually true in the real world. If you wait until all of the information is in, a competitor will beat you to market. The thing you must remember is that while *"Guts is cheaper than testing!"* is true, it is also far riskier. The tradeoff between risk and speed is one with which smart marketers will always struggle. In today's supercharged competitive markets, the choice may increasingly be to take speed and rely on a combination of "guts" and limited information.

Permission marketing

A few years ago, this would not even been a term in marketing vocabulary. Many classical marketing experts might debate its inclusion even now. The smart marketing person of the 21st century needs to know about "permission marketing" and how it is different from "old-fashioned interruption marketing".

This term was coined by marketing "guru" Seth Godin who helped build the powerful web portal Yahoo! into a mega-company and brand. Seth's 1999 book, *Permission Marketing: Turning Strangers into Friends and Friends into Customers* (Simon & Schuster, 1999) introduced some new terms and new concepts into marketing consciousness.

> "In a every market segment, only a limited number of companies will be able to secure permission."
>
> Seth Godin

How is this process of "turning strangers into friends and friends into customers" different than it has been for decades? Well, in many cases the goal is no different. In others, there is a dramatic difference. For years, marketers and their sidekicks in advertising tried to craft advertising and promotional campaigns that were "intrusive".

Intrusiveness means that you get the attention of the TV viewer, radio listener, and magazine/newspaper reader by interrupting them with a kind of a visual or audible slap alongside the head. Once you have their attention, you hope to convey a persuasive message that they will remember – and ultimately will result in their purchase of your product or service. At least that's the idea.

Seth comes at it differently. Permission marketing extols the principle that "paying attention" is a conscious act, requiring conscious effort. The best way to do this is to engage the person (target) in a dialogue – an interactive relationship in which they have either consciously or unconsciously granted permission to participate. After all, you are taking some of their precious time, which is in short supply and great demand.

To do this in the way permission marketing advocates, you need to know more about your target customer. No more "shooting with a shotgun" and hoping some of the people who are hit by the message are appropriate targets (guess where the term "*broadcast* marketing" came from). The key difference is that the Internet makes it possible to know more, with more accuracy and individuality, about your target customers than ever before. Permission marketing seeks to use that knowledge as the basis for starting the interactive dialogue leading to a sale and purchase.

> All permission is not created equal.
>
> Seth Godin

Now a few caveats are in order. Seth contends that "the old marketing will die" and that is a bit strong. But one thing is certain. Marketing will never be the same again since the birth and spread of the Internet. If you are smart, you will read that sentence over a couple times. The key issue is different *how*?

The old style of marketing – "interruption marketing" – will not go away. It probably won't even decline much. The issue becomes one of productivity and cost. With more new channels of media than ever, the answer is not just more interruptions. Already technologists have figured out how to zap the interruptions. VCRs, DVDs, TiVO and Replay Networks boxes help us ignore or delete the interruptions. New laws will inhibit annoying phone intrusions by telemarketers. Email filters clean out the spam. More such tools will be coming.

> What can we do to create a subscription model for what we are selling?

What I like most is Seth's idea to "find the niches that have the riches" and form a relationship with them. He calls it "subscriptions". A subscription is a continuing stream of interaction, which the recipient has agreed to receive and, when they want to, respond to. Good idea! Good economics too! This is not a magic solution, but it is a good use of new technology to cut through the clutter efficiently. Old-style interruption marketing is a "moment" and then it's gone. Advertisers hope the memory lingers on, and sales (or brand recall) eventually occur. Permission marketing is a process that, done right, goes on and on. It makes sense for a smart marketer to think about this seriously and try it quickly – what are you waiting for?

Annoyance marketing

Spam, junk mail, telemarketing, banner ads, and pop-up windows fall in the category I call "annoyance marketing". Unlike Seth Godin's permission marketing, annoyance marketing works on the principle that any impression is a valuable impression. I disagree with this. I think annoyances actually polarize prospects against the sponsor, regardless of the memorability of the ad or message. In rare cases the memorability will be so great that the customer will recall the brand and actually buy the product. I think this is the exception rather than the rule.

> "Being first adds up to little more than delusion and hype – it's good for duping investors and making founders and venture capitalists rich."
>
> Jim Collins

Spammers gain sales just like direct mail – the coincidence of a need and a solution at the right time and place. Junk mail has a low response rate, but it is obvious that its existence proves that it works. The smart thing to know about this area is to proceed with extreme caution lest you trigger a negative backlash. Also remember that the low relative cost and great reach are offset by a very low response rate.

Product development

The first challenge is to decide what product to sell to what market, and how (remember, markets are groups of customers with similar characteristics). The product should be one that gives you a reasonable chance of being competitive with or better than whatever is out there now, or can reasonably be expected to appear in the foreseeable future.

Feasibility analysis

The place to start the actual product development process is by deciding if you want to develop a single product or a whole line of products. Next comes the issue of what the products will do – specifically – and at what pricing (to a given market segment via an

> *"Think big, try small, then adjust and go like hell!"*

assumed distribution channel). This allows you to do a *feasibility* analysis. Feasibility means "Can you do that"? Does the know-how exist in your company? Does the technology exist or can it be developed quickly enough. Is the cost target even reachable and, if so, at an investment that is in the realm of what you can spend (or raise)? Feasibility problems have been the obstacle to fuel cell cars and widespread use of solar cells to generate electricity! They just are too costly, complex, fragile, etc., compared to current products. If the product is feasible, then the next question is whether it is *viable*?

Viability analysis

Viability means can you actually bring a product to market successfully and make enough profit to cover the investments needed so that you can keep doing it. Many products that are technologically feasible are not financially viable. This is a critical question smart marketers need to pose and answer *before* the financial types ask. Get help with the analysis if there is not a financial analyst on your team. If the product is only marginally viable, then you must be very sensitive to events that impact cost or performance during development. Minor cost or capital spending over-runs could move the product from viable to a loser, and result in wasted efforts, blown plans, and shattered careers.

Line pricing and specification

Once you have passed the *feasibility* and *viability* hurdles, it is time to actually design and engineer the product(s). This means you must consider how these new products relate to all of the current products that perform similar functions, which are established or imminent. A tip here: a common mistake is to take a snapshot of what is in the market at a point in time and introduce products which beat what is already there. This only works if no one else in the market is developing anything new or improving on what's there. The usual result

Q: Is there is a difference between "markup" and (gross) "margin"?

A: You bet there is.

- *Markup:* The amount added to the cost that results in the selling price. If you "markup" a $10 item by 25%, it sells for $12.50.

- *Gross margin:* The accounting term that defines the profit divided by the selling price. An item that sells for $12.50 and costs $10.00 yields $2.50 profit which, when divided by the selling price ($12.50) is 20% gross margin.

is a product that beat what *was there*, but is inferior to newly introduced/improved competitive products. Remember, this process is like shooting at a moving target. Anyone who has done that knows you have to "lead the target" – aim where the target will be, not where it is!

With those caveats, the smart product marketer lays out the product line in the context of competing products – your own and competition – because you'll probably cannibalize some of your own products' volume. It's better for you to do it than the competitor. Laying out the line means defining the key specifications, setting the hierarchy from low end to premium, making unit volume estimates by market segment and defining the pricing structure. Often the pricing structure is done only for the primary manufacturer. Big mistake. The pricing structure must consider not only what prices and margins the primary manufacturer will achieve, but also what the next step in the distribution channel will sell it for, and its profit margins.

"I don't go where the puck is, I go where the puck is going to be."

Wayne Gretzky

I have seen many high potential products get killed by a buyer who quickly figures out that the products may meet the manufacturer's (or importer's) profit targets, but fail to meet their profit goals. This is such a naïve mistake to make – don't fall into this trap. Walk in the customer's shoes to see how the product specs and pricing stack up from that perspective.

Mix and margin structure

I covered this concept in another chapter, so I'll only touch briefly on it here. This is the key to profitability. It is usually far easier to improve the profitability of a product line by shifting mix of sales from less profitable to more profitable items in the line than by trying to increase pricing on individual items. The sales mix of products in a line from opening price to top price will often determine the overall financial success of the product family. Most companies set pricing so that as features and specifications are added as the product moves up the line, profitability also improves. Some of this is just the math. Markups or gross margin percentages applied to larger numbers simply result in larger dollars, but the margin percentage must also increase at higher levels of the product line. Price pressure is usually greatest at the low end and/or the most popular parts of the line. This makes it critical to raise margins elsewhere to improve overall line profitability.

"Luck is opportunity meeting preparedness."

Investment and ROI

Wait a minute – isn't this a book about marketing? What is this investment and return on invesment (ROI) stuff doing in here? Isn't that what the "bean counters" take care of? The answer is, sure, the "bean counters" (accountants and financial types) keep score – but the marketing people are on the front lines playing the games (or should I say fighting the battles?).

It is hard to know if you are winning or losing a game without some kind of scoring system. Of course the first reaction is that's what "profit & loss" statements (income statements) are for – and that is true, but they're only part of the story. In most businesses, making a profit is imperative. Without a profit, the game is over when the money runs out. Technically, that isn't even true. *The game is over when the cash runs out.* Even if you would have made a profit by the end of the year, if the cash flow is not sufficient to get to the end of the year, the profit is an illusion.

All businesses require someone to invest startup capital (money) and as they grow, they require more working capital to keep operating. Startup capital is money from the initial investors, whether from individuals, venture capitalists, or banks. They invest this money in expectations of a return on that investment. Since they could put it in banks or bonds and earn a low-risk, predictable return of 3–5%, more or less, why invest in companies with risky new products/ services? The answer, simply, is the expectation of higher returns, commensurate with the higher risks.

This means that investors in companies, products, etc., will want at least a double-digit return on their investment – at least 3–4 times what a secure bank/bond investment would provide. Why? The risk. As high as 90% of new products fail – and by failure I don't mean not sell at all. I mean not sell at enough volume and profit to be financially viable and provide returns on the investment required to bring them to market. If your product line doesn't earn a profit big enough to provide that return, the investors will scatter like birds at the sound of a gunshot.

This is called failing to earn more than the cost of capital. Without going too far into accounting never-never land, the simplest way to describe the "cost of capital" is what it would/does cost to borrow, or otherwise obtain the capital, plus a sizable factor added for the risk involved. So, you see, there are several hurdles that must be overcome to get the money needed for developing, marketing, and launching a product line.

One popular measure of the concept of financial return is called Economic Profit or EVA (Economic Value Added®) a term invented by consulting firm Stern-Stewart. This EVA represents the value added, net of all costs, by the operations of a business over a given time period – usually a year. The important part of this measure is that the *cost of capital* (cost of capital = capital used × average cost of getting that capital) is deducted from after-tax operating income. If there are still positive earnings, then positive economic value is being created. If your earnings are not covering the cost of capital, then the economic value of the business is being depleted. The company will ultimately fail if this kind of trend continues over a long period of time, because it will be unable to keep financing its efforts. Many companies are adopting EP/EVA as the basis for financial performance measures.

"Buy low, sell high – not vice versa!"

Startup capital: The initial investment in a company or product line to fund operations until it begins generating cash flow and income. From the time of product idea conception to time of collection (cash inflow) can be as much as 9–18 months or more! Most people don't know that or don't believe it. It's true.

Cash flow: The actual flow of money collected from customers and investors and paid out of a company or organization to suppliers, employees, etc. Without a positive cash flow the business dies!

Working capital: The money needed to meet expenses (payroll, buy materials, etc.) while waiting to be paid by customers. Usually this covers items like *accounts receivable* (what others owe you for products shipped to them), *inventory* (raw material, parts, and finished goods), minus *trade accounts payable* (money you owe suppliers). This assumes the initial startup capital and any successive infusions of capital by investors were used to pay for the *tooling, property, plant and equipment*, and *product/marketing launch expenses*. Many dot-com companies spend most of this money on initial staffing and advertising.

Net profit: What (you hope) is left after all costs – *material, labor, overhead, selling, advertising, R&D, general and administrative expenses, interest,* and *taxes* – are subtracted from sales revenue.

> "Cash is like oxygen, run out of it and you're dead."

Return on investment: The return on the total invested capital. Usually calculated by dividing profits (either pre-tax or after-tax) by the total investment (usually a combination of borrowed money and shareholder investments).

Planned obsolescence

Economist Joseph Schumpeter described something he called "creative destruction". He was talking about the fact that it is necessary for businesses to kill off their old products and processes in favor of newer and better ones. Otherwise they will fall to competitors who do. An extension of this idea is the concept of planned obsolescence. No industry does this better than computer hardware and software companies. New models come out before the gleam is off the old one, and, of course, the new one and the old one are not quite compatible, so upgrades and more new software is needed. This creates a self-perpetuating stream of sales and growth.

Auto companies did this successfully with annual styling changes in the 1950s to the 1970s. Only when Japanese auto makers abandoned major facelifts each year in favor of more features and better reliability did the auto industry abandon annual model changes as a form of planned obsolescence.

In many industries, this is a good practice. Replace part of the product line each season and then every so often, make a big change requiring all customers to upgrade. Long lifecycle products and industries like capital equipment make this tactic tougher but possible. Even major machine tool companies obsolete the control units requiring the machinery owners to upgrade or be faced with finding parts of an obsolete unit.

Aesthetics and design in marketing

Creating differentiation in the competitive environment, especially in consumer products, is getting tougher and tougher. Deflationary pricing pressures exist in almost every category. Where price deflation is not occurring, more features/performance for the same price is the norm. As if this challenge is not enough, the boundaries between formerly well-defined markets have virtually disintegrated. Powerful competitors in next-door markets move over into your market and wreak havoc. What is a smart marketer like you to do?

I would like to propose one particularly powerful marketing tool for creating competitive advantage and differentiation: *aesthetic design*. By "aesthetic design' I mean the conversion, representation, and specification of an idea into a threedimensional, producible, and commercializable form, both visual and functional.

⊡

"Pretty beats ugly every time."

Great designs have two essential ingredients, which they share with great marketing programs: they meet needs/wants of customers, and they appeal to both the senses and intellect of the ultimate buyer. I covered the part about understanding customer wants and needs elsewhere, so I will concentrate here on how aesthetic designs can appeal to the senses and thus to consumers.

Visually appealing products have an advantage against less attractive competition. The evidence is all around us. Consider the following examples:

- Sight – Apple's iMac and iBook offer only a little new technologically but the aesthetic appeal of the "total visual package" is compelling.

- Sound – The Bose Wave Radio offers superior sound quality in a surprisingly small, pleasing design, at a large price (and profit).

- Taste – Altoids mints have a distinctive, strong taste – a unique, value-added package design and promotional theme that others are starting to copy.

- Touch – "Tactile" is in – Oral B toothbrushes, Gillette Mach 3 shavers, writing instruments with rubberized grips – all started their life cycle at premium price-value positions although some maintain this edge longer than others.

- Smell –Walk into Bath & BodyWorks, sit in a new car or think about aromatherapy and this appeal is obvious. (The aroma of fresh baked bread is used to actually help realtors sell homes.)

> "Ugliness does not sell."
>
> Raymond Loewy

The total marketing appeal is to a sixth sense – the one I call *"best value"* – when all of these elements and desired functionality are combined into a product. This is where aesthetic design is most effectively used by a smart marketer to get a jump on the competition. In another section, I deal with the packaging and merchandising – this is where the product gets its "selling clothing and coming out party"! The package may be the first, last, and only time you get to communicate your marketing message directly to the prospective consumer. Make it look great!

Copyright law – a field in flux

There are two reasons why it is important to be familiar with the basic principles of copyright law. First, US copyright law is a "federal" law and does not vary from state to state in the United States (although the interpretation of the law may vary in different courts). This book is protected by copyright law, but your brand may not be! Second, new Internet-based information-sharing programs like

Napster and Gnutella are rocking the very foundations of copyright law. The outcome of court cases surrounding Internet-based information sharing and copyrights may change this area substantially in the near future. See a patent and trademark attorney for up to date information.

Patent law applies in certain cases

Patent laws protect inventions and processes ("utility" patents) and ornamental designs ("design" patents). Utility patents may protect a product or process, but take a long time to obtain and do not protect a brand name – even if the product is the virtual embodiment of what the brand name has come to mean to consumers. Design patents can be a useful part of the total "web" of protection, but, like

Q: What are the major ways to protect (branded) products?

A: There are four major intellectual property laws in the US that protect various aspects of brands and branded products. Other countries have largely similar forms of legal protection.

- Copyright law, which protects original "works of authorship".

- Trademark law, which protects words, names, symbols, and "trade-dress", used by manufacturers and businesses to identify their goods and services

- Trade secret law, which protects valuable information not commonly known or available within an industry. (and usually comes into issue when people take knowledge from one company to another in the same industry).

- Patent law, which protects new, useful, and "non-obvious" inventions, designs, and processes not generally known and that has been kept secret by its owner.

J. Dianne Brinson and Mark F. Radcliffe,
Intellectual Property Law Primer for Multimedia Developers

copyrights, are more easily circumvented by making relatively minor changes to the design. A more effective form of protection is provided in the trademark laws under section 43(a) of the Lanham Act. This portion deals with a confusingly similar appearance known as "trade dress" which would cause a reasonable person to easily confuse the two products (or brand names/logos/icons).

Patents on software, e-commerce, and dot-com practices have raised a furor in the legal community. As this industry expands, these cases will be sorted out one at a time. Be careful what you rely on as "protected" for the purposes of marketing a proprietary product. The ground could fall right out from beneath you if a major legal decision changes the rules.

If this brand name (or image campaign) really works, how will we protect it?

Another increasingly common practice is to deliberately infringe on a patent and then contest the patent in hopes of having it ruled invalid. This happens often enough to be dangerous to patent holders who rely on them for marketing advantages. Check the solidity of your patents thoroughly with highly qualified legal counsel.

Trade secret laws may help

In recent years, as workers have become more mobile, employers have begun to appeal to trade secret laws to protect themselves from employees who leave and take critical competitive information to competitors. A trade secret is unique information of any kind that is valuable to its owner, that is not generally known, and that has been kept a secret by the owner. In the US trade secrets are protected only by state laws. Check what trade secret laws exist where you plan to do business, because they vary widely from country to country. One of the most highly publicized trade secret cases in recent years involved Ignacio Lopez, who was accused of taking boxes of confidential material – trade secrets – with him when he went from GM to VW.

Q: Are there some places to find more information on this kind of protection?

A: There are many of them – start with the US Patent and Trademark Office, http://www.uspto.gov

In most cases there are six factors generally used as tests to determine whether particular information is a trade secret:

- Extent to which the information is known outside the business.

- Extent to which the information is known by the employees.

- Extent of measures taken to guard the secrecy of the information.

- Value of the information to the claimant and its competitors.

- Amount of effort or money expended developing the information.

- Ease with which the information could be acquired by others.

Trade secret protection is earned automatically when information of value to the owner is kept secret by the owner. Trade secret protection endures so long as the requirements for protection – generally, value to the owner and secrecy – continue to be met. The protection is lost if the owner fails to take reasonable steps to keep the information secret.

Does someone else already own the rights to that name?

This area of intellectual property protection and law can be very valuable to marketing, but the laws vary by country and new Internet activities are causing rapid changes in interpretation of the laws. Most of the existing laws are being tested in court cases. Get a good attorney, who is well versed in this area. That is the smart thing to do.

Conclusion

We've covered a lot of territory in this chapter, most of it focused on bringing the product into existence and making sure you did your homework on why that product meets the needs and wants of customers. Now it's time to move on to telling the customers that we have "it", and fulfilling their demand once they know about it.

5 Advertising, Selling, and Fulfillment

> **The five smartest things to know about marketing**
>
> - You must have a plan
>
> - **Get close to the customer**
>
> - **Do your homework**
>
> - Remember relationships
>
> - Use the speed and reach of technology

Advertising and promotion/PR

No marketing book or marketing plan would be complete without a section on advertising and promotion. Lest a smart reader become confused, many advertising specialists talk as if the entire marketing plan is advertising and promotion – it isn't. But a critical element is the ability to communicate persuasively and effectively what it is that you hope to sell to the right group of prospective purchasers.

The communications plan

One of the keys to the marketing of consumer products is the means of integrating marketing and communications – how to inform and convince the potential customer to buy your product or service. There are an almost infinite number of ways, ranging from POP (point-of-purchase) displays and attractive packaging to email to conventional advertising via a variety of media.

All businesses have a communications plan – in some form. The question is whether it is an accidental reaction to situations, or a carefully considered one that is reduced to writing and communicated to all involved parties. The smart approach is the latter one, but I don't want to slow down the high-flying, fast-moving dot-com companies with anything that sounds like planning and organization. Just rent an office, launch a web site, make up a brand, and take a thinly done business plan to a hungry VC. Then fly over the target markets dropping new money out the window like a crop duster. Ridiculous? You bet it is. But that is what many of the dot-coms did. Those who have taken this uncharted, unplanned approach ran out of cash – and we know what happened then!

When you plan your communications, an orderly thought process assures no critical aspects are overlooked until the money is gone. The money is also allocated where it will do the most good – to support the strategy and products – and to generate revenue. To do a communications plan, first identify all of the constituents with whom you need to communicate: customers/prospects, investors, employees, suppliers, joint-venture partners, etc. Next list all the points and topics to be communicated: product info, features and benefits, unique points of differentiation, etc. Second, decide what the essence of your message is to be, considering that it may differ somewhat for different constituents. Then match the two lists, asking how is the most effective way to reach each combination.

"Failing to plan is planning to fail."

A matrix is a nice tool to use for this and you can even use it to support budget requests by filling in the costs at the intersections. Also ask yourself how materials and media developed for one audience can be easily tailored to another without compromising the delivery of the message. That is just smart planning and efficient use of resources!

A "dirty dozen" of changes predicted to be brought about by the Internet

- Paper directories are doomed

- Paper catalogs face an uncertain future

- The elaborate full-color brochure will become exceedingly rare.

- Classified advertising will shift to the web.

- The postal service won't be delivering as much mail.

- Financial services of all types will shift to the web.

- The parcel delivery business will soar.

- Internet retailing will become a price game.

- "Outernet" retailing will become a service game.

- Internet search engines will decline in importance.

- The Internet will change many aspects of telephony.

- There will be speed bumps on the Internet.

Al Ries and Laura Ries

Collateral materials

There are so many things I could say about these often overlooked items: letterhead stationery, business cards, pamphlets, catalogs, brochures, handouts, price lists, etc. These days, desktop publishing has taken away the excuses previously used to explain poor or inconsistent material except two – laziness and poor taste. These materials are like the clothing you wear on the important first meeting. They create your first impression and then speak volumes about you and your business. If they are of high quality, consistent style, well done, without typos or spelling errors, and using good quality images, it matters less whether the media is paper, cards, or electronic images. They all must say, "We are a quality company who cares about what we do." If they're sloppy, inconsistent, error-filled, etc., this same message about your company also comes through loud and clear.

"We only get one chance to make a first impression."

Take the time to invest in tasteful but not overdone design. Define a "style guide" for the business and communicate its contents so everyone with a computer and a color printer does not try to become a graphic designer. Unfortunately all are not equally skilled – and this is a very special skill. Remember the message and the image are the purpose, not the glitz factor. A memorable brochure because of its unique design is a failure if the company message is not understood and remembered.

How can we use print on demand and electronic media to improve the quality and lower the cost of our collateral materials?

An expensive business card of an odd size or on strange colored stock are attention getting at first, but may just be a nuisance that gets lost or doesn't copy well – thus failing its primary mission: to communicate clearly who the prospect just met. Always ask how collateral materials can be done more cost effectively, just-in-time, but without sacrificing quality. And, by the way, the smart thing to do is to save the expensive colored versions of brochures for the customers, and not "waste" them as attachments to internal memos or emails where the colors add cost or downloading/printer time without adding the corresponding value. A lot of money goes into these materials, so spend it wisely.

Announcements and public relations

Even though these are self-serving by their very nature, public announcements and press releases directed to the right list of people in the media, investor community, or even customers and suppliers can be one of the best advertising values in business. If publications find your press releases entertaining, interesting, and useful, the possible outcome is an editorial piece or an interview – and money can't buy that kind of advertising.

> "Ironically, public relations has a huge PR problems: people use it as a synonym for BS....Dishonesty in PR is pro forma...the best of PR people in PR are not PR Types at all. They understand that they aren't censors, they're the company's best conversationalists. Their job – their craft – is to discern the stories the market actually wants to hear, to help journalists write stories that tell the truth, to bring people into conversation rather than protect them from it."
>
> Rick Levine et al., *The Cluetrain Manifesto*

There is a definite skill to writing press releases and conducting public relations campaigns. There are many good guides to this practice on the Internet. One of the best is titled *The Care and Feeding of the Press*, compiled by Esther Schindler and members of the Internet Press Guild, and can be found at http://www.netpress.org/careandfeeding.html. It is both entertaining and informative.

Developing a network of recipients of such press releases, selecting invitees to press conferences, etc., are also special skills requiring the right network of contacts. A professional and well-connected public relations firm is a good investment in most marketing budgets, but once again, planning is required. The PR firm must know your objectives, your (and their) budget limits, and who you are trying to sell, impress, etc.

"There's nothing like good food and booze to get a good turnout at a press conference."

In the Internet community, this planned and cultivated notoriety is called the "buzz" – and it is treasured above anything but a really successful IPO (initial public offering), which it may lead to. If you work this area effectively, the results can be fabulous. My old rule of thumb is to expect $100 or more in equivalent advertising exposure for each dollar spent in good PR. Do PR poorly and you might as well shred the money.

Advertising

The vocabulary

Advertising is a critical element of any marketing plan. That makes it an important marketing topic, and one worthy of smart marketers' understanding. When speaking about advertising with ad executives, you can easily to get caught in a conversation with a set of terms that are completely unfamiliar. Ad people will talk about rating points, reach, frequency, SOA, SOV, SOM, and so forth. What does this all mean? It means that when you talk about the same things everyday, you develop a sort of verbal shorthand for terms. They are not that mystical! It is really important for you to know these terms, because an advertising agency or media buying firm might make promises, take your money and deliver on what it promised and that turned out to be far different than what your marketing needs were!

What is the Internet parallel for these terms? So far there is no clear agreement on this. Views of an ad should be consistent with visits to the site running that ad...but...how many people clicked through before the ad finished loading? Or how many saw it flash through

Q: What do those SOA, SOV, SOM terms mean anyway?

A: They are abbreviations for "share of" terms...

- SOA: *share of advertising* is the actual measured share of advertising dollars spent for competing products going after the same product/service consumers in the same media markets. In simple terms, what share of the ad media spending was yours?

- SOV: *share of voice* is the measure of viewership (or readership) shares as a result of a longer term campaign – in other words, how much of the "voice" of all the advertising run against that product/service and market did your advertising get?

- SOM: *share of market* is the bottom line – based on actual sales outcomes. In simplest terms, who sold what percentage of a given category of product/ service in a specified market segment over a specified time frame? This is what most advertisers want to achieve, because this is where money is made – both other measures are just how much is being spent for how much relative "noise" it makes.

just two of its four messages? How many were unique visitors versus someone clicking "back" and "forward" on their browser to review information on related pages? There are wide discrepancies between the number clicks on a site and the number of viewers who saw an ad on that site. Many sites count as clicks the number of frames on the opening page of the site. Hit it once and they count 5–7 clicks because there are that many frames that load. Confusing? Yes! Beware of *"figures that lie and liars that figure"*! Verify for yourself that your advertising is delivering the message you want – to the audience you want – as many times and with the quality you paid for.

Some experts contend that the Internet will force advertising to move beyond paying for impressions to paying for performance – a positive step indeed. J. William Gurley of venture capital firm Benchmark Partners takes a strong stance:

I am belligerently persistent on this one issue. I strongly believe that most web advertising will eventually be performance based. The most common yardstick of Internet advertising – CPM, which measures the cost of advertising for every 1000 "impressions," or viewings – will be left behind.

Whether this viewpoint is precisely correct is unimportant, because it is certainly directionally right on the money. When the measures are so doubtful, the pressure to base conclusions on performance is bound to build. As this "pay for performance" happens on web advertising, the pressure will build for it to be used on conventional media formats too. Ad agencies will resist, but it will come!

> "If you can figure out that core idea. . . . To be able to express a really, really fundamental idea about the way people act, the reason why people act, and how people hope to be, to really express that, that's just the sexiest thing in the world."
>
> from *GIG*, edited by John Bowe, Marisa Bowe, and Sabin Streeter

Hertz vs. Avis

An example of this concept of relative SOV vs. SOM is the case of rental car companies Hertz and Avis. More than 30 years ago, Avis launched its legendary "We try harder" ad campaign, but not much has changed since then – including its number 2 ranking behind Hertz. In recent years, Avis' image has suffered, arguably for no other reason than that it has been outspent and out-advertised by its rival Hertz, and discount competitor Alamo. Avis' SOV simply did not support its SOM!

Hertz spent $62 million in the first nine months of 1999, a period in

Q: What expectations should you have from an ad agency, and what might they expect from you?

A: This is not a simple one to answer, but here are the highlights.

What you want from an agency

- A top-quality marketer to handle your account
- Experience with your kind of industry (this is no place for OJT)
- Contact with and commitment from the top management of the agency
- Commitment of necessary creative resources to your account
- Clear understanding of the range of services it plans to provide – in writing
- Results – good ads, good media, good sales, etc.

What an agency wants from you

- Leadership that understands and appreciates its role
- Partnership and a long-term relationship
- In-house marketing support, top management commitment
- Information, shared both ways, freely and openly
- Compensation at the agreed upon rate for services to be provided
- An understanding of your "story" and strategy
- Assurance that you have the finances to succeed

What you should avoid

- Stealth services – if you can't see how it is being delivered it probably isn't – don't pay for it.
- Changes in key people or in the direction/ownership of the agency – this is a signal that all is not well.
- Informed misunderstandings – if you can't surface problems and issues and work through them constructively and collaboratively, there is some kind of deeper problem.

which Avis only spent $21 million. While Hertz is the market leader, its lead is not proportional to that spending differential. Add to that the fact Hertz used an inventive comparative advertising campaign with the theme "Not exactly", which did not single out Avis, but inferred that all other car rental companies did not measure up to Hertz in speed/ease of reaching cars, protection from inclement weather, and so forth. The result was that Avis service image suffered, in spite of the fact that there was no tangible evidence that Avis service declined in the least. Avis was simply outspent and out-advertised – and that's all it takes.

Target markets

Every marketing plan has (or should have) a target market. The target market is the audience you have identified that you want the ads for your product or service to reach. It is the market to which you want to sell your brand, value proposition, and goods/services. These target markets are often described in different ways. Here is a partial listing of some ways to segment target markets:

- *Age demographics*, such as "ages 13–25" or other age categories broken down into market segments or to match census data used for analysis.

- *Gender* – male or female.

- *Minorities* (using the US as an example) African-American, Hispanic, Asian, etc.

- *Job, career, or profession* – working mothers, two-income families, white-collar or blue-collar, etc.

- *Geopolitical areas* such as cities, states, provinces, counties, or other defined boundaries (a common term used in advertising is SMSA –

Who is our target market and how much of it will we reach with this advertising campaign?

Standard Metropolitan Statistical Area – the area surrounding a major city and measured/influenced by its media/advertising coverage).

- *Life-stage* which deals with the age and interest level of the consumer based on the stage of life they are in.

- *Activity* – a key form of segmentation based on the activity preferences of the group.

"Great brands are earned, not bought."

Scott Cook, founder of Intuit

Many other segments that might be of interest, such as parents of children in specific age groups, households with certain income levels, special-interest groups, retirees, etc.

Market segmentation is as varied as the colors of the rainbow. Any particular segment chosen in your marketing plan for penetration by your product can be your target market – *just make sure you and your ad agency and its media buyers agree clearly with you on who and what your target market is . . . and is not!* Nothing is sadder and a greater waste of time and money than good advertising going after the wrong market segment with the wrong media.

Target markets are usually reached by advertising in/on specific media. Women might be reached by cable networks (Lifetime), special Internet sites (oxygen.com), or magazines (*Women's Day, Vogue, Glamour,* etc.) – again depending on the target age, income, profession, etc. Most sellers of advertising media publish the specific demographics they reach in these terms.

Rating points and media

This is a measure of *reach* (how many of the audience sees or hears the ads) and *frequency* (how many times this part of the audience is reached by an ad during a specified time period). For example, in a

What will the reach and frequency of the campaign be, and at what cost per thousand (CPM) impressions?

one-week *flight* of ads, an ad seen by 50% of the target population has a *reach* of 50. If this ad is seen an average of 3 times by people in the target market, it has a *frequency* of 3. The target rating points calculation is 50 (reach) times 3 (frequency) or 150 target rating points for this one-week flight of ads. Change the word "target" to "total" (i.e. all of the population) and you get what is called "*gross* rating points". This means you may have reached a lot of people a lot of times, but tells you little about how you did against your target market audience.

Beware of advertising people who talk only of *gross rating points* (GRPs) and not of *target rating points* (TRPs). Gross rating points are measured by how many people of the general population will see the ad and how many times on average they will see it. This may have little to do with your target market segment, especially if it is a small fraction of the total population. Get the ad firm to talk in terms of TRPs – how many of *your* defined target segment will see the ads, and how many times during the time frame specified. That is what matters.

Is that target rating points or gross rating points? (The two are quite different and the difference is very important.)

Advertisers refer to *flights* in describing a particular set of ads over a specific time period with a strategic or tactical marketing purpose in mind. Obviously ads have different lifecycles. Internet ads may stay in place for days or hours. Magazines may linger on tables for days or weeks. Television ads are gone in 30–60 seconds. This is why the concept of permission marketing and "subscription" on a continuing basis is so appealing.

Cost – CPM

Another important advertising factor is the cost per thousand impressions (CPM). Advertising is communications. The less it costs to "reach" a lot of people, the more attractive it should be, but not always. This cost varies considerably for different advertising media

On the importance on discipline

"Developing a strong brand with a consistent message is key to a successful integrated marketing campaign. In order to stay consistent, discipline is required within the organization. On a daily basis, short-cut thinking will challenge brand discipline. Always stay focused on the long-term goal."

Gary Medalis, VP Advertising & Communications, Manco, Inc.

because of the quality of the impressions and the nature of the audience being reached varies widely. This is why network television advertising costs have not dropped as much as expected from the influx of cable TV and the Internet.

What forms of advertising and promotion will we use to launch and then support this new product, and what will it cost?

An important target market for many companies is the 18–35 demographic age group, which still watches a lot of (network) TV programming. They cost more money to reach because they are trendsetters, and advertisers want to reach them so badly. Unfortunately, the way they reach them is often done badly! Similarly, the cost of ads in magazines and publications that are sold cheaply, given away, or considered to be of low quality may be quite attractive – until consideration is given to the audience value assigned to the advertising impression made – then the price is appropriate.

Planning and measures

A wise man once said (or should have said) *"An ounce of planning is worth a pound of curing the problems later."* The marketing plan contains overall advertising plans, but there also must be detailed advertising plans and measures of advertising effectiveness. Without detailed ad plans knee-jerk decisions are often made. Without measures of effectiveness, there is no good way to manage decisions about future

Five lessons on advertising and the web

- Remember that no medium has ever replaced another. It isn't "either-or". Newspapers and radio survived the arrival of TV, and TV will survive the coming of the Internet.

- Great brands are about relationships, not just information. Internet advertising must have mystery and sensuality.

- Online agencies and old-line agencies should do what they are good at. They should go on dates – not get married.

- Welcome back the kids who defected to dot-coms. They'll come back wounded but smarter.

- Stop obsessing about technology, and start obsessing about ideas. The 'E' doesn't stand for electronic; it stands for Emotion.

Kevin Roberts, CEO, Saatchi & Saatchi PLC

adjustments. Did the ad campaign reach the target market audience? Did the product sell through? What were the reactions and recall of people who saw or heard the ads? Were the marketing goals and objectives achieved?

Failure to understand and follow these basics of advertising is what causes large, wasted expenditures for advertising that does little to build a brand or sell a product. The explosion of dot-com companies spending wildly to launch and advertise their new web "products" created a boom in advertising – until the startup capital ran out.

The "buzz" described earlier in the public relations section continues with advertising. Smart marketers know that you not only have to get the attention of the prospective customer, you have to hang onto them. That's expensive.

"Our problem today, however, is the growing percentage of the population that is functionally illiterate, able to read some words but unable to comprehend simple sentences, phrases or instructions."

Don E. Schultz, Stanley I. Tannenbaum, and Robert F. Lauterborn,
The New Marketing Paradigm

Another key marketing question to ask is whether the advertising's intent is to sell products directly (like infomercials do), to tie into retail promotions (like supermarkets often do), or to build brand awareness, preference, and loyalty over a longer time frame. Choosing this objective makes a big difference in how the marketing plan is structured, how a brand is portrayed in the advertising, how fulfillment will be done (a big one these days!), and what the expected ROI might be.

Creative and spending

Enormous sums of money are spent to advertise and build brands. Sometimes this is done with the greatest of wisdom. At other times it happens because someone gets carried away. Creative departments of ad agencies are among the most ingenious and imaginative people around. They can also spend money like water. The challenge is to maximize the creativity of the advertising without maximizing the money spent on either creation of the ads or the media costs to run them. Find out what ad campaigns like yours typically cost. Set budgets and manage the spending to get the necessary creative and media within the budgets allocated. The idea is not to see how much you can spend, but to see how much of an impression you can make on a planned budget. This is a special skill developed by effective, smart marketers.

If we are successful, how soon will we realize returns on our investments?

Spending control within a strategic framework is the job of marketing management. Be sure to carefully review all of the spending needs of a campaign or launch. There are more than just the advertising, creative and media costs. Talent fees for actors used in commercials can also add up fast. Getting product placement may be very expensive. Supporting customer promotional efforts can cost a lot. Depending on which kind of promotions they use, things like "slotting allowance" (fees paid to retailers to secure shelf space) or "floor planning" (financing allowances given to big-ticket merchants like car dealers to hold inventory) could easily exceed the entire advertising budget. There may be program costs like volume rebates, new store allowances, catalog page fees, and many other marketing costs that compete with regular advertising for funding. Consider them all and allocate your resources carefully. Clearly, having a prominent place for your product (and brand) in the mind of the consumer is a smart thing to do, but you must decide where and how to do that, and it can be very expensive.

> "The core of our dynamic business is the magical brand Coca-Cola which remains at the very heart of our entire enterprise."
>
> Coca-Cola, 2000 Annual Report

Tie-in and cross-branded/co-branded promotions

One of the more popular advertising devices of recent years has been tie-in promotions using cross-branding. Everyone who has been in a frozen yogurt stand knows about cross-branded promotions. You can get your frozen yogurt with crumbles of Heath®, Snickers®, or Butterfinger® candy bars, or with M&Ms®, or Oreo® cookie pieces. In each case the owner of those well-known brand franchises lent a bit of its prestige to the yogurt brand-owner – no doubt for a price, and for additional brand exposure at a bargain cost.

Tie-ins can also include licensing of names in hopes of transferring the cachet of one brand to another. The Eddie Bauer® version of the popular Ford Explorer SUV (Sport Utility Vehicle) is a strong brand tie-in that supports the image and reinforces both brands favorably. Lexus is in its second generation of co-branding. Lexus used Coach®

brand leather accents in a special edition previously, and did a tie-in with American Express Platinum credit cards. Bose® stereo sound systems are extra-cost options in many vehicles for the same reasons. It is smart to look for these opportunities as you develop your marketing plans. Properly done, they can be valuable, win–win partnerships. Be careful, however, that you don't append your brand to one that either doesn't fit well or could somehow harm/damage your brand/program.

How do the brand images and personalities of the two brands compare? Will co-branding help or hurt our brand?

The Sunday newspaper spills out a pile of FSIs (free standing inserts), many of which contain promotions intended both to advertise and to stimulate the sales of featured products. These are often used to get purchasers to try new products or purchase multi-packs of variations on existing products. At times free goods, trips, prepaid telephone cards, and many other items are offered as part of an incentive package tied to the purchase of some other item. Procter & Gamble, one of the traditional marketing legends, used these tools liberally and successfully. Some tie-ins require the purchase of multiple branded items to receive discounts. Others reward the purchaser with the popular "cents-off" coupons, which stores hate and consumers still seem to like.

Sponsorships and spokespersons

Another form of promotion that has grown in recent years is the use of event sponsorships and/or the use of famous people as spokespersons. There are different motivations at work in these two areas, but they use the draw of "fame and celebrity" as a strong appeal.

One of the longest-running sponsorships in the US is that of the Cadillac division of General Motors sponsoring the 45-year-old CBS-TV broadcast of the prestigious Master's golf tournament. While Cadillac continues to hang onto this unique property, and the famed Augusta National Golf Club, where the Master's is held, is among the most controlling and restrictive of sponsorees. The principle of "scarcity", which has been proven to heighten demand, is used to extreme lengths.

Master's tickets are carefully controlled and live attendance is limited to 40,000. Television coverage is limited to a mid-round start (vs. beginning-to-end for the other major tournaments), and other promotional conflicts are minimized. This is an excellent example of where an event, like a prestige product, could be overexposed and lose value. In this case, its controlled "underexposure" sustains the event's promotional value although it certainly doesn't maximize the short-term revenue potential to the Augusta National Country Club.

Q: What are the most important issues in advertising to launch products and support marketing plans?

A: There are two of them that stand above all the others:

- Make sure your advertising campaign is reaching the audience you want to know about your product and company, and that it is an audience that is likely to buy your product or service.

- Make sure the quality of the ad, the image of the message and the choice of media matches those features of your product, company, and brand.

Sponsorship of sporting venues is growing in popularity in the US. The past year's NBA (National Basketball Association) championship series was played at the *Conseco* Fieldhouse in Indianapolis, IN and the *Staples* Center in Los Angeles, CA. In fact, most new stadiums are named after companies instead of cities or people. Sponsorships of well-known sporting, and entertainment, events, combined with sponsorships of the venues and use of celebrity spokespersons, can lead to strong brand name reinforcement with target audiences.

Spokespersons are becoming increasingly expensive and yet more widely used. Golfer Greg Norman of Australia has long enjoyed sponsorship income that far exceeded his golf winnings. Tiger Woods signed a five-year contract for $100 million from Nike alone for using its clothing, shoes, and golf balls. Retired basketball star Michael Jordan, long a Nike celebrity, now pitches sports drink Gatorade among a raft of other endorsements. Priceline, the Internet "bidding–buying" service, uses actor William Shatner, of *StarTrek* fame, as its TV personality. His Priceline stock compensation is (or was) worth some $10 million!

How long will this person's celebrity be a strong enough factor to really support our promotions? Will it be worth what it costs compared to the alternatives?

Some celebrities are created or selected specifically for promoting a brand. This is the case of Wendy's (hamburger chain) Chairman Dave Thomas, KFC's Colonel Sanders (the late founder and its recent caricature), or the (non-human) examples of the Ever-ready (batteries) bunny, Taco Bell (Mexican food) chihuahua, or the sock puppet dog of Internet startup Petsmart.com fame.

At times, the appeal of celebrities is greater than their success in their chosen field. Women's tennis celebrity Anna Kournikova is one such case. She makes an excellent spokesperson for her many endorsees because she is attractive and attention getting. Her endorsement income far exceeds her winnings from tennis. Clothing deals with UK's Berlei and Germany's Adidas paid her upwards of $6 million in 2000.

Regis Philbin, an enjoyable and likable talk show host of morning TV similarly struck gold. His role as host of the US version of TV's *Who Wants to be a Millionaire?* has catapulted him, his show, and Disney/ABC's ratings into the stratosphere. Philbin then endorsed a clothing line patterned after his apparel on the game show and negotiated a weekly fee of nearly $1 million to host the show. After all, advertisers pay almost $10 million an episode for the 11 minutes of advertising time. Tie-in products such as home game shows, an Internet interactive game, and even music CDs are also yielding impressions and revenue.

Based on projected sales, what will the endorsement breakdown to on a cost per unit basis?

Boxer George Foreman was a formidable foe in the ring, but never held his championship titles for long. Now as a retired pugilist and boxing commentator, Foreman has struck it rich. He hawks Meineke Mufflers very effectively, but his endorsement of a simple cooking appliance (The George Foreman Lean, Mean, Low Fat Grilling Machine) and future line extensions netted him a $125 million contract from its manufacturer, Salton Corporation. Now that's a "knock-out" deal for "Big George".

This kind of memorable association with celebrities plays on the psychological appeal of persuasive attractiveness, and, while quite effective, has also become quite expensive (with human celebrities anyway). A 2000 *Forbes* issue (20 March) devoted nearly 100 pages to chronicling the celebrities behind this successful marketing tool. In an era when celebrity is so highly admired, this may still be a cost-effective way of building a brand's relationship with its purchasers. But there is a caution, because if (or when) a celebrity falls out of favor whether due to poor performance, waning popularity, retirement, or personal impropriety, the value of such an investment plummets. Remember what happened to O. J. Simpson! Fame and marketable celebrity can be fleeting.

Strategic selling and sales management

There is a lot of confusion about the difference between marketing and strategic selling. That's because the two are closely related. Let's go back to the basics from Roger Blackwell: *"Marketing is having what will sell; sales is selling what you have."* Strategic selling is making sure

> **Four keys to modern marketing**
>
> - Price – higher price signals quality;
>
> - Brands – trump quality, build on faith;
>
> - Packaging – makes it beautiful and appearances matter;
>
> - Relationships – most important of all because business is personal, all about people.
>
> Harry Beckwith, *The Invisible Touch*

that what you are trying to sell is what you have and vice versa – and framing it in the context of why the prospective customer should want what you are offering, in his/her terms.

In the beginning I stated that it was not only smart but also essential to have a strategy, and that the marketing strategy and company strategy had to be totally in synch with each other. Strategic selling is the part where the customer (or prospect) is also brought into synch with your strategy and plan and vice versa. It helps if the plan you have chosen is genuinely the right one for the customer. If it's not, you have an uphill, maybe impossible, selling task. But if it is, then framing the reason for buying what you are selling in terms of the benefits and advantages to the customer is the name of the game.

Does selling to this customer fit our strategic direction?

Do strategic selling well, and the whole marketing strategy compliments it. This is the place where it's also possible (and smart) to attempt to (figuratively) "drive a stake through the heart" of the competitors. If you can find elements of your product and program that cannot be equaled by the competitor, then victory is yours. At least victory that lasts until the competitor can come up with a new way to counter your strategic selling proposition. By this time you should have become close enough to the customer to have (jointly) worked out the next move – to a new, improved or different product – just as the competitor comes in "a day late and a dollar short". Get the picture? It's hard to hit a fast-moving target. Get your strategy and marketing really aligned with the customer, use strategic selling aggressively and keep moving.

> "In the modern world of business it is useless to be a creative original thinker unless you can also sell what you create. Management cannot be expected to recognize a good idea unless it is presented to them by a good salesman."
>
> David M. Ogilvy, founder Ogilvy & Mather

Sales support and presentation

Remember all that stuff about consistency in presentation, collateral materials, and so forth. Well, here's where you really need it. One of my old friends used a reminder I'll never forget: *"If you want to sell what John Smith buys, see John Smith through John Smith's eyes."* Presentation is critical. It tells the story, and must match the marketing plan, and dovetail with the selling strategy perfectly. Don't wing it! Practice it, rehearse it, debug it, and remove all the opportunities for things to go wrong. Make sure that everyone involved is knowledgeable about what are the key points of the presentation, who will make them, who will support them, how, when, etc., etc. Spontaneity is great, but nothing beats great preparation.

Once the presentation is done and goes flawlessly, then sales and customer support become top priorities. Samples that are promised must arrive at the right place, on time, fast, and perfect. Literature, specs, prices, terms, and all kinds of other information must be delivered promptly to exactly who expected to receive it – in exactly the form that is most convenient. Many companies still send hardcopy photos, specs, etc. when the customers need digital ones that can be used directly – or vice versa! Know what the material supporting the sale is to be and then "nail it" in terms of providing what is needed, when, where, how, and how much.

It is surprising how many companies drop the ball here – in the final part of the sale – and leave a crack in the door for a competitor to squeeze through. This would be like dropping the baton in an Olympic relay race when your team had a huge lead. That lead can evaporate in a very short time – especially in today's cyber-speed business world.

Account management

If there is a magic touch in business today, this is it. I have seen some of the fiercest buyers turned into lambs by deft account management. I don't mean manipulation or simple "schmoozing" either. A top-notch account manager has to be reminded periodically which of the companies' payroll s/he is on. Great account managers get to know the customers so well that they anticipate needs, synchronize the strategies of the customer and supplier, and keep everyone in the "home office" totally involved.

"We are those markets. We want to talk to you."

Rick Levine *et al.*, *The Cluetrain Manifesto*

Account managers must be great communicators, but they must also really understand the strategy on which the marketing and selling plans are based, and then make sure it matches the needs of their customer. The account manager is the leader of the business team that serves the customer. Companies like Manco and Procter & Gamble have raised this effort to a fine art in working with and serving mega-retailers like Wal*Mart. Study how the best do it, and learn. It is a lesson that any smart marketer needs to master.

Customer relationship management (CRM)

CRM is a new "buzz-word" for age-old processes translated to the new, computer/web-based economy. Its devotees describe CRM as *the overall process of marketing, sales, and service within any organization.* PRM or Partner Relationship Management is a subset of CRM, and is *the application of Relationship Management strategies and technologies to the unique needs of indirect sales channels.* CRM and PRM systems are supposed to help businesses develop and sustain profitable customer and partner relationships – and maybe they do. Companies are investing in CRM in hopes of gaining competitive differentiation in a world where products become commodities overnight. But there is no replacement for good old-fashioned customer relationships – between people!

Key functional areas of CRM include:

- *Marketing automation* – target the best customers, manage marketing campaigns, generate quality leads, and share the information.

- *Sales automation* – support the selling process from lead qualification to closing the sale.

- *Customer service* – resolve customer issues after the sale responsively, building customer satisfaction and loyalty.

- *E-commerce* – handling the transaction online, as a seamless extension of the sales process.

Information should flow easily between these functional areas, facilitating collaborative team selling and support. This can be accomplished with CRM suites or by integrating best-of-breed solutions. Increasingly, Internet-based CRM and PRM systems are the norm, providing a common platform to deliver applications for use by employees, partners, and customers.

Sales management

In recent years, many of what used to be the functions of brand and marketing management are now falling into the realm of sales management. As customer teams become more prevalent, more of the control and decision-making goes to the sales function. This makes it imperative that sales is knowledgeable about the marketing plans and strategies – but moreover, about the reasons behind them and the potential outcomes expected and not expected.

Sales management in the days of yore meant making sure the sales force made the calls, met its quotas, and knew the key buyers. Sales management in the 21st century is more like the COO (chief operating officer) of the customer interface. Not only must the sales goals be achieved, but also mix and margins must come in on target, and the logistical needs of fulfillment must be assured, all within the budgets for staff, technology, and expenses.

> "Sometimes you have to rise above policy and do what's right for the business."

Great sales managers take charge and take responsibility for making the numbers and keeping the customer happy in the process. Weak or poor sales managers always reach for the "price lever" too fast and push the "deal" button too often. No doubt price is a critical issue, but once a deal has been made, throwing more money at the customer to cover for other shortcomings or to stimulate demand when it is not intrinsically growing is a very bad, maybe fatal idea. You see, customers learn fast, and are easily trained in bad buying habits. If sales always comes up with extra discounts, more dating or hot deals near the end of fiscal quarters, what will smart buyers do? Of course – they'll wait until the end of the fiscal quarter to get the incentives, before placing orders. After this has been done – even once – it starts to become habit forming.

There was an era when "loading" customers with goods was a sales strategy, and some sales managers still employ this tactic. The saying

"A loaded customer is a loyal customer" still rings in my ears. It's true, to the extent that using the buyers' "open-to-buy" budgets and converting those into warehouses full of your goods will temporarily lock-in the customer and lock-out the competitor. But is it really a smart strategy? I say no! Carrying inventory costs money – no matter in whose warehouse and on whose books it is carried. Inventory is inflexible and demand is volatile. The best of forecasts and the resultant inventory is always wrong, just to varying degrees.

> Without a decent short term, there is no long term. If we always make the quarter, we'll always make the year – but mortgaging the future by pulling business ahead of its natural cycle or 'bribing' customers to take goods they don't need will backfire in the long run!

Once a company starts a practice of loading and offering "deals" to encourage excessive advance buying, it has done both its customer and itself a disservice. Procter & Gamble endured the wrath of Wall Street and the dismay of competitors a few years ago when it agreed with Wal*Mart to end the "loading game". Now, in retrospect, the benefits have been tremendous to both companies. The only downside was a brief "flushing" of extra inventory from the channels of distribution. Smart sales management knows that truly serving the customer within the broad guidelines of the company strategy and marketing plan is the way to win. Great sales managers instill this balanced sensitivity in their sales force.

Finally, the true masters at sales management understand the importance of good forecasting, proactive communications, and the power of mix and margin management. If no such management information system exists, they will seek out the right people and build it. If you are smart, that is what you will do too.

Forecasting and planning

I am almost reluctant to open this topic. In many companies, it is like the Holy Grail. "If the forecasts could only be more accurate, how much more effective our company would be." *But forecasts are destined to be wrong because they are predictions about the future.* Once production planning and operations people accept that fact and plan on how to compensate for forecast errors, then the pressure is on marketing and sales again.

There are differing schools of thought about whether it should be sales, marketing, or a separate function like logistics that is responsible for forecasting. My answer is *all of the above!* Sales is closest to the customer, and thus should have the best idea what the customer intends to order and why. That is its job; to bring this information to the forecasting process. This is especially true in the case of discontinuities like promotions, inventory adjustments, or anything else that could not be foreseen from historical information. Sales will only do this well if it is held accountable and that means measuring the accuracy of prior forecast predictions and attempting to determine the reason for the errors so they can be avoided in the future.

> "Forecasts will always be wrong – plan on it."

Marketing is closest to the "market". Thus it should add to the forecasting process an in-depth knowledge and awareness of market size, direction, competition, and environmental influences. If there are macro-economic issues that are either stimulating a market or depressing it, marketing must help factor those into the plans of customers (who are often the eternal optimists). I can't count how many times I heard numerous retailers tell us they were planning on double digit-growth and buying to support that level in a market that was barely growing at all. Something has to give in that case: either they take share from a competitor or find a way to expand the market – or most likely they forecast high and buy low. This is the origin of many costly inventory pileups.

Logistics professionals are specialists in using information to improve the availability and use of materials and to have the right thing in the right place at the right time. Because of this, many companies are enlisting logistics help as the "keeper" of the forecasting systems, incorporating input from sales and marketing both.

The smart marketer is the one who looks at forecasts in a total market context and helps blend the enthusiastic optimism of sales, the logic of logistics, and the pragmatic pessimism of operations/procurement. When sales are going well and increasing, sales almost always over-forecasts. When sales are declining, sales almost always under-forecasts. It is simply human nature, and the tendency to (rightfully) extrapolate the near term past into the immediate future.

There are only three potential solutions to serving customers in the face of imperfect forecasts:

- Inventory

- More lead time

- More, flexible production capacity

There are many good forecasting computer software programs. The smart marketer helps his/her company find one that is powerful enough to meet its needs, and simple enough that the people in all functions working with it can thoroughly understand what it is doing and how. I made a mistake early in my career of designing a forecasting system that was so gloriously complex that it took into account every imaginable factor. The problem was, when the results came out, no one – including me – could figure out what they meant and what was truly influencing them the most. Bad idea! Simple, yet effective forecasting programs like Demand Solutions® will run on

PCs, connect to your database easily, and use the most common and understandable "algorithms' (that is techno-speak for the mathematical formulas used to manipulate data into forecasts).

Shouldn't we be doing CPFR with our key customers?

The key point for marketers to understand is that while forecasts will be wrong, that is a poor excuse for not making them as good as they can be – and constantly working with sales, logistics and information technology to forecast all of the things that are forecastable! If this is done, it becomes the basis for moving into the field called "information logistics". *Information logistics* is the study of the movement of goods and information through a supply chain and the maximization of the use of all information sources for the best possible management of that flow of goods. More on this will be covered later.

Category and brand management

Good brand management is the most important factor in maintaining a brand's character, image, and integrity and keeping them consistent with the overall marketing plan and strategy. If you become a brand or category manager, you are entrusted with assets that are far more valuable than the company's buildings and equipment. These assets are the brands of a company that tell consumers what to expect, and assure them that they are safe buying your brand – a brand they can trust.

Brand creation and building

The job of brand management is to be certain that these eight principles are never far from the minds of top management and working levels alike. Not an easy task, but an essential one for success in brand management.

Another of the most difficult tasks faced by a brand manager, like the sales manager and the senior executives in any company, is the conflict between short- and long-term financial results. Wall Street investors' pressures for sales and earnings growth quarter after quarter, year after year can present serious conflicts for brand managers just as it does for sales managers.

> "What most marketers face today is a parity marketplace in which the only differentiating features are either logistics or communications."
>
> Don E. Schultz et al., *The New Marketing Paradigm*

Advertising is usually one of the largest chunks of discretionary spending in any consumer products company. Too often it is viewed as "expense" money instead of "investment" money. Expense money can remain unspent to prop up earnings in a lackluster quarter, and the resultant consequences are evident – something did not get done because it was not funded. Unfortunately, when advertising in support of a brand is the "expense" that is postponed, the consequences may not show up immediately but may be far more serious than is often realized.

Brand names take years to build in the mind of the consumer. Brands are not just about information – which can be conveyed quickly. Brands are about relationships – and those take time to build. As new brands flood into the market, all with the Internet overloading the senses and media ads screaming for consumer's attention, the older brands come under siege and many suffer. Whereas it took years or decades to build brands in the past, the Internet has made it possible to do so in much shorter time frames.

Brand mangers must fight like warriors to support and build their brand, especially if it is a leading brand. Only if those brands receive consistent support in advertising and promotion can they hold their own against the new upstarts. Capturing brand leadership doesn't mean keeping it. Brand loyalty is a relationship and, like all relationships, this one is only as good as the attention given to sustaining it. Once a brand is the leader, there is only one way for it to go – down. It is all too easy to fall into the trap of saving money, or increasing profits and earnings per share by diverting advertising intended to

Building a great brand depends on knowing the right stuff. Consider these brand-building principles carefully:

- A great brand is in it for the long haul.

- A great brand can be anything. Some categories may lend themselves to branding better than others, but anything is brandable.

- A great brand knows itself. Anyone who wants to build a great brand first has to understand who they are.

- A great brand invents or reinvents an entire category.

- A great brand taps into emotions.

- A great brand is a story that's never completely told.

- A great brand has design consistency.

- A great brand is relevant.

Scott Bedbury, *Fast Company*

support a brand to feed short-term earnings. This is a sure path to disaster and a devastating error.

The brand managers that manage the Coke brand (valued at $80 billion!) on a global basis have a huge job and tremendous responsibility. You probably know that Procter & Gamble and Frito-Lay (division of PepsiCo) are also two of the world's best brand management companies. Brand management is reputed to differ from other departments at P&G. It is far more intense, far more competitive, and staffed only by the best and brightest out of P&G's rigorous selection process. The same applies at Frito-Lay.

In the US alone, P&G offers eight different laundry detergent brands, six bar soap brands, four shampoo brands, three brands of tooth-

"What it lies in our power to do, it lies in our power not to do."

Aristotle

> "Top brands with the most longevity were in the food and beverage groups, while the most fleeting were clothing brands."
>
> Professor Peter Golder, Stern School of Business

paste, and two fabric softeners – and the list is constantly evolving. Each of the brands has a clearly delineated image and brand character, which differentiates it not only from competitors but also from other P&G brands of similar product types. Each brand falls into categories that retail customers have managed as closely as suppliers manage the brands. In recent years, the category management is shifting to a joint task, with suppliers increasingly providing category captains or category managers for retailers as part of their customer development teams.

How brand and category management works

When R&D or New Product Development creates a product, it is assigned to a brand manager, whose job it is to ensure the brand's success. The key challenge if you are a brand manager is often to battle for resources against other products and their brand managers! Unless a new product gets the attention and resources it needs, it may not make it – and after a couple of these, the brand manager will not make it either.

> "...consumers no longer aspire [just] to brands; brands – and stores – must aspire to consumers. If old brands don't give them what they want, consumers are much more willing to try something else. Consumers are now in the driver's seat, looking for a whole array of road markers – comfort, style, price, quality and good service."
>
> Carolyn Setlow, Group Senior VP, Roper Starch Worldwide

Since all of the brands in the company's stable are competing for a share of the same resources, brand managers must be effective advocates and internal sales representatives both for their brand and for related new products. Listening to consumers and documenting what they say they want and how they behave about what they really want is a key part of the brand manager's job. Because of this, brand managers spend a lot of time studying customers, analyzing market research data, observing consumer behavior, and finding the answers to what it is that consumers and customers need, want, and will buy.

What does our brand stand for and what do we want it to stand for?

Because of the competition, brand or category managers must be unusually resilient. Good brand managers understand that they must follow the rules, but occasionally they must know when to break the rules and make new rules. In this context, brand managers do not work in isolation. Neither do category managers. They must rely on support from people in other departments over whom they have no authority, and from whom other departments and/or brand managers are also requesting help. The success of a brand manager depends on finding out what consumers and customers want, selling the importance of their product versus all of the other competing new products in their company and then mustering the resources – people and money needed – to give their product its best chance at commercial success.

"Brand and category management is tough duty, and must be reserved for the best and the brightest. If you can't stand the heat, stay out of the kitchen!"

We are in the midst of the most dramatic change in brand management over the past two decades. So what can you do? Start by becoming an expert on category management! One of the major developments in the past decade has been the emergence of category management. Whereas brand management deals with all aspects of a particular brand, it has more of an inside-out focus. Brand management takes an inside-the-company viewpoint and seeks to maximize the brand's share, position and equity through managerial effort.

In category management you take the outside-in view. Category management is the discipline by which a single supplier or a small group of suppliers with a category *manager* essentially manage the shelf space in a retail store for the retailer. Category managers determine the number of product facings, the adjacencies and placement of related product families. Category managers also have strong influences in pricing, promotion, advertising, and merchandising for their category. Category managers often control the placement and promotion of competing brands and thus have considerable power in the distribution channel where they work. Retail store management must carefully manage the efforts of category managers or they can lose control of their own store shelves.

Category captains have similar roles in which they may do quasi-category management for retailers who are not ready or willing to relinquish the degree of control normally given to category managers, but want many of the merchandising and presentation/promotional benefits. This role of a category captain is also influential and can create a preeminent position for one supplier versus several competing brands. Used properly, these category captains can take a load off the retail store merchandising staff – but careful monitoring of the category captains is also critical lest the store management abdicate control of their own floor to suppliers.

Whereas brand management considers the performance of the brand itself, which may span multiple product categories, category manage-

> Clearly, the rules of branding are changing and now is not the time to become comfortable with a brand's historic position.
>
> James Gregory, CEO, Corporate Branding

> "...it is increasingly difficult to create advertising that stands out in the media world...they believe that being first to market...is critical to success. Thus they believe there just isn't time to get their advertising right...'haste makes waste'."
>
> David A. Aaker, *Strategy and Business*

ment considers the performance of an entire product category, which may span several competing brands. As a category manager, you would typically expect to be responsible for the sales, profitability, inventory productivity, and merchandising/packaging of the entire category of products. In this way, you approximate the inside brand manager's role acting on behalf of the customer instead of your own company.

The importance of a category manager's ability to understand the goals of both a customer and the supplier (including his/her employer) and balance those needs properly is one of the toughest challenges in business. The category manager or category captain may be working as an alter ego for the customer, managing categories which contain products from an assortment of competing suppliers only one of which is his employer. Resisting the urge to show favoritism to his own company's line is tough, but as one category captain told me, "I give away all the ones where the competitor has clear advantages, so my integrity and decisions don't get second guessed. We just get the ties and close calls, we still gain a big advantage."

Q: What is happening to brand power of major brands?

A: It is declining because of problems they have or the sheer weight of new brands entering the arena – more traffic for the consumer's mind to cope with.

As noted earlier, another development has reduced the influence of brand managers – the growth of sales management, particularly with the advent of customer development teams that service large, influential customers. Wal*Mart, the world's largest retailer, is the premier example of a retailer where customer development teams, often located in proximity to the Wal*Mart headquarters in Arkansas, have grown tremendously in influence.

Procter & Gamble was among the first major branded products company to adopt these powerful cross-functional teams and relocate them to Wal*Mart's hometown. This created an inevitable tension between sales management, customer service staff, forecasting/logistics, and brand management located together at the customer's site. No longer was the brand manager the controlling person. The power shifted to the sales managers who led the customer teams.

> "There is a need for inter-functional coordination between Brand management and Sales management due to the increasing emphasis on partnering and relationship marketing."
>
> Dr Richard C. Reizenstein, Department Head,
> The University of Tennessee–Knoxville College of
> Marketing, Transportation and Logistics

Customer partnerships and relationship marketing transferred the primary role to the sales management function. This does not mean that brand management was not important any more. It does mean that brand oriented roles were less influential in the overall decision-making process and strategies that result. Other marketing issues raised by such brand management diffusion are compensation comparisons between sales management and marketing or brand management personnel; forecasting control between sales, marketing, brand management and logistics; and last but perhaps most of all, communications gaps related to the power struggle that inevitably occurs. This area is still in a state of flux, and the final outcome is not clear. The amazing growth of Internet selling and marketing is beginning to muddle things still further. Suffice it to say, "Brand management ain't what it used to be!"

A brand name is not enough

Before leaving this topic, I must remind all of you smart marketers that a brand name is not enough to win in today's marketing mêlées and brand battles. Virgin CEO Richard Branson continues to inspire us with his swashbuckling innovation, and then demoralize us with the lackluster performance of many of his ventures. Virgin has an advantage going into markets where establishing a brand can be the single greatest investment. But, execution counts too. Branson's V2 Music was an attempt to relive past glories of Virgin Music, the company he sold to EMI in 1992. So far, that is all it is – faint memories of success. Beware of great names backed with weak ideas or poor execution: they are famous ways to fail.

Merchandising, packaging and POP (point of purchase) signage

Prior sections contained only a brief or topical treatment of this topic. How merchandising, packaging, and POP signage relate to the marketing efforts and strategy is so obvious there is a temptation to gloss it over and treat it lightly. That would be a big mistake. Visual images form a huge part of the consumer's decision-making process in a purchase – especially one in a cluttered retail environment. Studies have shown that over 90% of the sales in a typical grocery supermarket are generated by fewer than 10% of the items on the shelf. That other 90% of the items are clamoring for attention, hoping to join its more successful counterparts and become a long-term product facing on the shelf.

Thus retailer suppliers pay dearly for slotting allowances – fees for space on the shelf – and then execute the presentation in a variety of ways, from brilliant and to miserable. Usually the only decision-making information at the point of purchase for many items is contained on the package itself or on a very small shelf label. Smart marketers will pay attention to package design and merchandising if they hope to succeed in this cut-throat market.

Q: What are slotting allowances?

A: Slotting allowances are the decades-old payments made to retailers to gain desired shelf placement.

General merchandise retailers present yet another kind of challenge – variability in what is permitted and how it is executed. Some retailers like Target Stores severely restrict what a supplier can do in the way of in store merchandising, thus controlling the visual imagery of the shopping environment, and forcing suppliers to rely solely on packaging. Others like Kmart permit wide latitude in supplier merchandising creativity, then execute poorly in too many of its stores, resulting in a waste of suppliers' merchandising efforts and materials.

Wal*Mart and Carrefour, the world's two largest retailers fall somewhere in the middle of this range, permitting some supplier merchandising, but controlling where and how it is used. Drug stores are becoming mini-discount stores too, selling food, durables, clothing, and other items alongside cosmetics, pharmaceuticals, and medical needs. Merchandising clearly has a tremendous amount to do with success in these self-service channels of distribution.

"People like brands that entertain them."

Mark McGarrah, McGarrah/Jessee Advertising

In direct selling, such as mail order or Internet sales, the package may make little or no difference in the purchase decision. The consumer seldom sees the package until the purchase has been made and the goods delivered. Then the package can make a difference. How well it protects the product in shipment is critical. What kind of first impression it conveys may be important, as may any internal packaging or explanatory copy on the package's exterior about the use and benefits of the product.

Other channels present still different challenges. Warehouse clubs want large multi-packs, and often suppliers find this a way to offer them price breaks without destroying their overall industry pricing structure. Superstores may want the product touchable or usable to help the consumer in the purchase decision. Industrial products or pharmaceuticals packaging serves a much more utilitarian purpose, often protecting the contents from many kinds of harm – shock, moisture, etc. – while containing detailed information in the form of inserted literature.

Clearly a very important part of the overall marketing plan is how to package the product to enhance its sale while staying within cost parameters. After all, most packaging is just discarded after the product is purchased. How much value is added by the packaging, merchandising, and display in proportion to how it makes the product more desirable to the prospective purchaser? Determining that answer is marketing's job – your job, if you are the marketing person!

On "brand personality"

"The personality of your brand needs to be communicated in your integrated marketing efforts. It doesn't matter if your campaign includes packaging and point-of-purchase or complete communications. The activities must tie back to the brand's personality. Our site www.ducktapeclub.com shows the Duck's personality within the site without overt branding."

Gary Medalis, VP Advertising & Communications, Manco, Inc.

When a brand's image is a major part of the value being purchased, this adds yet another dimension to the marketer's job. There are at least two major schools of thought on this topic. One says always present your brand in a consistent manner, using the same icons, typography, etc. The other one says get attention and exposure wherever, however you can. That view is dangerous. Most companies should have a brand style guide – either formal or informal – controlled by the marketing, advertising, or the brand manager. This is a good idea. Following such a guide is usually a smart thing to do!

What is the most important message we can deliver in a few words or illustrations, which will attract potential buyers to our product over the others on the display?

Some experts contend that rigidly enforcing styles of documents and typography are foolish and restrict creativity. I disagree. There is an evident if unspoken quality about graphic works that are done consistently and tastefully. Unless the image of the brand is one of crazy, mixed-up, off-the-wall visual elements, the style needs to be consistent and the brand name or icon prominent. If it is an eclectic or offbeat image then the style needs to avoid being consistent. Doing either one well requires professional effort, and marketing management of how the desired result is to be achieved.

A commonly overlooked consideration in packaging graphics design is what I call simple readability. For products that will be purchased by people over 40 years of age, type size is important. If these people do not have their reading glasses with them, they may not be able to read your key message points. Simpler type styles that do not have "serifs" (the little lines at the top or bottom of letters) are usually more readable. If the product/package/merchandising is viewed from multiple distances, type sizes and messages must consider that.

For example, when I was in the bike business, the first view of bikes at retail is from 20–30 feet away. Point of purchase materials that are intended to attract consumers and differentiate between products must be large enough type and few enough words to be quickly readable – especially the headlines. Then when the consumer comes closer, the type face must be large enough and the message short enough for the consumer to easily and quickly get the message. Long paragraphs of information will almost always go unread. Smart marketers raise these kinds of questions. Also never forget the old adage, "a picture is worth a thousand words" and it will never be in the wrong language!

Marketing information

At the foundation of most good marketing departments is information and knowledge. Good information is a treasure, which reduces the risk and uncertainty. No amount of good information will completely eliminate risk and uncertainty! But bad information is particularly deadly. Decisions made with the best of analysis will be wrong. Money and time will be squandered. Results will be awful. Even good luck usually won't make up for marketing decisions based on bad information.

Market analysis and competitive intelligence

The place where information-gathering begins is with customers and in the market. After thoroughly considering what is known and can be learned from customers, the next stop is competitive intelligence and analysis. This is no place for shortcuts or intellectual laziness. A serious trap is to depend on "intuition or gut feel". *Don't!* As I pointed out before, a shortcut here is not the shortest path and may be the most dangerous one. A huge amount of information exists on most companies – market research, media reporting, POS data, public company financial data, import–export records, and the Internet. Find it and use it before competitors do.

Data mining and database marketing

Database marketing has been around for many years, but the power and speed of the Internet and low cost of computing and memory power has enabled more, faster, and more accurate information for use by marketing. Market segmentation, which used to merely target

Q: What do all of those marketing and advertising acronyms mean?

A: Here is a short list of the most common ones! If you are not sure – ask: there are no dumb questions in this area, just dumb moves by those who pretend they understand something they don't.

- CFAR: collaborative forecasting and replenishment
- CPFR: collaborative planning, forecasting, and replenishment

Both are terms developed to describe a new level of cooperation and information exchange between customers and suppliers.

- VMI: vendor managed inventory
- VMR: vendor managed replenishment

Both describe processes where the customer relies on the supplier to monitor in-store stock and/or warehouse inventory levels and then replenish according to agreed upon inventory and service levels.

- ECR: efficient consumer (or customer) response

A term for describing a system of quickly responding to demands for products, which originated in the grocery trade, (but has not spread as expected).

- POS: point-of-sale
- POU: point-of-use
- POP: point-of-purchase

The terms used for data usually gathered at either retail sales shelf or from scanners at checkout stations or at production reporting stations in a factory or distribution center.

- ERP: enterprise resource planning
- MRP: material (or manufacturing) resource planning
- DRP: distribution resource planning

All are systems (usually computerized) which allocate resources – typically inventory, people and money within parts of a business and then track the results of such allocations, both financially and usually physically by part numbers, locations, and quantities.

- 3PL: third-party logistics (providers)

Specialist companies to whom the various functions of logistics can be outsourced.

- SKU: stock-keeping unit

An item which is specifically identified within the information system by its number and physical configuration including size, weight, cube, contents, price, source of origin, and more.

Q: What do people do online that marketers need to know about?

A: A lot of different things happen when people are online, and marketers need to know about most of them! The following is just one of many such surveys.

Time spent online – How?	%	Time spent per month
Communicating	43	5 hr 12 min
Information gathering	27	3 hr 12 min
Entertainment	13	1 hr 44 min
Shopping	8	52 min
Finance	8	52 min
Other	1	7 min

Source: MediaMetrix and The Boston Consulting Group, *Infoworld*, 17 April 2000.

groups of customers that had common demographic or geographic characteristics, can now consider single customers, or communities spread around the globe, which have common characteristics.

Wal*Mart, the world's largest retailer, at this writing, had over 40 terabits of data stored at its Arkansas data center. From such immense data treasures, marketers can "mine" information that is like gold. When consumers use credit cards, the information about what they bought (by item and SKU), where (by retail store location and the customer's postal code), and even time of day and day of week purchased. Imagine being able to cross tab this data against sale prices, weather patterns, local economics, regional cultural preferences, etc., and you can begin to see the power of marketing information and data mining.

Wal*Mart is already using "cluster marketing" to aggregate what are otherwise seemingly unrelated groups of stores by using these pat-

"Smart markets will find suppliers who speak their own language."

Rick Levine *et al.*, *The Cluetrain Manifesto*

terns. This enables them to run promotions, adjust merchandise assortments, and tailor their offerings to match the desires of customers in previously unimaginable ways. Grouping and managing supply/demand from clusters of stores with similar weather patterns may not fit prior geographic cluster definitions, but will predict demand for weather-sensitive products much more accurately.

Mass customization

This term comes from the title of a book by Joseph Pine. Simply stated it means taking advantages of the economies of mass production while waiting until the last possible moment to add the features and specifications while tailor the product to the consumer. As Pine puts it, *"Mass customization means efficiently producing output – whether goods or services – only in response to actual demand."*

We used this approach on bicycles in my days at Huffy Bicycles, but did not know what to call it until Joe gave it a name. We made the structure of the product – frame, fork, wheels and handlebars – in mass production, flexible manufacturing cells and then added all of the decoration at the last minute based on retailer's orders. The paint, decals, seats, grips, pedals, etc., were all obtained from nearby suppliers on a short lead time basis. This allowed us to customize an assortment of what were (under the decorations and accessories) identical products into a huge variety of models and styles for different retailers and regions of the country.

"Mass customization is an oxymoron, which is like the putting together of seemingly contradictory notions, like jumbo shrimp and artificial intelligence. . . . The key is to embrace and transcend the paradox, rather than be limited by it."

Stan Davis, Foreword to *Mass Customization* by B. Joseph Pine

Q: What is postponement?

A: It means keeping major pieces of a product in semi-finished stages and postponing the assembly of the final configuration until needs are known. Hewlett-Packard makes extensive use of this approach for its printer production.

Mass customization is a distinctly powerful business model, and one which lends itself ideally to taking advantage of the capabilities of the Internet – but only if the rest of the business is aligned with that model from design through production to fulfillment.

For a long time, both marketing and manufacturing were "massified" because there was no practical way to make the volume of products and reach the variety of customers otherwise. That is no longer true. The Internet makes it possible to reach customers one at a time, interact with them, and fulfill their needs – and isn't that what we said value was all about. Customization of products is made possible by keeping a commonality at some stage or platform level and then adding the variability – postponing the customization – as late in the production cycle as possible.

Make every product different – and at the last moment? Are they crazy? How can anyone forecast that kind of demand? Easy – just forecast the quantities of the platforms and the quantities of the vari-

"I think the Internet will change the way people think about what they can buy. That said, the mass market isn't about to go away. One problem with customization is that it requires customers to do a lot of the initial legwork."

Richard Gerstein, VP Reflect.com

> "Mass Customization is providing a new basis of competition not only for American companies but for much of the industrialized world. When this shift occurs in an industry, success will come to those companies that can implement the new principles of competition faster and better than their competitors."
>
> B. Joseph Pine, *Mass Customization*

ous options and don't worry about the combination. If you have all the necessary components and materials those will be covered. Then make the product to order. In fact, there is even an element of compensating errors that may make this kind of forecasting easier and more accurate than trying to predict combinations. Chinese restaurants have been preparing meals this way for decades.

Modular product design, which is a key marketing decision at the inception of a product's life, enables the use of this powerful marketing tool as the product nears the hands of the end user. Failure by marketing and product development to consider how the differentiation is to be added makes the mass customization process difficult or impossible to use. Thus up-front decisions make product variety cost either very little, or very much. Marketing and product development must also work very closely with production, purchasing and logistics to build this mass customization capability into the competitive advantage it should become.

> "The focus on experiences has evolved out of two earlier phases of marketing: the attributes/benefits phase and the branding phase."
>
> Bernd Schmitt and Alex Simonsen, *Marketing Aesthetics*

Customer rules for a one-size fits one world

- The average customer does not exist – get to know us.

- Make our experience special: give us something to talk about.

- If something goes wrong, fix it quickly.

- Guarantee our satisfaction.

- Trust us and we'll trust you.

- Don't take us for granted.

- Our time is as important as your time.

- The details are important to us – they should be to you.

- Employ people who are ready, willing, and able to serve us.

- We care whether you're a responsible corporate citizen.

Gary Heil, Tom Parker, and Deborah Stevens, *One Size Fits One*

Dell Computer is one of the most familiar examples of mass customization in today's business world. The next step, according to Joe Pine, is moving from customizing the product to using the product or service to create a customized experience. For those interested in this concept see his *Harvard Business Review* article and recent book, *The Experience Economy*, written with Jim Gilmore.

Point of sale information

There is so much to cover on this topic that a couple of paragraphs will only scratch the surface. POS data is now available from most major retailers and distributors. Manufacturers have known for years what they use day by day – it is just that marketers never asked them. They were afraid the manufacturers would ask for still shorter lead times – and they would have – and should have. Delivery speed is a powerful competitive edge and it is a primary reason for using POS data. The accuracy of POS data from scanning used to be an issue, but refinements in scanning, pricing, and bar-coding technology is rapidly making that a non-issue.

> "Given the expansion in use of POS scanner data in stores, consumer databases, the new ability to track people's journey's through the net, etc., the challenge is how to harness this data for segmentation and targeting purposes. This is truly where information technology and marketing meet – how to mine the data that you have in order to direct 'rifle shot' marketing to specified target groups in your audience, versus 'shot gun' approaches using traditional media."
>
> Sarah Gardial

As microchips shrink smaller and smaller, these tiny identifiers will find their way into/onto everything and make scanning as we know it almost obsolete. Just as cars can pass through tollgates with the wave of a card or by merely slowing down, products will tell the checkout/control point what they are, and what they cost as they are moved from shopping cart or factory pallet to the consumer or the production line. Smart marketers of the 21st century need to plan ahead and expand their thinking about how to use this avalanche of information to their advantage – before their competitors do it. If you don't get and use POS/POU information from your customers, you're missing a great competitive advantage. Ask them for it right now! Then use it for their (and your) advantage.

Logistics and distribution

There are entire books about these topics, and there is little doubt that the overlooked discipline of the early Internet era might have been logistics. Fulfillment is the critical step that the Internet alone does well only when things can be downloaded. For decades, while the fields of logistics and distribution have been growing in professional competence and strategic importance, they have been underappreciated by marketing. The essence of logistics that a smart marketer needs to know is that logistics is all about fulfilling the customer's "bill of rights": *get the **right thing**, to the **right customer**, at the **right place**, and at the **right time**, with the **right cost**, and with the **right quality**!*

Sounds so simple, doesn't it. Well, it isn't. It is easy to say and hard to do. The problem is that forecasts will always be wrong – because they are guesses about the future. The production or sourcing of the items needed can be filled with problems – delays in shipments, machine breakdowns, parts/material shortages, people absent, weather delays, transportation problems, and on and on. Then add the complexity that all of these parts, people, and processes have to occur in a carefully choreographed sequence that might involve hundreds or thousands of suppliers scattered around the globe and it's amazing anything happens as it was planned. The smart thing to know is that most things that do meet the "bill of rights" happen because they were planned and managed by logistics professionals.

Logistics is about managing what is commonly called the supply chain or value chain. This supply chain is the network of companies and people that stretches from suppliers' suppliers through to the central manufacturer (who is often the primary marketer!), to the customers' customers. Include in this picture the employees and contractors of the various firms and you can imagine why this supply chain is actually a complex value network and why planning and managing it is difficult and important.

In addition to making sure the goods get there, minimizing the cost involved is important since the logistics usually add no "use value" to the product. It is just impossible to use the product if it isn't there. Different kinds of products present widely different logistics challenges. Consider yours carefully. Costs can be incurred in many ways, not the least of which is damage or loss in transit.

Here are just a few items and some typical problem issues:

• Furniture – bulky, easily prone to damage

• Chemicals – dangerous, subject to hazardous material regulations

• Fitness equipment – bulky, requires assembly to work properly

• Perishables – subject to environmental variations of heat, humidity, spoilage

• Software and jewelry – small, valuable, and theft prone

• Glassware and fine china – fragile and subject to breakage

This is just a small sampling, but you get the idea.

Information logistics

A new and increasingly important branch of logistics is one which deals not specifically with the movement of the product, but with the management of the information that determines which products to move where, when, why, and in what quantities. Without this information logistics function, forecasting, production planning, distribution, and customer fulfillment are all disjointed. With information logistics, each step in the supply chain can be linked and integrated for the best results. Leading companies such as Warner-

Lambert, Procter & Gamble, Manco, and many others are working along with retailers like Wal*Mart to pioneer the field of information logistics for improvements in productivity, sales, and in-stock positions while minimizing inventory and transportation/distribution costs.

A little humorous riddle: "Why is material that travels on ships called *cargo*, and the material carried by trucks called *shipments?*"

Information logistics will ultimately permit you to *pull* the necessary goods through the supply chain based on near-real-time consumer demand. It is almost always necessary to forecast the overall demand, the mix, by customer, by product, by geographical region, etc., and then cross-check these individual forecasts against a macro market forecast. Once this is done, use information logistics to accumulate data to either support or refute the conclusions, then check how accurate you were, assess the probable causes for the errors and do it all over. You will improve as you go through this process. As you develop this process, it is mandatory to collaborate with your customers to improve the results and raise their involvement in developing the forecast and studying how you can jointly continue to improve on it. That is the way forecasts will become as accurate as you can make them. This is the natural companion to the customer/brand relationship process called category management.

Physical distribution and transportation

As long as a physical product is part of your marketing program, it requires a system of physical distribution. This usually means warehouses or distribution centers, which handle and/or store the product and then pick/pack, mark, and ship the goods based on customer orders, or demands from other parts of the distribution system. Once the products have been unitized or packaged, it is necessary to route them onto various modes of transportation – trucks, trains, planes or ships/barges. These modes, sometimes used in combination, transport the product to intermediate or final end-users.

By now you may be saying, what does all this have to do with marketing? The answer quite simply is a lot! **Marketing plans must consider how the logistics of fulfilling demand will work and what they will cost. This area was a fatal flaw of many dot-com company start-ups.** The downside of poor or failed logistics and delivery can be devastating, while doing it right means it goes almost unnoticed!

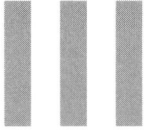

III The Defining Markets

6 Industrial Marketing

The five smartest things to know about marketing

- You must have a plan

- **Get close to the customer**

- Do your homework

- Remember relationships

- **Use the speed and reach of technology**

You can't make something from nothing

It's tempting to jump right into writing about marketing of consumer products and services because it's easier for most people to relate to those. Rather than do that I want to start by covering the marketing of industrial products and services because most consumer products depend on industrial products for their creation/production.

Plastic, paper, and metal parts of consumer products can't come into being without the machinery, molds, dies, and the machine tools to make these molds and dies, as well as a plethora of other industrial parts and equipment. Automobiles, computers, telephones, health and beauty aids, household packaged goods, and all kinds of consumer services depend on industrial products to provide the means of production and delivery.

Marketing industrial products and services has a lot in common with consumer marketing, but there are some unique aspects to it. Industrial products are usually purchased to meet definite specifications or to perform specified functions, which meet the needs of the buyer in a particular way. Whereas consumer products might appeal to more of the creative/emotional right side of the buyer's brain, industrial products more often appeal to the left side of the brain – the logical-analytical part.

Traditional distribution meets the Internet

Many industrial products have historically gone through intermediate distributors who fulfill the needs of the end-users rapidly from their inventory. This meant that marketers had to convince two levels of distribution to purchase and carry inventory of their offerings. This also happens in retail/consumer goods marketing where the retailer is an intermediate distributor on the product's journey to the consumer end user. But marketing to industrial distribution is more analytical and driven by some different competitive issues.

"The whole business of industrial products and services is one which gets almost passing consideration in most marketing texts. However, this is a huge part of the economy."

Sarah Gardial

There are many who believe that the Internet era and the emergence of "marketplace exchanges" will revolutionize this field of commerce, and perhaps it will. The Internet has given birth to hundreds of exchanges which are web sites that permit buyers and sellers to exchange information, share bids and quotes, and complete purchase transactions, all electronically. These exchanges serve specific industry groups and will signal the end of business as usual. There are some that predict they will also mean the end of traditional (physical) distributors. That's probably not going to happen, but it will certainly require the surviving distributors to change the way they do business, to take more advantage of info-mediation, and to trim their overheads and the profit margins on which they can operate profitably.

Do we know all of those who influence the buying decision?

Purchasing exchanges for B2B (business to business) commerce are arguably the most profitable and effective early adopters in the Internet era. Old-line companies like the Thomas Register, known for its large array of directories from which purchasers could find potential suppliers, and broad line industrial supply distributors such as W. W. Grainger have all scrambled rapidly onto the Internet and carved out strong positions.

Wholesalers can succeed in the new economy

US-based office products wholesaler United Stationers is working hard to bridge the new and old economies and prove that there is a viable place for distributors in the new economy. Small office product stores can access United's 35,000 SKU inventory purchased from more than 500 suppliers. Their orders placed before 4 p.m. are delivered the next day, and if desired, United will pick, pack, label, and ship to one of its customers directly from one of 66 distribution centers with 99.8% accuracy – and in the same, one-day time frame. That is an old economy wholesaler moving at new economy speed.

"Joint press releases don't make money."

Yobie Benjamin, Ernst & Young

Wholesalers like United Stationers also act as backups to contract stationers and office products superstores, providing a large catalog of the less frequently needed items that contribute as much as 10% of the superstores' sales. In addition to these efforts, United Stationers is the fulfillment agent for over 100 web sites that sell office supplies, including such well-known ones as Dell Computer. These kinds of success stories illustrate that old-style industrial distribution and marketing is not being bypassed by the new economy.

> "In a time of rapid change distributors and distribution channels tend to change faster than anything else. It is also on distributors and distribution channels that the 'Information Revolution' is likely to have the greatest impact."
>
> Peter Drucker

Who are you selling to?

A good place for the marketer to start is by knowing whom the real manufacturer or distributor actually is – when it may not appear that way. For example, Coca-Cola (the beverage company) doesn't bottle most of the Coke it sells – subsidiaries that are part of a company named Coca-Cola Enterprises do that. This means that to market the machinery and supplies used by bottlers of Coke, you would need to target Coca-Cola Enterprises, not Coca-Cola (the marketing company and owner of the secret Coke formula).

How do we add value – and is the value we add worth what we want to charge for it?

Dell became the biggest PC supplier by displacing Compaq, and by selling computers to both individuals and companies. As Dell continues its growth, and expands into servers, it will run into new competition from companies like Sun Microsystems. The marketing of servers to corporate customers is a lot different than marketing and selling PCs to consumers. There are still buyers, but the buyers are not the end-users. The buyer represents a lot of invisible users, and this gives the buyer a disproportionate amount of power/influence and insulates the seller from contact with its end-user customers. This is usually the case with industrial products marketing.

Pleasing several masters

One thing I learned from my stint operating an office products company is that getting unbiased feedback directly from end-users was

> "Today an increasing number of entrepreneurs start companies with little more than a gut feeling that someone will eventually need or want their product. This form of 'ivory tower' capitalism is quite dangerous."
>
> J. William Gurley, "Startups, Beware:
> Obey the Law of Supply and Demand"

very difficult, and yet marketers depend on such feedback to refine their products and programs. The idea of a "gatekeeper" who filters information both ways is a key concept to understand and deal with. In many cases, end-users do have influence in the form of specification control, so there may be several different buying influences that must be satisfied to make a successful sale. These influences may not even agree on what makes a good supplier or a desirable offering. The immediate buyer wants a low price. The technical systems specifier wants a lot of capability for the money. The end-user wants fast, flexible delivery and easy-to-use, reliable equipment. Industrial marketers must please all three, plus their respective financial and distribution groups.

B2B exchanges

"Can you tell me and show me exactly how that will work, and who else is using it?"

The list of planned or announced B2B exchanges and marketplaces seems to grow daily and the number is now well over 1000! Some will succeed and make the marketing of industrial products very different from what it has been in the past. Many of them are dreams that will never come true, and only time will tell which is which. The position of a smart marketer is to check out the substance behind the announcement. How will this new exchange or marketplace work? Who will it serve? What kinds of products or services will it list, trade, sell, etc. In other words: think! Don't just react to such announcements. If there is a realistic chance that the exchange or marketplace will come to fruition, then get involved early and find out what is expected and how you can participate profitably.

Which ones will work?

There are some kinds of web alliances that make so much sense they are bound to work. The Internet is an ideal medium for purchasing many industrial products and services, especially where there is wide variety but low volume of any single item. It is the world's largest, most comprehensive catalog, and its interactive nature allows a fast, easy exchange of specifications, RFQs (request for quotations), and quotations between purchasers and prospective suppliers. Not only can this be done on a global scale, but also it can be done with lightning speed, expansive content, and pinpoint accuracy – and all transmitted electronically in a blink.

"A [second] risk to the supply-driven startup is the relatively low barriers to entry. Let's face it: If you can think up a concept in your head, there are probably five other people who can dream up the same concept."

J. William Gurley

There is always a question of the credibility/viability of this invisible supplier who submits the lowest bids. Does it have the infrastructure to fulfill the order on which it bid? Is it a "real company"? What are its competencies? Most exchanges are now providing a means to prequalify bidders' capabilities – after some early débâcles of bogus bids and incompetent bidders. Smart marketers keep close track of their competitors, both current ones and these potential new ones. A part of an incumbent suppliers' marketing must be to create some buyer insecurity about the risks of switching suppliers.

The Internet is also a great tool for interactive tracking. That is why alliances like the one announced by four large railroads are likely to be successful. It makes great business sense for companies like Union Pacific, CSX Corp., Norfolk Southern, and Canadian Pacific to invest in Arzoon (an Internet company based in San Mateo, CA) to create a new service by which rail customers can procure, execute, and track freight movement using the Internet. These are competitors, but the service doesn't exactly pit them against one another, except indirectly. It complements what they do. This one should work as should many others like it. It is a smart form of marketing collaboration.

Industrial marketing *is* different

But people are pretty much the same. The question this raises is how can marketers most effectively promote and advertise their products in the Internet era? The answer might be "not all that differently than before"! Smart marketing to industrial customers and prospects requires clever blending of the old and new technologies and methods. Catalogs, "snail mail", email, trade shows, sales reps, telemarketing, CD-ROMs, filesharing, and e-commerce must all be used in combination and tailored to the needs of customers in a chosen market segment.

"I know that all of the jazzy stories generally tend to be consumer product based. But, as things move to B2B e-commerce, there ought to be some really great stories to tell, and relationship marketing will be key with this category."

Sarah Gardial

Smart marketers of industrial goods must make sure that the major distributors in the product and geographic market segments they want to serve will be able and willing to offer the product to end-users – either by carrying inventory or providing some form of rapid delivery service. This means that marketing to intermediate distributors whether they are real (physical) or "virtual" is an important part of the smart marketing plan for industrial marketing.

Although industrial goods are purchased primarily on specification-based considerations, the influence of human factors and emotions cannot be ignored. The emotional concerns of anxiety and fear (insecurity) will drive many industrial purchase decisions in the direction of risk avoidance. The consequences of not having a critical component or raw material can be very great, and the buyer knows that. The smart marketer must know that too, including what risks the buyer may face! It is simply smart marketing to play to that insecurity. Then you must deliver on the promises you make – having what they need, when and where they need it, and at a suitably competitive price.

Do we have all of the latest specifications of what we want to sell and is there anyway we can influence them to our advantage?

This means that the marketing of industrial products and services, like its counterpart consumer goods and services, requires a smart marketer to do his/her homework. This homework consists of gaining a clear understanding of what the current (or prospective) customer needs (or will need) and making good decisions in product planning. The homework also includes investigation of unserved market opportunities since your largest untapped new potential market is among purchasers who don't currently buy from your company.

New and old customers – opportunities and pitfalls

Companies too often tend to look only at current customers and have a poor understanding of potential customers with whom they do no business. But things change and times change. What's hot and what's not changes too. Maintaining current customers and keeping them very happy is a smart thing to do, but for significant growth, it is usually necessary to blend growth from current customers and new customers.

Some of the most common problems that industrial marketing encounters have to do with over-promising and under-delivering.

To illustrate just how dramatic this change is, over the last forty years there has been a huge movement in the 20 largest companies in the US. Half of them disappeared off the list in that time and there was a huge movement from natural resources companies in industries like oil and chemicals towards information/communications companies, both hardware, software and information providers. Smart marketers acknowledge such seismic change in the long term, and never take anything for granted in the short to medium term no matter how permanent something appears to be.

Unlike retailing, where there are other stores, and product purchase alternatives, industrial situations often have no easy alternative available in the case of non-delivery. Customers for these kinds of products usually depend on them to support their means of production/delivery. If you fail to deliver and shut down a major assembly line/process or knock a major telemarketing/customer service callcenter offline, no amount of marketing skill will minimize the problem. If you promise performance that is not delivered more than a few times, and that'll probably be the last time you get to make (and break) that promise – at least to that customer. If you misunderstand the specifications or pay too little attention to critical details, there'll be no need for glossy catalogs, a clever web site, or fancy trade show exhibits.

> "The best place to grow is with current customers – but it is hard to grow fast in a slow growth market."

The smart marketer understands that in industrial products and services marketing, the most critical success factor is delivering exactly what was ordered, exactly when it was ordered, exactly where it was ordered, and having it perform exactly how was specified. Success in marketing of industrial products and services is dependent on success in execution.

Channels of distribution

Different channels of distribution demand different marketing methods and strategies. Now there's a profound statement! The funny (funny surprising, not ha-ha funny) thing is that this principle is overlooked way too much of the time.

The vaunted business schools too often teach cases that deal with highly visible consumer products marketing because they are easier to develop and better known for their highly publicized successes or failures. Industrial products marketing and wholesale distribution is dull – but it can be quite profitable. Machinery parts and raw materials suppliers are (yawn) unexciting. Try to make any of those

Q:What is an example of old economy industrial marketing doing well with new economy practices?

A: There are many, but one of the most prominent is W. W. Grainger Inc. – here is a recap on its efforts

W. W. Grainger, which was founded in 1928, is a $4.5 billion company located in Lake Forest, IL, USA that sells over 200,000 no-frills items like nuts and bolts, motors and fans, keyboards and floor mats. These items have been listed in a thick paper catalog for years. These catalogs sit on the shelves of purchasing and plant maintenance people everywhere.

Now Grainger's huge catalog is accessible on its web site or on CD-ROM. Grainger merged its OrderZone.com unit with new economy rival Works.com. Grainger's sites racked up sales of over $100 million in 1999, a figure that will more than double in 2000. The order size on the web site is twice what it experienced in its traditional business and much of it comes in after normal business hours. Its distribution system is already in place giving it a competitive edge on upstarts.

Grainger's early initiatives like TotalMRO.com to support maintenance departments will help it gain the first-mover advantage in the marketplace. Right now, the "bricks and mortar" part of the business is subsidizing the startup of the "clicks and mortar" part – but not for long. Don't be surprised to see this old–new economy company becoming as much of a necessary fixture in industrial supply during the 21st century economy as it was in the 20th.

exciting consumer products without a solid wholesale and industrial infrastructure and you'll experience exciting – in an unpleasant way. Ditto for delivering services like fast food, banking, entertainment, and so forth. One of the first questions to ask when locating a manufacturing plant in a less-developed country is "What is the industrial infrastructure?" Companies like Tyco, Emerson, Danaher, and many others make good money, year after year, making, marketing, and selling these "dull" industrial products.

Q: What issues do B2B/industrial products companies need to consider when developing a marketing and advertising strategy

A: There are four major questions that must be answered as you craft
this strategy.

- How large is your target audience – and how will you reach them?

- How mature is the business – and how much ad "traffic" will you
have to contend with?

- Is there competition (now) and how fast is it moving? (And if there is
not, quit reading this book and go take advantage of it, because
there will be soon enough.)

- What role will co-marketing or joint marketing play – is it necessary
to connect your marketing and advertising strategy to those of
others?

All of the basics of marketing apply to industrial products as much as
they apply to consumer products. The major difference is that
instead of convincing retail buyers, you must convince those "steely-
eyed", analytical industrial buyers – and their specification-oriented
engineers.

In fact, some of the most prominent consumer marketing companies
are going after what used to be industrial and commercial markets.
This is clearly the case with the multi-billion dollar Home Depot
chain. While it built its success as a traditional retailing business, it is
rapidly encroaching on the sales of traditional wholesale lumber
yards, plumbing and heating distributors, electrical distributors, car-
pet and wall-covering distributors and more. The same applies to the
wholesale clubs. When Sol Price initially founded Price Club, the first
of its breed, his idea was that it would be a distributor for small businesses first and a retailer second. Now in Costco and Sam's Club, the

current US industry leaders, it is hard to tell where one stops and the other starts. This means that the marketing disciplines and approaches for wholesale/industrial begin to blur with those for the retail/consumer distribution. Industrial buyers are consumers too: smart marketers need to remember this!

> "There is no such thing as a 'free' lunch."
>
> Anonymous

Trade shows and trade publications are major marketing tools for industrial distribution. So are local and regional shows and conferences. Seldom does this channel use TV advertising, and only occasionally does it appear in expensive consumer magazines or newspaper ads. A much smaller share of its budgets go to advertising and thus a larger share is allocated to other forms of marketing. For years, ubiquitous handouts like notepads, pens, keyrings, mouse mats, etc., have been silent salesmen for the industrial products supplier. But these carry little marketing content beyond the company name, telephone number, and web site. Of all the channels of distribution, this may be the most effective for the Internet to reach because of high technical information content in the sale/purchase decision making process. Learn how to use the speed and reach of this new media tool on this old market and you can win.

Wholesale distribution

These are the aggregators and disaggregators for local and regional (and in a few cases national) markets. A wholesale distributor either carries inventory to service its customers, or knows how to get needed items there fast to meet the customer's needs – which can be critical at times. When production-processing equipment is down, nothing gets made. That's when the industrial wholesale distributor comes to the rescue. The same goes for construction machinery. Take an asphalt plant or a paving machine out of service for a few days, and big dollars go out the window.

Beyond construction machinery and equipment, there are many

other fields that often get overlooked. While less than 3% of the US labor force are involved in farming, it is still a large industry. Such a huge industry cannot be ignored in other countries around the world. How does it get sold, marketed, and served? I'd bet the marketing folks at John Deere, a leading US maker of farm equipment, spend a lot of time thinking about this. In addition, this old industry is learning new tricks – Internet tricks to be specific. Online exchanges and new web sites such as farmbid.com, farms.com, directag.com, farmstech.com, netseeds.com, and xsag.com help farmers save money and time buying seed, feed, chemicals, and much more. Some sites even offer livestock auctions.

In many respects farming is like a manufacturing business – and a capital-intensive one. When a large piece of farm equipment is broken down, production either stops or suffers mightily – just like in a factory. Getting the necessary parts is a big business! The message for smart marketer is don't limit your thinking to obvious industries. Go after the overlooked ones, where the competition may be less intense and the opportunities far greater.

Direct sales

Many industrial manufacturers sell directly to end-users. In this situation, the marketing function must accumulate data and use information technology to identify, find, and economically call on current and prospective customers. Advertising can help in this case, especially if there are popular trade publications or shows. Trade associations and their membership rolls can be a valuable source of prospect lists. Increasingly, data warehouses with easily accessible records of past and present customers can help aim marketers in directions that are most likely to yield results.

In the past, direct mail campaigns have been used extensively in direct selling, but as the volume of junk mail increases and the cost per response increases, this media is falling out of favor. As more and more companies go online, Internet and email direct selling will grow in prominence. Some well-designed and targeted early efforts are already yielding responses rates much higher than direct mail campaigns. The bottom line is that direct selling can be both cheap and effective *if* you have a good customer database and the technology to use it effectively.

> "The sales force get the first order. The plant (and its performance) gets the ones after that."

One of the largest direct selling efforts in this new century is that of selling professional services. Computer services like those provided by EDS, IBM, and hundreds of others make up a huge business. The large accountancy and consulting firms like Accenture, PriceWaterhouse Coopers, McKinsey et al. are among the largest, most aggressive, and influential direct sales companies – but their "products" are all services delivered by thousands of highly skilled professionals. A smart marketer can learn a lot by studying how these companies position their efforts and attempt to differentiate themselves from largely similar competitors.

OEM (original equipment manufacturer) sales

In many cases, the process almost works backwards when OEM sales are involved. Marketing people usually think in terms of finding the customer to make the sale. For OEM sales, the name of the game is *being found by the prospective purchaser*. Usually there are only a few ways to know that a prospect is planning something that may need what you have to sell. You may know of a lot of prospects but the frequency of their orders are so low that calling on them to get orders is often not economically possible. The key, then, is to be "well-known for something".

When marketing does its job right in this field of OEM sales, the potential customers know about the suppliers and seek them out. Not only is this a more efficient process, but it is also a lot easier to get the order when the customer comes looking for you. Many companies exhibit at trade shows for just this reason – to be "known" and to be "found" when the need is imminent.

What is our "claim to fame" or what are we "known for"? Or are we known well enough?

For decades, companies like the Thomas Register (now also available online) have made a business of helping OEMs find suppliers in their volumes of listings sorted by industry, products, geography, etc. The key to success is for the marketing efforts to make the company and its capability known and respected in the first place, and for the company to have lived up to its reputation by reliable, cost-effective delivery of what was sold. Then the ability to meet the specifications, bid competitively and get successive orders by servicing the first ones well is what creates success.

Because of the proliferation of B2B exchanges in industry after industry, this entire field will go through a cataclysmic change in the next few years. Even when it does, being known and respected will be the critical first job of OEM marketing.

Non-profit marketing

All kinds of institutions must do marketing, and some of the most challenging applications are for not-for-profit organizations: charities, schools, churches, civic organizations, educational institutions, and more. Competition in this area, like many others, is more intense that ever – but not because of the Internet!

Organized charities

The marketing of charitable causes is big business. The range of these organizations is so great that a simple listing would fill many pages. There are global-reach organizations like the American Red Cross, the World Health Organization, UNICEF, and many others. These organizations gain funding from many sources, but the marketing challenge they face is the same as many well know brands – keep their names and messages in front of their publics on a consistently effective basis.

The huge number of organizations formed to raise money in search of a cure for specific diseases grows almost daily. From the American Cancer Society to the many campaigns for AIDS or Alzheimer's, to antiabortion groups, these appeals are worthy – yet often suspect. One of the primary concerns about not-for-profit appeals is where the money goes. A key measure of a charitable organization is how much of the money goes for the actual purpose intended, and how much is consumed by administration and, yes, marketing too! Thus marketing in these organizations has yet another dimension to be concerned about. They must sell the cause but support the credibility and reputation of the organization at the same time.

Local and regional charities raise funds for their causes through a variety of marketing methods. These range from direct mail campaigns (not all that efficient: a low 1% response rate), to door-to-door canvassing (not very effective since so many people work, volunteers are hard to find, and local regulations prohibit solicitation), to targeted fund raising events like festivals, bazaars, walk-a-thons, bikes, runs, outdoor historical events. You get the message – the range is immense. Each such event requires marketing. Many of the best, most creative marketing efforts are directed at these charitable or non-profit activities, and often done on a volunteer basis.

Churches and schools

Places of worship have existed for centuries, relying on the religious beliefs and faith of their congregations – and on financial contributions. For some, this income is still the primary one, but for others a much broader range of activities requires marketing. Church bazaars, and Catholic bingo games are long-standing means of fund raising through community building activities that also yield a profit – whoops – "a surplus of revenue over expenses". Remember that these are not-for-profit organizations. That means the terminology used is different. What businesses call profit, these organizations call a surplus of revenue over expenses or favorable revenue to expense ratio. Even small, local fundraisers require basic marketing skills.

Public schools in the US came into being in the early 1900s as factories and working parents became more common and children could no longer be effectively educated in the home. Throughout the world, schooling takes differing forms. What is called "home schooling" in developed countries has seen a resurgence as public school quality has diminished. But, through the ages, there have been private schools, which were the province of the elite, the wealthy, and the landed gentry. Private schools may be not-for-profit, but they better have a favorable revenue to expense ratio or they won't be around for long – unless they have a rich endowment. This means that schools must do marketing.

This is especially true of colleges and universities. If not for reasons of economics, then reasons of image, prestige, or political pride require that schools market themselves. And market themselves they do – just check the back pages or special sections of nearly any business publication. Competition between colleges and universities is intense, and these institutions must build brand names and images for themselves just as any company might for its products. Many alumni are premier marketing spokespersons and fund-raisers for schools, but this is still marketing in one of its highest forms.

Community service/civic organizations

Social change, the increase in hours people work, urbanization, and (yes) increased communications technology has decimated membership in community organizations. This means the remaining ones must compete harder for members and a reason to exist that will sustain them. That means they must market "what they are about" and why people should join, contribute, and participate!

With the increase in two-working-person or single-working-person households, and the time pressures of today's world, membership in community service organizations has declined dramatically. Some community/ civic organizations like the United Way act like charities as they perform consolidation and administration services for communities, raising money and then allocating it to those organizations that serve the community's needs.

The three most important questions all winners ask themselves:

1. What do I want?

2. How am I going to get it?

3. When am I going to do something about it?

Mark Gibson, "Going For It!"

Others like Goodwill Industries and the Salvation Army (in the US at least) perform different functions, helping the disabled or disadvantaged become self-sufficient or less dependent on society in general. Still others including fraternal orders – Elks, Moose, and Lions Clubs – and organizations like Rotary International raise money and perform services for communities in which they live, based on the efforts of their members. Some reach out on a global basis to do good works, but all are suffering from declining membership and participation. Each of these organizations relies on marketing at one time or another to spread word of its efforts or its needs.

There are organizations that specialize in fund-raising campaigns for non-profit organizations. This area is a very challenging form of marketing since the rewards for the money spent are often vague, intangible, and realized at much later dates. The smart marketing person would be wise to volunteer for such an organization for two reasons: (1) it will do good for the community, charity, church, school, etc., and (2) you will learn a lot about the most challenging form of marketing – raising money for non-profit organizations and their causes.

Government marketing

Government marketing is almost an oxymoron. After all the government only buys what it needs right? Wrong! The government is still operated by people and people are influenced by marketing regardless of the position they hold and responsibilities they have. The problem in marketing to government organizations is that it is often necessary to suspend logic and adjust to the realities of the situation. I know governments should be logical, well-controlled organizations, which respond more predictably to good marketing. Don't believe that for a moment. Government organizations are ultimately controlled by either a huge bureaucracy or a political organization or (worse yet, and most common) both.

> "Never attribute governmental behavior to malice when it may be attributable only to sheer stupidity or ignorance – but sometimes it may be malice too!"
>
> An experienced Washington DC lawyer

The challenge when marketing to government organizations is a lot like industrial marketing – find who the key decision-makers are and market to them, in their own peculiar language. This is not always easy since there are "hidden agendas", specifications, and contract conditions that must be met, but these are always open to some interpretation. People do that interpretation. Don't forget or ignore that fact. The government in most developed countries is one of the largest spenders. Smart marketers make sure they get their share of that spending.

7 Consumer Marketing

Everybody is an expert

Everybody likes to talk about consumer goods marketing because we are all consumers and thus we all have a feeling that we know what we are talking about. And we do – but not completely and certainly not professionally. Marketing of consumer goods and services is arguably the most competitive, most demanding, and potentially most rewarding part of marketing.

This field of marketing is serious business, and the opening discussions about the marketing plan are worth mentioning again here. With the time pressures for fast decisions and actions, it is terribly tempting to "hip-shoot" or make "gut calls" on critical decisions. Smart advice is "don't do that"! Common sense goes a long way but it doesn't replace solid research combined with observation and analysis of what consumers want, what they have been buying and what they say/feel.

> "To the consumer, perception is truth....If perceptions are reality to consumers, then the perceptions which the marketer delivers must be consistent through all forms of communication or the consumer will simply ignore them."
>
> Don E. Schultz et al., *The New Marketing Paradigm*

Gut or intuitive decisions often rely on accumulated experience, which can't be easily articulated, but exists nonetheless. This kind of basis for a decision is useful, but a smart marketer realizes that there is an unknown factor in gut or intuitive decisions – the emotions and current situation of the decision-maker. What is at stake? What are the risks for the decision-maker? Is s/he objective, or can they be, given that their future, their reputation, even their livelihood might be at stake.

Know your customer

Smart consumer products and services marketing starts like all others – know your customer. Choose the targeted markets and segments wisely and carefully, and then do your homework. Find out about competition – what they do well and what they do poorly. Understand your consumers, not just on an aggregate average, but individually. What are they really buying? The old saying of years ago was that *"Black & Decker wasn't selling $9.99 electric drills, they were selling the ability to make holes cheaply and easily."* Too often, marketers use old experience on new problems. The line from Abraham Maslow's work comes to mind: *"When you have a hammer and know how to use it, every problem looks like a nail!"*

The longer a person is in a job, the more situations come up that are similar to past ones. Yet, each one is different – a different time, a different set of circumstances – even if only slightly. Using past experience without improved understanding, new learning, and adaptation will almost always result in mediocre or wrong solutions. Maybe they will only be a little bit wrong – if conditions are only a little bit different – but there is precious little room for error in today's business environment. Use old tools carefully, and constantly keep "sharpening them".

The pressure for rapid decisions, which leads to the kind of problems I just described, will not likely get any better. It will get worse. Time for deliberation just keeps shrinking. The smart marketer does his or her homework ahead of time whenever possible. The smart marketer also makes a sound marketing plan and then follows it, adjusting it as new information becomes available, but not skipping steps or taking risky shortcuts.

Find the right mix of old and new

The keys to successful consumer products and services marketing are constantly evolving. The new economy offers challenges and opportunities based on a mixture of bricks and mortar, clicks and mortar, and Internet marketing. A smart marketer carefully considers the differences in how and where products and services are offered, purchased, and delivered/used. A really smart marketer knows that this is a constantly shifting scenario and is continuously making adjustments based on new knowledge.

A costly shortcut at Huffy Bicycles – Crosswind

One of the greatest errors in my career came from just such a shortcut taken about ten years ago. A new bicycle we were developing for our featured, TV-advertised product was the victim of that shortcut – its name was *Crosswind*. It was a beautiful, deep metallic purple bike, and had a new Grip-Shift™ shifting system that was a lower-cost version of the most popular high-end model. We had proprietary rights to this shifting system for our market, and we fell in love with our own innovation – a dangerous practice to say the least.

Our normal process was to do comparative market research on new TV products to validate their consumer appeal versus competing products and our own prior best sellers. But this bike was in a whole new category ("hybrid or crossover" bikes, hence the name *Crosswind*) since it was not exactly a mountain bike and neither was it a lightweight racing/touring bike. Thus, we decided to test it against other "hybrid or crossover" bikes, even though there were not many competitors in that new category.

Part of our normal process was to test each bike in a mall-intercept style of consumer survey, asking them which one of four or five in a group they preferred, where models in the groups were all about the same price. (*Caution: Market research on what people will pay for something is notoriously unreliable – unless they are voting with money!*) Well, this bike beat all of the competitors in its class by a wide margin. We were ecstatic. But, in our haste to get the new product to market, and in the interest of saving a little time and market research money, we took a shortcut – we skipped one of our normal, final validation tests.

The normal final step was to mix different kinds of products of similar price-value levels together to see how the new ones fared in "mixed company". This step was most representative of retail settings since all kinds of products are mixed there for consumers to choose. Since we skipped that step (taking a shortcut), we did not find out that our sleek, beautiful hybrid bike, *Crosswind*, would have fared terribly when put up against bulky, well-equipped mountain bikes. Unfortunately we discovered that *after* launching the product and finding retail sales were awful. We ran an early flight of TV ads in one market to see if it was just that consumers didn't recognize the product. Nope! They just didn't see the value compared to the other products.

That shortcut and the hasty decision to take it cost us dearly. We mortgaged valuable retail placement space for *Crosswind* – and it didn't sell. That meant giving retailers "markdown money" to lower the price until the value looked right – which was a lot lower than we thought! Since we had scheduled and promised TV advertising, we were compelled to run it – to no avail.

Until the price was right, consumers just passed *Crosswind* by and even with markdown money retailers are slow to reduce retail prices. Then there was all of the backup inventory in our warehouses that was built to support TV-driven sales, and finally, we had huge quantities of unique components that were not usable on any of our "standard" products.

This simple shortcut cost us millions of dollars, untold amounts of management time, and damage to our credibility as product innovators (our record for the prior 7–8 years had been one of unparalleled success for our TV-advertised products). This is a good lesson to smart marketers everywhere: *watch out for shortcuts* – they can be the longest path between two points and are filled with pitfalls.

For example, software is ideal for sale on the Internet because it can be downloaded immediately. Instant gratification must not be underestimated as a part of the purchase process. Stores work well for things that must be physically seen and touched or used prior to the purchase. Items like books and music or video CDs are suitable for either traditional retail or Internet purchase because the actual item will vary little from what the purchaser expects – if they are familiar with it. Waiting for a day or two may be acceptable. For large, complex items traditional retailing usually wins, especially if the purchaser wants to use it as soon as they get it.

" 'Free' is a tough price to beat!"

If a purchaser is not familiar with a book, a traditional bookstore may win the retailing battle for that purchase because it offers a chance for browsing the book – and to have a cup of coffee at the same time. Music stores that offer the ability to listen to CDs may have a marketing edge and those that don't, may not – unless the desire to have it "right now" is strong enough. Downloads of music via MP-3 and Napster have emerged as a serious threat to conventional retail formats. What other products might be threatened similarly? What should a smart marketer do? Pay close attention to the compatibility between the wants and needs of the customer and what the product and its distribution format offers. Match those two well and you win! Mismatch them and too bad, you lose!

Tangible vs. intangible products = services and benefits

Most products are tangible. You can pick them up or touch them, feel them, and assess what they are all about. Lumpy objects are somehow easier for us to value. We can use our senses, and thus marketing such objects is based on an appeal to the senses as described in Chapter 4. What I want to cover here is the intangible "products", which are usually services of some kind, or the benefits of products which are not necessarily evident just by looking at the product. Marketing such intangible products and their benefits is a very different process. The same principles of value and customer satisfaction still apply – but how they apply is altered.

The marketer must understand what it is that the end-user is buying and deliver on the implied promise of performance, however clear or unclear it might be. In many cases this promise is part of the advertising or is printed on the packaging. In others it is simply implied. Take a couple of extra-strength Tylenol and pain should either be reduced or go away. Only if there is no perceptible difference might an end-user question the efficacy of the medicine – and then they would likely attribute the failure to improper use/application.

"Sell the sizzle not the steak."

Another useful idea about intangible or imagined benefits arises from research done several years ago. I've forgotten the source, but not the conclusions. A test was conducted on ski jackets, One jacket was tagged "down filled"; the next one was tagged "100% goose down filled"; the third one was tagged "100% Arctic goose down filled". Consumers consistently expected and were willing to pay more for the jacket as the tags became more descriptive of the contents of the jacket. They expected the "100% Arctic goose down filled" one to be much more costly – and worth it – than the "down filled" one. Even though all admitted that they realized that all of the down filling came from geese, the more descriptive the name, the more valuable the feature of the product. This concept can apply to a variety of

Hard vs. soft benefits – at Scotts and L. R. Nelson

Many years ago, I had a conversation with Lee Herron who was then CEO of Scotts Lawn Products. I was an executive of L. R. Nelson, which made lawnsprinklers, and we were discussing the difference in how our two product lines were marketed and perceived by consumers. Herron pointed out that when I sold a Nelson lawn-sprinkler, the end-user could readily evaluate (in his/her opinion) whether the sprinkler did what was expected. It whirled or sprayed water in about the expected pattern over an area approximately what the carton copy promised. As long as the sprinkler continued to work mechanically and do about what was expected, the end-user was likely to be satisfied with it. If it failed, the failure was likely to be fairly obvious. It might stop working, leak, spray in unintended directions, etc.

The Herron drew a contrast to what Scott's sells. He pointed out that Scott's products, while tangible enough (bags or bottles/cans of something) produced much less easily measurable results. If an end-user buys a bag of grass seed and spreads it on the lawn, and grass comes up, s/he is most likely satisfied. There is no easy way for the end-user to know how much grass should have come up. The same goes for fertilizer or weedkiller. If the grass turns greener, then it is assumed that the fertilizer worked. If weeds die, the weedkiller worked. If not all the weeds die, it's imagined that those might have come up after the application. If the greenness is not uniform, perhaps the application rate of the spreader wasn't uniform.

Thus tangible products can have varying tangible but vague benefits. What Lee Herron was telling me is that Scotts' customers can be satisfied without knowing whether the product performed exactly as intended or not, unlike my sprinkler customers, who could immediately see if the sprinkler stops moving or springs a leak.

products and is entirely legal as long as it does not misrepresent the truth.

Perishable products/yield management

A similar, yet different marketing situation is presented by perishable products and the use of yield management. You may think I am only talking about fresh fruit or fish. I'm not! I'm talking about unused capacity that once past its usage date can no longer be sold: airline seats, hotel rooms, rental cars – and factory production capacity! The

> **Great advice: "Build great partnerships with customers (wholesalers, retailers, consumers)"**
>
> "Learn as much as possible about the consumers of your products – their needs, wants, and product ideas that they may not have been able to articulate, but which they would like. For instance, consumers could not articulate the fact that they wanted a fabric softener that could be used in clothes dryers but when Bounce® was introduced to them, they loved it!"
>
> W. W. "Wally" Abbott

name given to the practice of maximizing the use of these kind of perishable products is "yield management". Smart marketers for these perishable items must not only create demand for the product or service, they must do so at the right times and in the right amounts – a considerably more challenging task. Variable pricing for the same item (like an airplane ticket or hotel room) has become a typical and accepted pricing practice used in yield management marketing. Higher demand equals higher price and vice versa.

Retailing

Retailing is all about location, location, location…and information, information, information which drives proper planning, strategy, store format, profit/volume models, mix/assortment decisions, and many more topics. Then comes execution of the plan, the Achilles heel of most retailers.

Location is important because it means the store is where its target shoppers would like it to be. Busy intersections are great for high traffic stores like gas and convenience stores, drug stores, etc. Locations close to large residential neighborhoods are great for home

> "The essential mission of retailing has always had four elements: getting the right product in the right place at the right price at the right time."
>
> Clayton Christenson and Richard S. Tedlow

improvement centers, hardware stores, video stores, dry cleaners, and neighborhood grocery stores. Large stores like Wal*Mart's Supercenters, Carrefour, and Home Depot stores are best situated in locations that have excellent highway access making them convenient for a large number of customers who travel by auto.

The difference between a good location and a bad one can be something as simple as traffic patterns and the ease/difficulty of turning across a busy highway. Highway changes that result in changing traffic patterns can dramatically alter the desirability of a retail location. There are many factors that dictate retail store locations including demographics of the area, growth patterns, traffic patterns, competitor's locations, etc. All of these are important keys to retail success.

What do they do better than us, and what can we learn from that?

By now, the smart marketer is saying, "OK, but why go into all of this retail location stuff?" The answer is *because most of it applies inside the store just as much as outside* – and most marketers are very, very interested in what goes on inside the store. (They don't put batteries and breath mints by the checkout lines and gas stations near busy intersections for no reason!)

Locations also have direct influence on industrial distributor success. You will notice they are usually located in a convenient area for their customers too. Customers are customers, and will get things where they are the most easily, conveniently, and obviously available. Obvious conclusion – sure – but don't ever forget it.

Retail stores all operate on largely similar principles. They buy merchandise as cheaply as they can and present it in a merchandising style consistent with their "format". Kmart or Tesco presents goods in a "general merchandise discount store format" – bulk displays, located with like categories together and appropriate signage and price information, since floor sales help is almost non-existent. A camera shop or electronics/ computer store may be densely packed with goods, but usually offers floor sales help in the selection, and thus has only representative samples on the "displays" or in enclosed glass cases. Department stores like Marks & Spencer or Nordstrom will offer goods in a stylish, fashion-oriented display that is either artistically tasteful or lifestyle oriented. No-frills warehouse clubs stack it high and sell in volume – at very low profit margins. The goal: once you get the customer inside, make sure they buy something.

> 85% of people are right-handed and turn right when they enter a store. Are we considering that?

Profit and turn format formulas

Each of these retail formats has a formula which relates the margin at which they can succeed, and the inventory turns which they must achieve to permit their margin to earn an acceptable return on the invested capital they employ.

- *Discounters* usually aim for around 25% margin, and hope for about five inventory turns. *Multiplying 25 × 5 = 125.*

- *Department stores* more likely aim for 35–40%+ margins, and will be satisfied with three or four inventory turns due to the greater range of styles and sizes. *Multiplying 37.5 × 3.5 = 131.*

- *High-end boutique/specialty shops* might aim for 50%+ margins ("keystone" pricing is what this is called – doubling the cost – or equal to 100% markup) but must live with only 2.5 inventory turns due to the uniqueness of the assortment. *Multiplying 50 × 2.5 = 125.*

> "If it ain't turning, it ain't earning."
>
> A retail executive

- *Warehouse clubs* only make a 10% gross margin, but typically only have ±30 days of inventory on hand, for 12+ inventory turns. *Multiply 10 × 12 = 120.*

- *Internet retailers* can work on as low as 5% margins, because they carry very little inventory – just enough to have the goods come in and go out, and some are even direct shipped by manufacturers. Their inventory turns will be as high as 25! *Let's do the multiplication again: 5 × 25 = 125.*

Do you see the trend emerging? All channels need to earn returns that are in a similar range and this can be approximated by multiplying the gross margin times the inventory turns. This is not precise because there are widely different investments in the selling environments between department stores and warehouse clubs, but, as you can see, those are at the two extremes. Comparisons of actual results from major US retailers showed a wide range – from 80 to 170 – and not surprisingly, those at the low end were having financial problems, while those at the high end were doing very well.

The fact that Internet retailers and warehouse clubs are built on a "negative working capital model" favorably influences their ability to earn good returns even with significantly lower profit margins. What's this "negative working capital model" I am talking about? Simple: working capital is the money you need to pay employees, to pay suppliers for goods, to carry inventory, etc., until the purchasers pay you. If Internet retailers or warehouse clubs can sell the goods and collect from their customers (which they do) before they have to pay their suppliers, they don't need any working capital for that purpose. In fact, it becomes a negative number – they collect before they must pay. Large retailers like Wal*Mart are striving to achieve this in its discount store/supercenter division by accelerating inventory turns and stretching supplier payment terms. Wal*Mart is more than 63% of the way to having sold and collected from consumers for goods before paying for them!

When retail stores fail to make the required combinations – margins times inventory turns – they eventually fail (financially), unless they can find a source of cheap working capital to sustain them. This is why product mix and margin is so important for the smart marketer to understand.

Direct sales

"There's a sucker born every day."

P. T. Barnum

One of the toughest calls in today's environment is when, if, and how to sell direct when you are already selling to the intermediate customer. This is commonly called *channel conflict*, in which you essentially compete with your customers. Giant retailers like Home Depot have made it eminently clear that they take a dim view of suppliers who try to sell around them via the Internet. In fact, they have threatened to drop that supplier's offerings – and probably will – if any are foolish enough to take that risk.

The starting point for this topic goes back to the discussion of strategy – who do you want to sell, what, and how? If you want to sell retailers, then selling direct will almost certainly raise their ire, and complicate your life. If you want to sell direct – fine – the retailers are no longer your primary customers. They are your competitors! You better decide this one early and firmly. A little waffling here can be deadly.

If there are products you want to sell that the retailers do not want to carry, enlist them as partners in a direct selling effort. Get them to be part of the sale, and then maintain your role as their supplier – not their competitor. If they say, "go ahead and sell it direct" *be careful*. This is still making you a competitor and will come back to bite you in the end. The market can only generate so many sales in a given product or service category/segment. Any goods that you sell direct are coming out of the same market category your customer is selling. In my book, that makes you competitors.

And there are no such things as "friendly competitors" – that is an oxymoron. If the product or service is in a totally different category, segment, etc., still proceed with caution. Each type of sales you expand into adds complexity to your business. The more things you try to do, the less chance you will do them all well.

Trends, fads, and foolishness

One of the most serious challenges in marketing is deciding what is a trend versus a fad. Trends are longer-term directions taken by industries and segments. Fads are short-lived whims that usually waste more marketing resources than they are worth. Once this evaluation has been made, then comes the decision about committing resources. In the toy industry, video games have been a growing trend for the past few years. However, some faddish video-like toys have come and gone in a single season, leaving nothing but a shelf full of closeouts and a ledger of losses.

Tools in the marketing toolkit

No section on retailing would be complete without a mention of the many promotional tools marketers use to separate consumers from their money. Influencing consumers in favor of buying your product instead of the competitors' is one of the key jobs of the smart marketer. Let's just go through some of the most common ways this is done:

> "You can lead a horse to water, but you can't make it drink."
>
> Anonymous

- *On sale* – the most common and still one of the most powerful tools. The sale price usually represents a discount from some previously established retail or regular price. Caution: Sears got in big trouble because they failed to establish the regular retail prior to claiming that the item was "on sale" for a substantial savings.

- *New and improved* – the famous line used by consumer goods marketers for years. Procter & Gamble has taken products like Tide detergent through dozens of product changes that made it "New & Improved" over and over.

- *Discounts and bonuses* – the familiar cents-off coupons, percent-off sales, bonus packages like "buy one, get one free" or for 1¢, extra-size packages which give larger quantities for no higher price; these are all examples of incentives offered to consumers to get them to buy.

- *Introductory specials* – the cellular phone industry is using this one ad nauseam in efforts to capture customers, including giving free phones as a bonus for signing a lengthy service agreement.

- *Free trials* – common on large ticket items especially if sold via a medium where trying the product is difficult or impossible. Products like air-cushion mattresses and large pieces of fitness equipment use this approach. Try it for *x* days and return it if not satisfied. (Of course these are very awkward things to return!)

- *Rebates and free/cheap financing* – these incentives are used with large ticket item sales, such as autos, mobile homes, furniture, etc. TV merchants like QVC use multi-payment plans, which bundle the financing into the price.

- *Infomercials* – those intrusive and persuasive shows that seem to be on when there is little else to watch, hawking wares that are "too good to be true" – and they usually are! Money-back guarantees and 30–90 day free trials are common in this kind of impulse-purchase marketing.

- *Come see it and buy it* – a common tool to sell vacation homes, timeshare properties, and other resort properties is to provide either a cheap or free stay at the property in return for listening to a sales pitch.

(!)

"Never underestimate the motivational value of money."

There are many other kinds of sale incentives, so this list could go on for pages. The ones above are just some of the most common and widely used.

Blurring boundaries

In retailing, like in most other industries, the smart marketer needs to realize that the segment boundaries are blurring more and more. What do I mean by that? Consider aWalgreen store. You will find food, clothing, and selected durable goods, as well as all of the normal drugs and sundries. There will also be a full photo lab for one-hour film processing and a convenient drive-through pickup window.

"My biggest weakness in life is that I can't say no."

Richard Branson

Wal*Mart is opening "Neighborhood Markets" which are sized comparably to stand-alone US grocery stores (40,000 sq. ft.), but stocked with a blend of grocery, drug, and general merchandise. Wal*Mart, Target, Kmart, Carrefour, Meijer, and others are building 200,000 sq. ft. behemoths that stock everything a full service grocery store and a huge general merchandise discount store would carry – plus much more. Most include services like hair salons, optical stores, fast food restaurants, auto service centers, garden shops, etc.

How does a marketer segment the market when such blurring of boundaries is growing? More carefully than ever, by understanding the differences and specialties of each format in great detail and then targeting/serving those that match your strategy. Sometimes the hardest decision will be who and what *not to sell*!

Lessons from marketing wins and losses

In this section, I review several well-known consumer product companies with icon-like brand names, and draw lessons for smart marketers from what they have done or failed to do successfully. You see, it is easier to do post-mortems and explain successes and failures after you know how they turn out. Unfortunately you won't have the luxury of 20–20 hindsight when you are making marketing decisions. But after all, that is what you'll get paid the big bucks for! Let's go!

A success story: Volkswagen/US

This is a classic success story of a company that resurrected its product line and brand from the scrapheap in the US market. In 1970, VW sold 570,000 vehicles in the US. Its Beetle, Minibus, and Kharmann Ghia sport model were the symbols of the sixties' generation. Then disaster struck. The serious German management could not understand these crazy Americans and how they "made fun of" VW cars. So, the Germans stopped selling the fun products and introduced a suitably serious product line to the US. This was a bad mistake!

> "It ain't what you don't know that'll kill you. It's what you think you know that ain't so!"
>
> Will Rogers

VW sales plummeted to a low of 49,500 units in 1993. This was a brand and a company that was almost out of the US market. Not only was the VW brand damaged, but also its upscale Audi line was the primary victim of the accidental acceleration scare. Then someone got smart at VW. VW knows how to make good cars, so it started with that skill, added some whimsy for the "crazy Americans" and some sizzling style for the upscale baby boomers, and *voila!* – the new Volkswagen.

Led by the rebirth of the Beetle (but on an Audi-like platform), VW began its resurgence. The new, redesigned Audi line parlayed sophisticated styling and all-wheeldrive into a solid niche position among the big luxury auto makers Mercedes-Benz, BMW, and Lexus. Then VW "knocked off" its own Audi styling to make the Jetta and Passat models to sell alongside the Beetle. In 2003, VW sold 603,000 cars in the US (source: conceptcar.co.uk) and this growing level of sales was fueled by its "DriversWanted" advertising campaign, emphasizing the combination of visual uniqueness and excellent drivability.

VW is once again a solid player in the US market. Why? *Because it decided to sell what its customers wanted to buy and not what it wanted to sell. Then VW built on its technical strength to make sure that was what it delivered.*

A failure: Levi's

This legendary maker of denim jeans is a brand that almost became a generic name for this style of clothing. Unfortunately, it lost its way as a marketer over a number of years and slipped badly. Sales declined from $7.1 billion in 1996 to $5.1 billion in 1999. Profits plummeted and plant closings multiplied as Levi's tried to restructure itself to maintain profitability in spite of declining sales.

"...change in the way companies operate their business is often precipitated by reaching a high level of pain."

George E. Palmatier and Joseph S. Shull, *The Marketing Edge*

Worse than the financial woes is the fact that Levi's lost its appeal to its two most important customer groups – teens and baby boomers. The company's marketing was insensitive to customers at a critical time when styles were changing and competitors were squeezing from both directions. Designer jeans from Polo, Tommy Hilfiger, Gap, Diesel, and many others took the premium business. VF Corporation's Lee and Wrangler brands captured the growing discount store volume, while Sears and J. C. Penney's private label goods squeezed Levi's on popular priced jeans.

Then Levi's made a number of confusing marketing moves in the area of Internet retailing. Overconfidence about the power of the Levi's brand name led to this débâcle. These moves included launching its own online stores (remember the warning about competing with your customers) and then bailing out of that web venture and turning the distribution over to (just a couple of) department store web sites. This probably hurt Levi's image, credibility, and trade relations more than it hurt sales. The Levi's web site was not pulling in the key teen purchasers anyway, and it's "bells & whistles" design made it slow-loading for those teens who did try to access it via dial-up modem lines.

Not only was Levi's suffering from marketing woes of losing touch with its prime customers, it also had product and production problems. Levi's desire to keep its production in the US increased its costs, and did not yield the offsetting benefits of responding fast to trend changes because marketing was missing the trend changes in the first place. Then some key Levi's customers, like J. C. Penney, lost share of retail market to stores like Gap/Old Navy which carried its own brands. As if this was not enough, Levi's tried some "knee-jerk" marketing recoveries.

Levi's tried to recover the favor of the teen market, but its teen attitude "Silver Tab" ads were offputting to older consumers. Its "Engineered Jeans" unusual cut and not-too-evident features were a tough sell in today's largely self-service retail environment. Levi's missed trends like flared jeans, cargo jeans, and stretch jeans, many

How consumers make buying decisions

1. Problem (Need) Recognition

2. Search

3. Alternative Evaluation

4. Choice

5. Satisfaction or Dissatisfaction

Dr Roger Blackwell

of which appealed to the aging (and growing) baby boomer segment – the second largest market for its products.

In June 2000, Levi's announced a continued sales decline of "only 6.4%" after reporting double-digit decreases in recent quarters. Operational improvements provided improved earnings in spite of decreasing sales. In the words of one analyst, "the sales declines are decreasing" – faint praise! New CEO Philip Marineau said it better, "To be honest, this is no quick fix." The question is how do you stop and reverse a downhill slide? The answer is great marketing, or more specifically "by having what people want to buy" and then selling what you have in the places where they shop!

By 2003 Levi's sales had recovered to $4.1 billion, though this was still 43% less than their performance eight years previously.

The lesson: *Never, ever take your eyes and your ears off what the your customers are doing and saying (wanting and buying), and watch out for getting "caught in the middle", in a squeeze play between higher lines "cachet" and lower lines "value".* That middle ground is a tough place to be.

School is still out: Nike

Nike is the king of the athletic shoe market, but the king is getting old, and a palace revolt is underway. Led by a rejuvenated European brand, Adidas, the palace revolt is coming from many directions. Outdoor shoes for hiking cut into the athletic shoe (sneaker) market. So have the orthopedic sandals epitomized by Birkenstock and Clark's comfy yet casual styles. As Nike spends millions on athletic endorsements and institutional (or is it attitudinal) advertising, it is under fire for the labor practices in its Asian factories.

School is still out as Nike attempts to market its way out of trouble. It is trying to compensate for the shift away from athletic shoes with its

ACG (All Conditions Gear) product line of outdoor wear. An appeal to women athletes, both the advanced ones and midstream active women, is intended to tap that large market. That may be its wisest move yet, since this is a huge and lucrative market segment.

Meanwhile Nike cuts costs and inventories as its retailers struggle. Nike's paid endorsers still represent the cream of the athletic crop, led by young golf star Tiger Woods. Nike continues to use showcase stores in prestigious shopping locations like Chicago's Miracle Mile on Michigan Avenue, and outlet stores in most of the newer outlet malls. But this form of competing with its customers may give an edge to competitors like Adidas, Reebok, New Balance, and others when selling to major retailers.

Time will tell on this one. *Lesson to take away: It's perilous at the top of any industry and there is only one way to go – and that is down – and all of the competitors are trying to take you down.* It takes constant vigilance and intense competitive marketing efforts to stay on top! Mistakes are costly.

> "Online advertising has to be integrated holistically into a brand's overall marketing plan. A consumer should feel like the same brand is speaking to him, whether it's market research, online advertising or an e-commerce click-to-buy interaction."
>
> Vivienne Bechtold, Procter & Gamble's director of I-Knowledge

Making the turn: McDonald's

Here is one marketing story that will confound the theorists. The question is whether McDonald's, the world's largest restaurant chain, is making brilliant moves or is a "day late and a dollar short". McDonald's created the fast-food hamburger industry, and is clearly the industry behemoth. Its store count is up to 31,000 worldwide at the end of 2003. It has undertaken major steps to abandon its outdated "batch-mass production" model of making sandwiches in favor of its "custom cooking system" which is more of a "mass customization/assembly line" system. The problem is that stores are struggling to learn its use while keeping up with peak demand. Waiting lines are growing, and in this industry, that's bad. Will the learning curve kick in soon? Who knows?

McDonald's has at least awakened from its corporate marketing paralysis and begun doing new things. The new cooking system was a big one. Customers want it "their way", which competitors Burger King and Wendy's already provided (but fortunately Burger King still has its gun loaded and aimed directly at its own feet.) This will give McDonald's operators time to learn how to use the new cooking system. Meanwhile, McDonald's advertising is attempting to convince consumers that making sandwiches "on-demand" is their idea! If this works it will be a major coup!

Now taste is another issue. While McDonald's focused on healthier sandwiches, Wendy's made them taste better. The key marketing call here was what people want – better tasting or less fattening/healthier food. The answer, I'm afraid (for McDonald's), was better taste. While everyone in developed countries is watching dietary content of meals more than ever, a person who is really concerned about this doesn't choose a fast-food burger place anyway. Greasy French fries with a lowfat burger are simply an edible oxymoron. At least the new McDonald's sandwiches are more focused on "tasting good".

Diversification at McDonald's has more or less failed. Why? Because, as Al Reis and Jack Trout constantly remind us in their books on positioning, *"once you have a position in the mind of the consumer, it is terribly hard to change it"*. And you shouldn't try anyway. McDonald's is hamburgers and fries, breakfast and lunch – but not dinner! (These

"In the same way we distinguish personal attention from inattention, we can tell the difference between a commercial pitch and words that come when someone's life animates their message."

Rick Levine *et al.*, *The Cluetrain Manifesto*

new acquisitions are dinner places.) Why fight it. Simply make the best-tasting, fastest, most consistent, and inexpensive hamburgers and fries.

McDonald's new 'Plan to Win' strategy refocused the business back into its old success story, with, of course, a new Chairman and CEO.

> " . . . many managers and marketers have forgotten what provides value to customers; what truly satisfies customer; what turns them on. . . . Value is provided only by satisfying needs."
>
> Bernd Schmitt and Alex Simonson, *Marketing Aesthetics*

There is a lesson here: *Understand what you are in your customers' minds and don't try to be something else – it'll just confuse them and drive them away – and be the best one of those that there is. Above all, understand what made you successful and build on it, but don't rest on your laurels.*

Many other lessons, but so little time to study them There are dozens more stories like these, but in the interests of space and time, I'll just hit the high points of a few.

Starbucks

It's a relief that Starbucks is abandoning its misguided web/lifestyle venture and getting back to what it's good at – which is not necessarily just coffee, but being the coffee, food, and experience/place. *You can make brief (misguided) excursions from your core business, but as soon as you see it is not working, get back to what made you successful in the first place.*

Wrigley's Gum

The prime audience, kids and teens, is getting pulled away by other "oral treats" – the answer: reinvent yourself and "freshen your breath, and your product line"! Nostalgia only goes so far. *Knock off yourself before somebody does it to you.*

> "Our view of strategy has changed from the classic Coca-Cola versus Pepsi market share fight to how do you shape the emergence of the new opportunity areas, whether its branchless banking, satellite telephony or genetic engineering."
>
> Gary Hamel

Coke

Maybe it's still "the real thing", but its mistakes chronicled in the worldwide press have made it a "real mess". Problems with the corporate image can hurt a brand. So can dilution (pun intended) by other kinds of drinks – which Coke is doing as it expands its product offerings to cover 232 brands, some of which are far outside its "cola" franchise. In many of these brands it has a much smaller advantage in mind-share over competitors. Fortunately, like its partner McDonald's, Coke's entrenched world brand position will let them muddle through. *If you're going to sell wholesome products, be a wholesome company, and then stick to your knitting!*

PepsiCo

Pepsi is not just a beverage company – in fact the larger part of PepsiCo's revenue and profits comes not from soft drinks but from salty snacks. Does the name Frito-Lay ring a bell? This dominant leader in snacks is PepsiCo's jewel. Frito-Lay controls about 40% of the world market for salty snacks and contributes over 70% of PepsiCo's profit. Former CEO Roger Enrico got rid of the drain of PepsiCo's fast-food chains and spun off capital intensive bottling into an independent public company.

And, while Pepsi is still second to Coke in colas, its Mountain Dew edged out Diet Coke for third place. Pepsi's Aquafina bottled water brand is also number one, and Pepsi's Lipton Iced Tea brand has a whopping 16-point share lead over Coke's Nestea. PepsiCo's Tropicana Pure Premium is the US's largest selling orange juice, and recently passed Campbell Soup as the third largest US grocery brand.

But not everything PepsiCo is doing is a winner. If you read my book *Smart Things to Know about Brands and Branding* you know I predicted that Pepsi "One" (a one-calorie cola) would be a resounding "ho-hum", if not an abject failure. I still think so. If Pepsi had spent the ad dollars on its core products of Pepsi and Diet Pepsi against a faltering Coke, it would have enjoyed much greater success. Spend this money on your strong existing brands, until a whole new market segment is found.

> "The way you build a brand and create enduring value has more to do with the day-to-day execution by tens of thousands of people on the front line than it does with the brand manager with the hot idea."
>
> Roger Enrico, CEO PepsiCo

Tommy Hilfiger

Overexposure will kill an upscale brand's cachet. As soon as every-body can get "it" at most retailers, it loses its exclusivity and that was what "it" was all about in the first place. Ralph Lauren knows that and manages it better than anyone. Tommy Hilfiger doesn't. Watch for the real Tommy stuff in discount stores inside of a year. Let me say it again: *Overexposure will kill an upscale brand's marketing cachet. As soon as everybody has it, it loses its exclusivity and that was what "it" was all about in the first place.*

Gucci Group/Yves Saint Laurent

The Gucci brand first, and now Yves Saint Laurent were victims of overexposure. Both are being pulled back, which is a wise move. These are status brands with unequaled cachet – until they were overextended and overexposed. Tom Ford and Domenico De Sole are cutting licenses back dramatically and adding exclusive shops and increased consistency of collections worldwide in order to reclaim the image of these two great brands. Great move. The lesson again: *Exclusive brands are hard to get and expensive – keep them that way.*

Miller Lite

Who knows what they are up to? Who cares whether it "tastes great or is less filling"? The models are cute and the sports figures engaging, but what is the marketing hook? Having a beer is a celebration, a relaxation, and a social event. Why is this so tough to advertise? Marketing beer is hard because the differentiation is so marginal. In blind taste tests, what percentage of people could identify their own beer? About half – the same as random chance. You have to appeal to the serious beer drinkers (who consume the most beer, by far), and they are there for celebration, relaxation, and socializing. *Always remember what your customer (really) wants from your product – not what you want!*

Virgin . . . whatever

Virgin's greatest problem is that it is unfocused. The brand does not confer credibility on all of its widely disparate companies until they prove they can live up to its promise – which many of them have not. Virgin is a reflection of its founder – personable, exuberant, but unpolished. The longer Richard Branson keeps putting the Virgin name on businesses that are failing or doing poorly, the more damage he does to it for the future.

Saturn

I probably should write a whole book on GM's marketing mistakes, but who would read a 1000-page book? GM is doing a fine job of trying to confuse customers about the only car that it has in its lineup whose customer satisfaction exceeds the Japanese imports. GM came to market late with the new, larger Saturn model, and first positioned it as an alternative to the ho-hums in the Japanese product lines like Nissan Altima, and what did they get? A bigger ho-hum. Recently it is being slotted against the Honda Accord and Toyota Camry. Do these guys have a death wish? These are the consensus finest family sedans in the world. Even thought the new Saturn is a nice car, talk about creating high expectations. Then dealers are given money to use on "advertising and promotion" – as in rebates – *ugh*. What happened to the highly successful theme of "The Saturn's Family"? What happened to "Caring about its Customers"? Of course we know – only GM could liquidate market share and confuse/damage a customer franchise so fast and so well (or is it badly?). Lately the Saturn ads have positioned it as a cheap luxury car. Next thing they'll do is make a Saturn with a Cadillac grille and call it a Cadillac. Don't laugh, it's happened before. Lesson: *If you want to know what to do in marketing, study GM and then do something different.*

"If you try to become everything to everybody, you risk becoming nothing to anybody."

IV Trends that Are Shaping Marketing

8 Marketing and the "Monster"

The five smartest things to know about marketing

- You must have a plan

- Get close to the customer

- Do your homework

- Remember relationships

- **Use the speed and reach of technology**

Marketing in the era of the Internet

The monster in the title of this chapter is the Internet. We all have heard the phrase "The Internet changes everything." Or at least that is the popular mantra. Well it does – or at least it changes so much, that everything must change to accommodate it. Life will never be the same again – nor will marketing. Maybe so, maybe not – it depends on the situation!

How on earth can I write just a single chapter about this incredible

"Through the Internet, people are discovering and inventing new ways to share relevant knowledge with blinding speed. As a direct results, markets are getting smarter – and getting smarter faster than most companies."

Rick Levine *et al.*, *The Cluetrain Manifesto*

topic? How does all of this affect marketing? The Internet is like the monster in a science fiction movie – it is all over the place, enormous, growing by leaps and bounds, and capable of incredible feats of power. Like mythical monsters, everyone is talking about it. The media is full of it. Different people describe it as a great force for good or evil. All agree that it is awesome and some prefer to say fearsome. The books are coming out faster than anyone can read them – or heed them. Yet, in keeping with Smart books, I will try to give you at least this one chapterful of *Smart Things to Know about Marketing* – and the Monster – specifically slanted to the Internet's monstrous impact.

When massive change occurs, the first rule is always to consult a "guru". I chose Peter Drucker, who is my candidate for being considered the Albert Einstein of business for the 20th century.

"We live in an economy where knowledge, not buildings and machinery, is the chief resource and where knowledge workers make up the biggest part of the work force. . . . A great thing about knowledge is that it – like today's pension and 401(k) plans is mobile and transferable. It belongs to you, not your employer. And it is highly marketable today."

Peter Drucker

Now, if that is not sufficient motivation for you to become a smart marketer, and to accumulate as much knowledge as quickly as possible, I don't know what is. And, if the emphasis on speed is not enough, I'll add my own view, echoing that of Gary Hamel – we are in the midst of a revolution in which the victories will go to the swiftest and the smartest but above all, to the *well-prepared revolutionaries*. Why? *Because the Internet changes the speed and reach of marketing, but it does not change the fundamentals*. Success depends on attacking, but with a good strategy and a sound plan and then superb execution of the basics.

The power and potential

First, how big is the Internet, and how many users are there, using it how often? Nobody knows! That's a fact. It's really big! That's something everyone agrees on, and it's growing really fast too. Sound like lines from a science fiction movie as the "monster" is described? Sure does!

> "Today, a company can gain a competitive advantage via the Internet. Tomorrow, it will be standard equipment."
>
> Vaughn Baker, Valu.net

Before you say your brain is not up to dealing with all this, remember that the human brain has a computing power of 20,000,000,000,000,000 CPS (calculations per second) while the best our most common PCs can do is 2,000,000,000 CPS. So, for the time being, we still have an edge of 20,000,000 times on our PCs – although at times we don't feel that way.

There are more than 250 million active web sites, and page counts are still growing fast, by perhaps as many as 2 million pages per day. Every day another 200,000 new Internet access devices and 150,000 web users jump online. Some estimates say there are over a billion people using the Internet, but what does "using" mean? Does that mean used it once? Used it regularly? When I send a robot shopping for me, do all of the sites I never see because they didn't have what I want count me as "using them"? Probably! Did I? I'm not sure. This is sort of like the old question, "If a tree falls in the forest and no one is there to hear it, did it make a sound?" No one can quite agree on how to define "using it", so the statistics are approximate at best. But they are *huge* regardless of their exact accuracy!

"Unless a new technology solves consumer problems better than their current solutions, the technology will ultimately fail."

Roger Blackwell and Kristina Stephan, "The Retail Paradigm"

I guess I "used" these sites or my robot did, anyway, so let's count them, even though I never saw them and don't know which ones they are. How about when I click back and forth on my financial research site looking at stocks? How many times do I get counted? I am only one unique visitor – which is the term now being used as the best indicator of web traffic. Clicks (or hits) which were used early in the web's media lifetime are misleading. If there are five frames on my home page (there are), then if you click on www.mariotti.net, do I count you as one click or five? You may not even wait for all of them to finish loading if you find the button you want and it has loaded. You just click on through to what you were looking for.

All of this matters a lot to marketers. It is important to know whether you really captured the eye and mind of a potential purchaser of whatever you are marketing. How long I stay matters too. The techies refer to that as the "stickiness" of a web site and its viewer. If I was trying to buy something, did I? Did I put it in a shopping basket and then abandon it – a common experience for web-based sellers. More than two-thirds of shopping baskets are abandoned and the sale is not completed. I guess those sites were not sticky enough!

How can we use the Internet to serve our customers better, and beat our competitors to doing it?

And we can do all this really fast. To complete a transaction that might have to travel 5000 miles between a group of seven or eight network hubs, switches, and servers takes only a few seconds. What takes the most time is for the site to load onto your computer. That's where a lot of merchants lose their prospective customers. Slow loading sites, no matter how "cool", tend to lose impatient web surfers/shoppers.

On web sites that are fun and functional...

"Utilize your web sites to help deliver your product and brand promise. Don't put everything you want to say on a package or display. The product web sites – www.duckproducts.com and www. loctiteproducts.com – help consumers with product information and project advice. The fun site, www.ducktapeclub.com, drives the brand and entertains Duck tape users and web site enthusiasts.

Gary Medalis, VP Advertising & Communications, Manco, Inc.

An invisible monster, big and getting bigger

So what do we have so far? This really big, really powerful, rapidly growing monster that is really fast, and that we can be all over without ever seeing it or knowing where we have been. Sounds even more like a sci-fi monster now. Marketing people must learn to cope with all this. It is a viable form of media. In the decade to come, it's probably the most critical form of media and we are all neophytes. How on earth do you decide what it is worth, what it should cost, and what benefits come from using it? Now you understand the problem.

Have you visited the site and looked at it or used it yourself?

When you buy traditional advertising, there is a measure called CPM (cost per thousand) which measures cost based on how many people saw your ad. On the Internet they talk about capturing "eyeballs", and what those are worth. The answer – at its current stage of "eyeball" capture – is "not very much" and it's very hard to quantify at that. Content sites like AOL and portals like Yahoo! are the best formats to capture eyeballs. They are frequently visited, and revisited as web surfers search for the real destination. Value sites like amazon, Travelocity, eBay, etc., which are actually visited with an intention in mind – to buy or sell something – are the next best. Because of these blurry uncertainties, the future of Internet advertising will move to a new "pay for performance" model.

But, it is still unclear how much these kind of "good quality eyeballs" are worth compared to traditional ads. A TV ad runs for 30 seconds, and you may catch 5–7 seconds of that. Is that equal to a 5–7 second pause at Yahoo? Maybe, if the intended message gets through. TV's animation capability is able to convey far more complex messages than the Internet (at its current rate of video transmission), so the TV ad wins. Maybe the Yahoo stop is more like a 5–7 second dwell on a simple magazine ad. When the 27 million TVs (and the 19 million VCRs and 10 million audio systems) sold each year become truly Internet enabled, then the phenomenon of media "convergence" will take hold and these considerations will all become a blurry mass of audience-users, viewers, surfers, or whatever.

When we get to B2B (business to business) web sites, there will be more "stickiness". Visitors usually want something specific – an "electronic errand" for lack of a better term – which keeps them there a bit longer and makes the ad delivery better. But how much better is it? No one has yet figured out how to measure it. If someone tells you they know that answer, question them hard. I'd bet they are oversimplifying things.

How big is a lot?

Let's go back to trying to see how big the monster is and how fast it's growing. Maybe that will help us assign some value to advertising on it or doing market research using the Internet.

Overall, it's easy to imagine 250-plus million active Internet users, and that number is growing rapidly as personal computers spread into the poorer but more populous countries like China, India, Indonesia, Malaysia, etc. But which ones are your target customers?

> "You'll see a transition (on the Internet) from information to relationships. Great brands can't exist just by providing information. The great ones have a mystery and sensuality. Our task is to create the mystery and sensuality on the Internet. Right now we're failing hopelessly, just hopelessly."
>
> Kevin Roberts

Remember marketing is about segmenting the market to find the targets for what you want to sell. Shooting with a shotgun is easy, but inefficient, and so is Internet advertising, but *wow*, what a speed and reach it has!

What about the most popular sites, and their traffic? It probably makes a difference whether the Internet use is from home or work – and that is something a smart marketer needs to understand.

Good luck in knowing how many people you are reaching, and at what cost. "A lot", but how do you know with any accuracy how big "a lot" is? What did you get for your money?

"If we can't calculate it, let's guess at it and then start improving the accuracy of our guesses."

The Internet has permeated both home and work. Beyond a doubt, the power and potential of the Internet is huge, and the challenge of using it for smart marketing is equally large. This power is one of the forces behind the so-called "new economy" which drove the US stock markets to new heights and even greater volatility.

Hundreds of established executives and even more middle managers have bailed out of so-called "old economy" companies for the thrill and potential riches of Internet-based "new economy" companies. As they do so, the realization quickly hits them that they are not really sure what it is they have undertaken to tame or control. A few win and are liberally publicized. The majority fail and either sink into obscurity or rebound to find new jobs. When the term "burn rate" (i.e. the rate at which they "burned through" cash in a startup) is considered a positive résumé factor, you know lunacy is not far behind!

The Internet's impact on brands and advertising

The Internet has made possible some things previously thought impossible. One of these is building a brand that is essentially a household name in just a few years. Legendary brand builders like Coke, Marlboro, Mercedes-Benz, and Kodak took decades to build their brands. Yahoo, amazon.com, eBay, and America Online have done it in less than five years.

What does that say about the value of traditional brands? It says they are threatened by faster growing competition more than they ever imagined. Yet, in spite of this, brands endure as the most powerful tool in marketing for conveying the desired message to prospective customers.

> "People are throwing money at businesses that wouldn't pass simple due diligence screens five years ago."
>
> Jim Breyer, Accel Partners

The book listing *The World's Greatest Brands* published just a few short years ago by Interbrand, and listed in my book *Smart Things to Know about Brands and Branding*, is changing very rapidly due to the influence of the Internet and the acceleration of change in global business. Once you know that, you have an advantage on those who are still in denial – assuming that "this too will pass". It may pass, but like the aftermath of a plague of locusts, nothing will ever be the same again. Either get ahead of the curve or find a foxhole and hope it doesn't turn into your (or your company's) grave!

Clicks and mortar vs. bricks and mortar

Marketers the world over, along with writers, consultants, academics, and every other type of expert (that may or may not include

> Did you realize how fast the Internet spread to 50 million users in the US? It only took one-tenth the time radio took and one-quarter the time the PC took to reach that many people!
>
> Time to reach 50 million users (in the US):
>
> | | |
> |---|---|
> | Radio | 38 years |
> | TV | 13 years |
> | PCs | 16 years |
> | Internet | 4 years |
>
> *Source:* US Department of Commerce

investors and analysts), are pondering the future of "clicks and mortar" vs. "bricks and mortar". In other words will the Internet make traditional retailing obsolete? The more outspoken Internet advocates have predicted such a dire fate for traditional retailing. Just like the experts at the turn of the last century who predicted that if nothing were done, the projected growth in the number of horses pulling buggies would leave the world knee deep in horse manure, they were wrong!

The Internet is a wonderful marketing tool and a very effective selling tool. It will not replace regular retail because retail shopping is

> Q: Who has done unique things in the European market as a new economy company doing old economy sorts of things?
>
> A: A European company doing neat things is Egg!
>
> Egg was "hatched" in late 1998 providing direct financial services and attracting customers with its higher than normal interest rates on savings. In 6 months, Egg had 500,000 customers, and $7.5 billion. Egg is now up to 3,000,000 online customers.

Marketers need new skills

1. Skills in building the company's reputation

2. Skills in managing the customer portfolio and database

3. Skills in creating images, experiences, and solutions – not only products

4. Skills in building a network of win–win partnerships (employees, suppliers, distributors)

5. Skills in building brands

Dr Philip Kotler

not just a shopping tool; it is a social and recreational experience. Internet marketing will put some pressure on traditional retailers, and traditional retailers will put pressure on Internet marketers too! That is the way it has always worked.

E-commerce – B2C

One hot term that is cooling off now is B2C (business-to-consumer) selling and marketing. Decades ago, the mom & pop stores took orders in person or by phone and delivered them to homes. They yielded to lowcost chains of supermarkets like the Great Atlantic & Pacific Tea Company. The small stores either disappeared or sought different market niches (delis, butcher shops, bakeries, etc.). The Sears and Wards stores and their impressive catalogs came next, serving everyone, everywhere using the US Post Office as the delivery mechanism. For years, mail order has been a strong form of B2C selling in Europe via old line firms like Quelle, and newcomers like Viking Office.

"To take full advantage of the potential in E-business, a company's leaders must lead differently, and people must work together differently....The challenge for established companies is not only deciding whether to embrace the Internet; it is understanding new requirements for running the organization that a move to E-business involves."

Rosabeth Moss Kanter

These were followed in the US by the great department stores and malls, which spawned suburban sprawl and automobile accessible discount stores. Parts of Europe are following this pattern, albeit somewhat more slowly. Within this same time frame catalog showrooms, superstore category killers, and warehouse clubs all emerged and matured. Each new retailing development created a new set of challenges for marketers.

You must understand the dynamics of the new forms of selling, and manage them accordingly. That is what marketing is all about. Although this varies by country and market, globalization continues to invent new hybrid forms of selling and marketing. If you think you can master just one current form of retail marketing, you are in

Some great advice from Seth Godin

- "Consumers have power."

- "Marketing CAN be learned from books."

- "Test and measure!"

- "There is very little magic involved."

Seth Godin

Q: Everyone seems to be spending money to get customers, but how does the customer acquisition cost for web-based businesses compare to regular retailers?

A: Higher: in fact, double the average rate for Internet-only retailers, and 3–7 times as high as old-fashioned catalog retailers!

for a short and painful career. Brands can now be built more rapidly. New markets can be tapped and expanded more rapidly. And competition unlike anything ever seen before can emerge equally rapidly. The whole race goes on at a faster pace, in more places around the world, but the principles are still the same. Find a customer with a need and fulfill it better, faster and more consistently than the competitor. Then do it over again and again.

The rules of marketing are not suspended because the company is a dot-com or because communications is via the Internet instead of a telephone. That is why a substantial part of this book deals with basics of marketing. When clicks and bricks come together with the customer's needs and a sound marketing plan, then they will succeed at using the Internet as a selling medium. Until then, it's all hype and hope!

"Of course, some products are less suited to electronic sale than others. While Internet retailers excel at getting the right product in the right place at the right price, they're at a disadvantage when it comes to delivering physical products at the right time. When shoppers need products immediately, they'll head for their cars, not their computers."

Clayton Christenson and Richard S. Tedlow

"Ultimately, shoppers will migrate to the retail channel that offers the best combination of convenience, price and added value. It will be rare that any consumer will shift all their buying of any one kind of product to the Internet, just the same way that there are relatively few people who buy all their goods from catalogs."

Robert Scally, "Clicks-and-mortars have the
right stuff to dominate the Internet"

E-commerce – B2B

The hotter topic in Internet commerce is the business-to-business (B2B) format. Used correctly, this is a wonderful new tool. For MRO supplies, office supplies, travel plans, tracking of shipments, and much more, this is a great advance. The new rash of purchasing "exchanges", however, is another thing entirely. Some of them make good sense – usually where there is a compete absence of a sourcing infrastructure. Some, like those announced by the auto or retail behemoths, have yet to prove that they are functional, viable, and legal. Let's consider how these may impact marketing.

It is hard to read a business publication these days without reading a story about yet another purchasing exchange. Auto companies, retailers, steel companies, chemical companies, and many more industry groups are joining forces in the formation of digital, Internet-based marketplaces. So are many major companies like GE. According to a mid-2000 issue of *Forbes*, over 1000 such exchanges have been announced. Its ranking of the top 200 gives a clue to the inevi-

Q: What kind of stuff really sells on the Internet?

A: All kinds! The current estimate for retail sales in 2004 is $36 billion.

"The incremental cost of an online transaction is essentially zero."

table consolidation and shakeout that must follow such an explosion of growth. The one certainty about these exchanges is that on them, the best deals and lowest prices will become transparently and startlingly evident. Marketing will take a distinctly lower priority but will actually become *more* important in such a commodity-oriented environment.

A secondary consequence of the online marketplaces is that the companies which use them wisely – suppliers and customers both – will realize large transaction cost savings. Transaction costs for purchase orders average $100–150 per order. If the participating companies use the full power of an Internet-based system, including electronic funds transfer and elimination of payables/receivables transaction costs, then those costs could be cut by up to 90%. Marketing's involvement in such exchange-based transactions will be minimal.

But marketing's job won't go away. How do users decide which exchange and which suppliers to choose, and why? Sounds like a marketing challenge to me. Such exchanges may threaten longer-term investments in R&D, advertising, etc., which are the cornerstones of marketing. The focus will be on the short term, and the fast buck. The resultant "auctions" will generate intense competition and savings – but for how long? Getting that fast buck out of transaction costs is fine. But, the transaction costs for a purchase order, even at $200 (double the $100 average so often cited) is only a small percentage of the total value of the order. If these costs are eliminated entirely, savings of a few percent might be realized.

What kind of traffic do we expect and can the site and servers handle it at acceptable response times?

Then come the ripple effects of making the best price and best deal evident to all, with little or no marketing, little differentiation, negligible new product influences, etc. Suppliers who are currently charging the highest prices will get squeezed – until they can no longer reduce prices to maintain volume – because price will be the dominant tool in the marketing mix that these exchanges consider.

Q: Why is everybody flocking to e-businesses anyway?

A: The reasons vary, but mostly to either get new sales or dodge competitive pressure.

Top 10 reasons for building an e-business

Generate new sales	62%
Competitive pressure	53%
Customer pressure	52%
Cost savings	46%
Internal efficiencies	45%
Better staff productivity	44%
Value chain integration	26%
Product differentiation	25%
Partner pressure	24%
New prospect base	23%

Source: Meta Group cited in *InfoWorld*, 27 March 2000

Companies in markets such as continental Europe will be faced with wide visibility of the pricing differences by country, and pressures to harmonize pricing at the lowest common levels. Then those suppliers that are not efficient, lowcost producers will first cut overhead, then cut corners, next cut quality, and, finally, fail.

Only the strong will survive. Prices will find their level just like water does. The hypothetical savings attributed to exchanges will look great at first, as the inefficient and high-priced suppliers are squeezed, and as the large suppliers and customers find price parity. The interesting part of this concept is that the purchasers taking advantage of the marketplace exchanges will also reach parity – at least temporarily. Their competitive advantages, many of them based on marketing or differentiation, will be gone – lost as the "widely known best deal" is exposed on the web. The strategic positions that once were the province of the largest or most astute buyers will now

> "After three years of living and breathing B2B, I firmly believe the final retail model will seamlessly integrate traditional and interactive activities. The techies will learn that each industry has its nuances that require a street level understanding of their industry; and the bricks folks will not be able to ignore their consumer customers any longer."
>
> Vaughn Baker

be available to many – but not for long! The strong, efficient suppliers will find a pricing floor, below which they cannot go, and they will start to "take sides" – picking which purchaser they choose to serve for other than price/volume based reasons.

Whenever an industry group approaches its business with a lowest common denominator approach, the strongest competitors and most competent (well-managed) companies will revolt, either openly or quietly, and re-establish their superior positions. The new economy won't change this. It will simply accelerate the speed at which it happens, and amplify the severity with which it eliminates the weak and ineffective. The marketing programs will regrow themselves like trees after a forest fire because they are an important value added in business to business relationships.

> "Internet companies are organisms that feed off money, opportunity, and people."
>
> Henry Blodgett, Merrill Lynch Internet analyst

Where competition is rife and capacity plentiful, price-driven auctions will thrive. Marketing strategies and plans must recognize and account for this. Where there is growth in a market segment, there will be greater potential for increases in sales and profits. Where there is stagnation and maturity, the fight for survival will be bitter and bloody. Where there is slow, fat, or sloppy execution, the culling will be brutal. Where there is superior execution, strong brands and cost/quality/speed advantages, the winners will emerge as always. When this happens, marketing will be necessary to lead the way to the future.

Internet or "dot-com" marketing – one-to-one contact and real-time marketing

There are some areas where the Internet has enabled a form of marketing and selling that has been previously impossible – or at least impractical or not economically viable. Never before has it been possible to market to individuals on such an interactive and instantaneous basis. Smart marketers will take advantage of the power of such a marketing system. Further, the ability to do so in real time has added yet another dimension to the potential of Internet marketing.

> "One of the biggest things that's going to happen is a lot of people are going to come back from dot-coms bruised, battered, shaken-up and broke, their options not worth a box of Charmin."
>
> Kevin Roberts

Centuries ago, products were sold on a one-to-one basis, from the local craftsman or trader to the end-user. Now we have moved back to the realm of the one-to-one sale because of the power and reach of the Internet.

The Internet enables that direct one-to-one relationship to be established again. It also enables communities of people with the similar interests to be assembled without regard to geographical locations. This is a big new opportunity. In the past, markets had to be aggregated on a geographical basis so the distribution and marketing communications could be done for that area. Radio and TV stations (prior to cable and satellite TV) also served defined geographic markets.

Marketers defined these areas as SMSAs (Standardized Metropolitan Statistical Areas) and could measure key marketing information about the customers in these areas using statistical sampling and published data. This allowed targeted marketing and coordination with distribution and retailing. Print publications could also be targeted on SMSA data. Consumers in similar geography could be grouped into market segments with similar desires, needs, resources, and demographics/psychographics.

Now comes the Internet and potential purchasers from Syracuse,

New York, USA; Madrid, Spain; or Shenzen, China can all be connected electronically as a new marketplace community. These geographically diverse consumers can be combined into markets worthy of pursuit via the Internet when no such market could even be imagined in the old world of physical geographic market segmentation.

> "…last year it was B2C and earlier this year it was B2B, and now its P2P – you need to see a path to profitability.
>
> Frank Quattrone, MD, CFSB Technology Group

If Internet customers want to customize their purchases of music, travel, clothing, or computers – now they can. Marketers must consider this in their marketing plans. Whether these markets fit the strategy of their companies is a separate issue. The fact is that now they can be reached and either collected into a larger market or served interactively one at a time. The concept of "permission marketing", which was covered in Chapter 4, is a variation of this power. By getting the permission of customers to be "targets" of marketing efforts, companies can create a less intrusive, more user-friendly marketing program. Converting this permission into some form of subscription is an even more powerful extension of permission marketing.

> I wonder what the competitors are doing while we are waiting around for decisions, doing nothing?

To cite a brief example of how this might work. If a consumer likes a certain brand of trash bags, and uses one (on average) every two days, then why not "subscribe" to a service which simply ships a package of 15–20 bags to the home each month (along with a variety of other predictable, non-perishable household needs like cleaning suppliers, tissue, etc.) and bills the consumer just as they would for electricity or water. Dairy companies used a variation on this approach decades ago as the milkman made home deliveries of fresh milk, butter, eggs, etc.

Privacy and security

This is not the place for a broad discussion about issues of privacy or security on the Internet. That would take volumes and be out of date by the time this is printed. What is in order here is the admonition

What community of customers and prospects can we reach profitably using the Internet that would have been impossible to reach using old techniques?

that these areas will cause serious problems to a marketer if not understood and considered. Privacy in the Internet context means managing the intrusiveness of the message to match the tolerance levels of the prospect and exercising discretion in the use of data gathered from online customers.

Privacy fears can hurt marketing efforts. Why? Abuse of the privilege is why! Carefully consider how much the customer or prospect wants to hear from you about your sales pitch or marketing message, and don't violate this privilege. Consider even more carefully what information you gather from customers and how you use it. Doubleclick.com is one of the leading Internet companies which got in trouble with consumer advocates by its planned use of consumer information. Fear of legislation caused them to rethink their marketing plans. Although marketers have treasured and used information about their customers/consumers for years, the Internet has brought concerns about this use to a whole new level.

The security issue is a more insidious one. Since there is a great deal of proprietary information moving on the Internet, the likelihood of security problems is great. Hackers can find out alarming amounts of information. Information about people, pricing, product launches, customers, programs, that would never be left lying around public places is often sent thoughtlessly via open email, discussed on cell phones in public places, or posted on insecure web sites – or even discussed in (insecure) chat sessions.

"Marketers must become communications vigilantes."

James Daly

The people questioned in the statistics about credit card security were not asked how they felt about giving their credit card information on the phone to an unseen, unknown individual. Neither were they asked how they felt about an unshaven young waiter or bartender disappearing with their credit card for 5–10 minutes, with no idea of what they intend to do with it (beyond charging for drinks or dinner). The security risks of using credit cards on the Internet if the sites use secure servers are no greater than many other risks. But if consumers perceive the risks to be greater, they will act accordingly. Smart marketers know that "perceptions are reality" for prospective consumers, and plan accordingly.

Unprecedented speed and global reach of a whole new era (revisited)

There is so much speed of change, and so little history about marketing in this Internet phenomenon, that traditional time frames of data gathering are irrelevant or at least not useful. This puts pressure on how long it takes to do homework. It also creates pressure in the form of very little margin for error. It used to be that costs were calculated, and prices were set and if there was an error, the margins just came out lower. That's not true any more. People now realize that the market sets prices and the only relationship to costs is the one of whether there is any profit left after the sale. This lead to one of the most perplexing issues raised by the Internet: *selling things for nothing – free*. How on earth can anyone make money at that? The answer is, most don't!

> How are we defining our market segmentation? Is it geographical? By product? By end-user? Or what?

No section about marketing in the Internet era can overlook the pricing issue of "free". Much has been written about how the "doctrine of the Internet" is that many things are "free" – especially information. There is nothing wrong with giving away valuable information for free – well almost nothing. What's wrong is that it is hard to make money when you give things away for free. Aha, say the Internet gurus. We will make money elsewhere. Aha yourself, you say back to them – where and how? We'll sell advertising, they say. You say "baloney" – show me! No one has yet figured out exactly how much money – or *if* profit can be made from selling advertising on the Internet, because no one really knows what Internet advertising is worth – at least not yet! "We'll build our brand," they say. Fine, you concur. But what exactly will that brand stand for that will make

> How can we find out and use information about our customers and consumers without offending them or abusing their trust? We need their permission!

Q: How much confidence do people have in the security of credit card transactions on the Internet?

A: Not too much – almost half of the people are *not* confident!

Completely confident	4%
Very confident	18%
Somewhat confident	32%
Not too confident	22%
Not at all confident	24%

Source: The Gallup Organization cited in *InfoWorld*

a profit so you can stay in business when your startup capital runs out?

Business is a game where the score is kept in money. If you do not make a profit and create a sustained positive cash flow, the game clock runs out and you don't get to play any more. Financial service companies are struggling with these issues. Selling financial news is not very viable since so much is offered free by online investment sites. Stock

Q: What new kind of marketing approaches has the Internet spawned?

A: One of the most interesting is "viral marketing".

In viral marketing, the message is spread across the vast network of the Internet – like a virus in humans – by "carriers" who are already "infected" with the worth of the idea. This is a form of referral or advocacy-based marketing that is potentially very powerful. It makes businesses more dependent on the goodwill of their users/customers. Any company that uses viral marketing must provide top quality and service – because its users are vouching for it with new prospects.

trades cost less than $15 and the price is still dropping. A few sites even offer free trades. Ancillary fees are under pressure. What next? Where will the revenue come from to pay the bills?

If we give it away "free", how will we make money?

Long-distance phone costs are also dropping fast, heading toward zero! Internet service providers are still selling connection services and web site hosting, but free services are springing up all over the place. Will this continue to be a viable business model? Let's watch NetZero.net and see if (or how) it figures out the issue of making enough money to stay in the game, while offering free services. Travel sites like expedia.com, travelocity.com, and priceline.com are still hanging in the game, but for how long?

But it's so easy to start a web-based business, you say. Fine, but this just means more competitors entering an already overpopulated

A brand must be more than a name

- Brands originated as a trademark serving as an identifier

- A brand must be at least able to trigger a set of associations (features and benefits).

- A brand also stands for an anticipated process (McDonald's, amazon.com).

- A great brand has personality attributes and value attributes that trigger emotions.

- A great brand represents a widely understood and credible *promise* of value backed by an organization able to deliver it.

- The ultimate brand builders are your employees and operations, not your marketing communications.

Dr Philip Kotler

arena. Low barriers to entry mean overpopulation and then natural selection starts – the strong win and the weak lose, disappear, or are gobbled up by the strong. Old economy competitors who get their act together will crush the new economy upstarts more times than not. Merck-medco.com, the old-economy, prescription filler, books eight times the prescriptions that drugstore.com does from one-quarter the visitors! That is a 32:1 advantage for the established company who wakes up and has a good web presence. This will happen over and over.

Just as old-economy companies are catching onto using the Internet, the more progressive Internet-based companies are now testing physical store initiatives. Yahoo! opened a promotional store in New York City's Rockefeller Center to encourage passers-by to try Yahoo!'s shopping site. Just as catalog-based companies like Gateway Computers turned to retail stores to broaden its reach, Internet companies are experimenting with hybrid formats. How these will work is uncertain, but multiple marketing formats carry the threat of too much complexity and not enough focus. Beware!

Just one more comment on confusing information before we leave the issue of global reach and speed. Correlating the number of global web users and the success or failure of an Internet venture is tricky business. First there is the definition of what value to assign to a click, a hit, a unique visitor, etc. The range of data variation on this issue is staggering. According to Neilsen, a statistic for Go2Net's unique audience says it is 3.7 million; MediaMetrix says it is 11.3 million. Wow! Try deciding which of those numbers to use for your marketing planning or analysis.

Then there is the question how long people stay? How "sticky" is the site? Yahoo.com gets high marks at keeping people around for an average of 26 minutes, while Disney's go.com network comes in at 13 minutes and AOL.com, the grand-daddy of consumer sites, is

> "The sooner the customer of the online and offline world are treated as one, the better."
>
> James Daly

> "Let's not try to be good at too many things at once – let's get good at them one at a time and build each upon what we learned on the last one – but do it fast!"

> "It is apparent that online retailing and its costs are closer to catalog retailing than to location-based retailers. After decades of experience in the direct-to-consumer business, why do catalog sales still only account for about 3% of total retail sales?...Catalog retailing is not particularly profitable."
>
> Roger D. Blackwell and Kristina Stephan

third at 10 minutes. That is if you can believe the data! The smart thing to do is to cross-check information as many ways as possible before depending on it A checklist is always a nice way to wrap up a section like this.

A 13-point checklist for web-biz

☐ *Focus:* Define the *purpose* of your web site and e-business at the start. Is it to sell goods, to sell services, to link to other sites that do, etc.?

☐ *Fast*: Be *frugal* at first – don't spend a fortune on the first web site, but move fast. Get it up and refine it as you go, adding necessary features and functionality. In the Internet era, *"Wrong, fast is better than right, slow"*, says Marc Andreeson, co-founder of Netscape and youthful Internet guru.

☐ *Simple:* Keep it *simple* so it loads fast and is easy to navigate. Web designers love complex, fancy, animated sites. Buyers don't. If I have to wait a minute or more for a site to load via modem, I find another site.

☐ *Flexible:* Provide easy *search* capabilities. No one wants to meander through a site map or dozens of pages looking for a needle in a haystack. Visit your site and pretend you are a customer – then do what customers would do. Look for something. Find it and try to buy it, use it, download it, etc.

☐ *Friendly:* Lose the scrolling, blinking flashing banner ads unless you absolutely *must* have the income – they are *really* annoying! Also lose other extraneous animated graphics that add loading time to the site and slow down its primary purpose. Banner ads have a dismal click-through rate, yet account for a large proportion of online spend – what a waste!

☐ *Functional:* When you are ready to take orders, be able to take orders – simply, easily, fast. This is a simple statement but it is also a common flaw in failed web marketing. That means taking credit cards, and completing the order without using more than two or three screens. The majority of shopping carts are abandoned unpurchased! Why? The site is too hard to work with.

☐ *Fair:* Give the customer one last chance to say *yes or no, add*, or *delete* items. This will reduce returns and disputes, and, done well, may even increase sales by asking if there are related purchases that have been forgotten. If an order is entered, provide an easy tracking system, tracking number, send a confirming email, etc., in case an inquiry is necessary.

☐ *Fulfill:* Be prepared to *fulfill* the order effectively, efficiently, and fast. This means either you or someone must have inventory (or rapid, flexible production capacity), and the people to pick, pack and ship the purchases. Picking orders is not terribly complex, but it is terribly important in fulfilling the customer's "bill of rights".

☐ *Deliver – I:* Have a good *delivery* system, preferably with web-based tracking. Have backups if there are known risks of problems – overload, weather, strikes, etc.

☐ *Deliver – II:* If you are selling a downloaded product, break it up into *pieces* that are logical and viable. Anyone who has had a huge download interrupted by a communications glitch knows why this is a good idea. Multiple concurrent downloads are better than one big one.

☐ *Up-front:* Take care of all this *up-front*, before you "open up for business". You wouldn't open the doors of a retail store (old style) with no goods and no way to let the customers pay for them and take them along – would you?

☐ *Measure: Measure* results and adjust. Be prepared to constantly and regularly update your systems based on what you learn. This is a fast moving target.

☐ *Learn and leverage:* Learn from others, finding competitive and uniquely different sites and "borrowing" their best ideas. Look for what they do better than you, not vice versa. Then leverage what you learn to get better, fast!

In other words, ask yourself what the customer would *wish* for – then provide it.

"The problem with the top is not too much perfection, but too little perspective.... Legendary, long-lived companies are intensely outward-looking."

Kevin Kelly

9 The Globalization of Marketing

The five smartest things to know about marketing

- You must have a plan

- Get close to the customer

- Do your homework

- Remember relationships

- Use the speed and reach of technology

As the world becomes a more global village, multinational companies will operate in all of the major economic spheres in a near interchangeable fashion. Most companies these days, and certainly the more prominent ones, are global or multinational companies. They are buying and selling pieces and parts of each other until it is hard to decide where the country of origin is – or was – or even if it matters. Examples are everywhere: Vivendi, Diageo, LMVH, Unilever, DaimlerChrysler, Henkel, America Online, Wal*Mart, and dozens more. The ones that are not actually selling or buying each other are forming partnerships or alliances to work together on joint product or marketing plans.

Yet, in spite of homogenizing forces like the euro, satellite and cable television, satellite telephone communications, and the spread of the Internet, centuries of culture will hang onto many of its unique and sometimes sacred beliefs and customs. Smart marketers will need to understand these cultural heritages to realize how to penetrate these markets. Determining how to tell the story of their goods and services in a culturally diverse yet somewhat uniform manner will be a global challenge of the 21st century. This chapter will only touch on a few of the keys to this huge topic of marketing globally – especially those of culture, communications, the influence of the Internet, and currency/ exchange-rate considerations. Some of these will exhibit a high portability of practices, while others will not. The smart marketer must be sensitive to these issues.

The globalization

The world is an ever-shrinking place: advances in communications, information technology, and transportation are making it seem much smaller. Technology can move around the globe in a few seconds. Training and professional management have become the means to transform less-developed countries into fearsome competitors in a very short time. Smart marketers understand this and act based on this understanding.

"The key thing is not just to plant flags. It's to make sure you build a business, customer by customer, day by day."

Peter M. Thompson, CEO Pepsi-Cola International

Market boundaries are changing faster than geopolitical organizations can redraw their borders. Cultural biases will change very slowly, but new trends spread by the electronic power of television and the Internet can overlay on old cultures very rapidly. The key to global marketing is to understand the cultural underpinnings well enough to realize when these new ideas are having a dramatic impact on how consumers and customers in global markets will behave.

John Anderson, an international consultant, with experiences as an executive with Gillette and Rubbermaid, always reminds me that global marketing, and in fact global management, is about 80% the same principles and practices regardless of where it occurs. The key is to realize that *there is 20% different*, and figure out *where that difference exists*. To achieve leverage and benefit from economies of scale, smart marketing must take advantage of the principles and practices that are 80% the same regardless of the country, while recognizing which ones make up the 20% of difference that determines success or failure.

> "Marketing is the most important area where managers must work together with local market managers. Without this cooperation the transfer of product knowledge, company culture and marketing strategy will not occur. The result will be unfocused strategy, the development of 'renegade' country fiefdoms and the waste of resources."
>
> John Anderson, international business consultant

Another problem with global marketing is that it is too often directed by people who have never been there – at least "not really". Arriving at the airport to be picked up by a limousine and taken to a hotel for meetings, having cocktails and dinner with people from that country, and moving on to the next county is *not* "being there"! "Being there" means spending enough time in countries other than your own to see, feel, sense, and internalize the discernible differences that make up the 20% difference and the critical success factors. This is not done by attending a couple of trade shows, taking a trip or two, or during a few days visit. Americans are arguably the worst in this respect, and are widely regarded as provincial, arrogant, and ignorant of world cultures.

A combination of these "business trip" visits and trade shows/conferences with longer periods of less structured time, traveling alone, shopping, dining, and interacting with local people, in the various countries is necessary for senior executives to gain a sense of global markets. Then comes the importance of accepting and valuing input from local management (and expatriates) as the marketing strategy is being developed and decisions are being made. Different cultures have widely differing customs and practices. These can range from meal times to social interaction and unwelcome familiarity. Even affluent, educated Americans are accused, often rightfully, of practicing poor cultural manners.

> "We have come to realize two truths about the global economy: First, the global economy is all about open markets and competition. The winners will be companies and countries that best understand competition and how to avoid falling prey to their competitors' strengths while exploiting their weaknesses....Second, the global economy is all about skilled managers and leaders. The market will punish mistakes, so you must avoid making them."
>
> Al Ries and Jack Trout

There are other errors to avoid in global marketing. One is the overcomplication of the efforts in the beginning. There is more to global marketing than simply reprinting the entire line of product catalogs and packaging in different languages. Lifestyles vary. Beliefs are different. Even the nuances of how things are said in commercials or on packages can vary from the expected outcome. Mexican Spanish differs from what is spoken in Spain. Canadian French is different from the language in Paris, France. Chinese is not a single language but many different ones, with regional dialects.

> "As companies go global, they must observe the principle of specialization and narrow their product lines. Big, diversified companies must get more focused."
>
> Al Ries and Jack Trout

To understand global marketing properly, you have to understand the heritage and culture of countries. At the same time, you have to understand these countries' societies and relative position in the global economy. This combination means that most global marketers need help from the very outset. When Japan attempted to penetrate the US automobile market, its first efforts were misguided and futile. The reason for this error was that the Japanese failed to understand the motivation and desires of the American auto buyers. American companies attempting to penetrate Asian or European markets make the same kind of errors.

When American auto producers attempted to penetrate Japanese markets, they failed because they neither understood the Japanese import system of commercial restrictions and protective mechanisms, nor did they tailor the product for Japanese needs – right-hand drive, smaller vehicles for the crowded conditions, and much more. American retailers faced similar difficulties as they attempted to penetrate Japanese markets. They were faced with Japan's large store regulations, which gave small local merchants a heavy influence on the ability of new, large stores to enter their cities and areas. Most European retailers have encountered difficulty transporting their stores to the US market successfully.

China – and Taiwan before it – have gained huge penetration in the open world markets due to their low manufacturing costs, and high product awareness from either local use (like bicycles, clothing, etc.) or imported marketing/product knowledge (many other products).

Q: If Anheuser–Busch is the largest brewer of beer in the world, who is second largest?

A: Belgium's Interbrew! Surprised? Most people would be.

One of the products of globalization is that world leaders pop up in the most surprising places. Thanks to a series of 17 acquisitions in 11 countries, Interbrew now owns brands such as Rolling Rock, Bass, Labatt, and Stella Artois. While Anheuser–Busch, Miller, and Coors own 80% of the large US market, a battle is brewing – not just the beer.

What the Chinese and Taiwanese failed to understand when they went after the European markets is that unlike the open American market, the Europeans collaborate to create entry barriers. As soon as the very low priced products began to enter the major European markets, the influential local companies and countries banded together to pass new, higher tariffs. These higher tariffs neutralized the Chinese cost and price advantages and protected the local markets. (This is what tariffs are designed to do!)

Culture and communications

Global marketing also must recognize the differences in lifestyles, transportation, and communications around the world. Large stores were slower to catch on in Europe, and food supermarkets never did become established in many areas because the cultural predisposition was to "go to markets based on daily needs". Many European residences had neither the space nor the appliances suited to mass purchase and storage of food and supplies that is the norm in the US.

American marketers attacking European and Asian markets were faced with a broad range of country to country differences in tariffs, standards, and regulations. European marketers attacking American

"Heaven and hell in Europe" – a cultural lesson

This anecdote was told about 10 years ago by a former US Secretary of Commerce in explaining how understanding cultures in different countries was so important to global business expansion.

Heaven in Europe:

- English are the police
- French are the cooks
- Germans are the engineers
- Swiss are the administrators
- Italians are the lovers

Hell in Europe:

- Germans are the police
- French are the engineers
- English are the cooks
- Swiss are the lovers
- Italians are the administrators

If you smile at this story, you understand a little of major European cultures. If you don't get it, ask a European to explain it to you!

markets found the standards much easier to deal with than the peculiar (to them) preferences of American consumers and retailers. Smart Asian manufacturers enlisted the help of American marketing firms to design, market, and launch their products. Only in the past decade or two have the major continents begun to converge in preferences and performance standards, and there is still a considerable gap.

Chinese consumers could never consider buying the large packages of laundry detergent (and many other products) that are common in the American stores. The Chinese have neither the means nor the need for such "bulk" quantities – thus packets sized for a single load of laundry had much greater appeal. Conversely, bottled drinking water was much slower catching on in the US where municipal water supplies created safe, potable water. In less developed countries, or older European countries, bottled water was a preferred form of drinking water.

> "Let's use icons on the product. 'A picture is worth a thousand words,' and it can't be in the wrong language!"

Brands in Europe developed over the decades, indeed even centuries, within the boundaries of individual countries or regions. Until the advent of satellite and cable television there was no means for pan-European brand advertising, and even then the culture and language differences still present formidable obstacles to broad scale advertising. In large, populous countries like China and India provincial dialects and cultural differences make them far from homogeneous markets. This factor, combined low incomes, make these apparently attractive markets far more difficult to exploit that might be expected. Carrefour, the European retailing giant, blanketed China with scaled-down stores – 23 in 14 cities – and sales are strong. The cliché *"think global and act local"* is more appropriate than ever in these markets.

When the majority is the minority – globally

The 21st century is the one where the majority becomes the minority – in the US anyway. Caucasians from Europe and their descendants were the primary settlers of the US and thus are the majority from an ethnic viewpoint. In a few decades, that will change. Why? Because immigrants to the US and other developed countries are flooding in from less developed countries all over the world. And, overall, these immigrants are more prolific. In the US, Hispanics are nearing 15% of the population; in 25 years, African Americans will approach that same percentage, and Hispanics will grow to 25%.

Over that same period Asian Americans add 5%. Then throw in what we still call a minority although they were here first – Native Americans – with an assortment of other global immigrants, and by the time today's babies enter the workforce, the US will be only 50% Caucasian. The increase in interracial marriages and the resulting blends of children will further blur that figure into a meaningless statistic.

Marketing to that medley of racial and ethnic backgrounds will require all kinds of new, smarter thinking. Minorities eat out more often than the Caucasians. They tend to have bigger families and younger households, which can mean a boom in kids' clothing, and starter home sales. Media, autos, financial services, and communications (remember, their families are far away in most cases) will be changed – perhaps radically. Marketers need to understand this and be prepared to gain their rightful share of these new markets. Some are. Some are not.

> "We do business where we live – we live where we do business. You'll never be the real thing if you're from out of town."
>
> Coca-Cola 2000 Annual Report

The Internet, Benetton, Toys R Us, and Wal*Mart

The Internet, is dramatically increasing the convergence rate of market preferences in countries around the world. The cultural differences will not evaporate, but the easy access to "global best" products and worldwide pricing via the Internet will hasten the broadening of preferences and purchases. Two American retailers and an Italian one broke many of the trails for marketing internationalization. Benetton was an early global influence in retailing, spreading stores around the globe selling its trendy sportswear everywhere. Although it faltered and had to retrench, its legacy remains. Other European fashion retailers are now located in prestigious shopping centers the world over and especially in the US.

> When asked by an American manufacturer, "How long will your bicycle last?" the answer of a Chinese manufacturer was "For your lifetime – at least"

Toys R Us was an early global retailing pioneer, spreading its massive toy stores into all of the major markets in Europe and Asia during

"Effective marketing is innovative, refreshing, relevant and – more than anything, real. It's not enough to record radio spots in 40 languages; we produce music for those spots in 140 distinctly different versions, each carefully adapted to what's popular in local markets."

Coca-Cola 2000 Annual Report

the 1980s and 1990s. Even though Toys R Us has also faltered somewhat, it is still the dominant global presence in toy retailing.

Next came Wal*Mart, the world's largest retailer. Wal*Mart began its international expansion in North America – Canada and Mexico (with Cifra), but spread rapidly into South America (with only modest success to date), Europe via acquisition, and China. This behemoth of retailing has met stiff competition in South America and parts of Europe, especially from large, well-established global retailers like Carrefour. Over time, Wal*Mart's march around the world will be unstoppable, but companies like Carrefour will present larger obstacles than Wal*Mart is accustomed to.

The outcome of this inexorable expansion of Wal*Mart will further globalize markets with similar merchandise and practices. The extent to which Wal*Mart or any invading retailer adapts to local markets vs. local markets adapting to what it brings is still not resolved. What is resolved is that once a retailer like Wal*Mart enters a market, the market will never be the same again. Smart marketers need to con-

"According to Forrester Research, 85% of e-tailers are unable to fulfill international orders due to the complexities of shipping across borders, yet it is imperative to deliver to global destinations."

Phil Wilkerson, Chief Technology Officer, GlobalFulfillment.com

sider the implications of this on their global marketing plans. Any company that is the world's low-cost buyer and distributor of products with $250 billion sales (now) and aspirations to reach $1 trillion in global sales by the year 2015 bears careful watching. Wal*Mart will likely become the largest retailer in most of the markets it enters within a decade after the entry. Carrefour is likely to hang onto the number two spot. Plan on this and figure out how to capitalize on it – or at least how to survive in the face of it.

> "The key trend affecting marketing strategy is the global economy and marketplace. Products and brands are moving worldwide."
>
> Al Ries and Jack Trout

The Internet, like Wal*Mart and Carrefour, will not go away. Plan on how to capitalize on that too. Fulfillment is a challenge for Internet sales, since the physical goods must be moved across oceans, continents, and borders – each of which presents different challenges. You must learn how to do this effectively, or your best Internet marketing efforts could be wasted. You must also move fast or a giant competitor like Wal*Mart or Carrefour, even if slow moving at first, will beat you to the markets you are targeting and out-muscle you. If you cannot figure out the fulfillment puzzle, get help. Either in the form of international logistics consultants or third-party logistics partners, help is readily available. Don't wait: do it now – before someone else does!

Currencies and exchange rates

One of the common excuses for earnings shortfalls these days is some form of exchange rate fluctuation. Global marketers have to

> "…using technology to help meet customer needs in any corner of the globe is required. Ultimately the Internet's true benefit is its ability to connect companies to customers or businesses to suppliers, regardless of geographic location, currency or language."
>
> Phil Wilkerson

Q: What is the big deal about exchange rate calculations?

A: If you don't understand them, you can make big, expensive mistakes doing them!

Liars may figure, but figures don't lie!

- Let's say I am buying an electronic product that costs 600¥ in Japan. At 120¥ = $1.00US exchange rate, I must pay $5.00US for it.

- Then let's assume the exchange rate goes from 120¥ to 100¥ for $1.00US. This is a swing of 20¥/120¥ or 16.7% change – right?

- With the exchange rate at to 100¥ = $1.00US, I must now pay $6.00US for it. My cost has gone from $5.00 to $6.00 an increase of $1.00 on my original cost of $5.00 – a 20% increase!

- If I only pass on 16.7% increase from my earlier calculation, I lose 3.3% – which may be most (or all) of my after-tax profit.

understand exchange rates and currencies. Many think that they do, but they don't; others do and they usually win. As companies expand globally everything from setting price points to decisions on when to change pricing is dramatically influenced by currency exchange rates. The popular US price targets of $9.99 and $99.99 change when there is a translation to euros, yen, pesos, or Hong Kong dollars and vice versa. Fluctuations in purchase cost and selling price due to local exchange rates can wipe out profits, and destroy market launches in a blink.

Pricing is a distinctly local phenomenon. A common error is to assume the price can just be imported with the products and converted into local currency. This is a foolish error, but a common one. Another of the typical errors is in calculation of how percentage swings in exchange rates affect costs and prices. Everyone is taught in school that the percentage of change is the amount of change divided by the starting number. In math that is true and in single currency situations it is too. In exchange rate calculations it isn't always true.

Japan and retailing

I used Japanese currency in the prior example because this small, yet prosperous and highly developed industrial power has suffered volatile up and down swings in its currency (and economic system) over the past two decades. The Internet promises to have profound effects on Japan's economic and cultural future as it makes information about prices and sources much more widely available to the Japanese people of the next generation. The Japanese government and banking system controlled the behavior of its economy and companies for years – until its recent collapse due to liberal credit and unwise investments. Japan faces an era where its protected economy must open up to foreign competition or fail of its own internal weaknesses. Global marketers must proceed with caution, but get ready.

> "Global marketing plans most often ignore the market potential of countries in favor of pursuing cultural clusters of markets with similar language and customs."
>
> John Anderson

The Japanese competitors will not be pushovers, as US office superstores Office Depot and Office Max discovered in the past couple of years. Even though the Japanese stationery industry was archaic, and stores usually charged "full price", the US stores made some typical mistakes. Stores were too big and "too American" for Japan's tightly clustered cities and insular population. Product errors were common. Japanese office products differ from those in the US: binders have two rings, not three. Japanese culture abhors the desktop storage of paper files and queues of paperwork. Many office products sold in the US are bins, trays, and sorters designed to do just this. Unlike the US and Europe, offices in Japan are open; partitions are the exception. Office products which fit three ring binders or store paper and hang on partitions ignore these differences and fail. Cultural factors ignored lead to marketing failures.

Japanese stationery maker Plus Corp. formed a division it called Askul (which means in Japanese "it will come tomorrow") and targeted the same customers as the US office superstores – small businesses that were not getting the discounts enjoyed by the large companies who buy in bulk. When US stores opened, Askul cut prices and catered to core customers more than ever. Like South American retailers' reaction to Wal*Mart, Askul asked "Why should we concede our business to the Americans?" Askul ran customer loyalty programs, launched an Internet business, and fought the new market entrants. Thus far, Askul is winning with major sales gains of 77% over a year ago in spite of the new market competition.

Toys R Us and Gap stand out as American retailing successes in Japan, but not without going through a painful period of learning and adaptation to the nuances of the market. Sporting goods retailer Sports Authority made the same error as the office products stores – "too big, too American" stores. Its Japanese partner, Jusco, is now opening smaller stores stocked with more targeted assortments. Remember the popular saying, *"Think global, but act local."*

Expect competition

A common error in global expansion is to somehow expect that the local entrenched competitors will tremble in fear and become paralyzed into inaction while the new entrant comes in and snatches market share. Nothing could be further from the truth. Entrenched local competitors will fight for their lives and businesses. Expect it, plan on it, or get beaten by it.

As a general rule, if you can do it, attacking is better than defending when competitors come knocking at your door. The attacker can at least choose the playing field and how the contest starts out. The defender is left reacting – not a good position to be in.

> "Companies marketing outside their home market continue making a basic mistake over and over. They continue to expect consumers and markets around the world to react to their initiatives just like they do in their home market. The single most important skill an international marketer can develop is cultural sensitivity and empathy."
>
> John Anderson

Culture, culture, culture – and BigBoy

If the key to retail success is location, location, location, then the key to global success is culture, culture, and culture. Understand it and accommodate it or fail. A simple story illustrates this so well, I'll close this chapter with it.

BigBoy is an US-based chain of restaurants, which specializes in typical American fare of hamburgers, fries, and chicken in (American) familystyle settings, using a large statue and picture of a pudgy-faced little boy as its icon. After observing numerous American restaurant chains entering the market in Thailand, and being contacted by a Thai entrepreneur, BigBoy (owned by Elias Bros., Warren, Michigan) decided to franchise restaurants in Thailand.

It seems they had been convinced that simply opening the restaurants would be enough to assure that people would come and buy the food. *Wrong!* First of all, the BigBoy statue spooked many of the Thais. They asked if it was a Chinese Ronald McDonald or some evil figure. Others claimed that the "room energy" was bad. Many preferred sweet satay, a noodle bowl, or grilled squid from street vendors instead of a greasy hamburger at five times the price. Peter Smythe, head franchiser for Big-Boy in Thailand summed it up pretty well, "Here I was trying to get a 3,000 year old culture to eat 64 year old food."

In an act of desperation, before closing the doors and yielding what was left to creditors, Mr Smythe added a couple of cheap Thai items to the menu, and customers started trickling in. While BigBoy restaurants are still far from successful, they are still open and trying to find a menu that suits both the cultures of its market and its theme. BigBoy had made the typical mistakes of rushing in without considering the cultural fit at all. Local suppliers couldn't supply its basic needs such as buns because they were "too complicated". Unlike McDonald's, which brings its clout and global supply network with it, BigBoy had to find one within the country's culture and infrastructure.

> We may understand it here, but will they understand it there – or will they misunderstand it?

Then there were the menu adjustments. Not only Thai dishes were added, but European ones as well – to cater to European tourists. As Smythe sums it up, "We thought we were bringing American food to the masses, but now we're bringing Thai and European food to the tourists. It's strange, but you know what? It's working." The marketing message is clear: understand the culture, then make your globalization plans, not vice versa. If you don't understand marketing to the culture, get help from someone who does. The alternative is to fail.

Conclusion

Globalization is proceeding at an accelerating rate, fueled by technology – the Internet, telecommunications, computing, bandwidth, satellite entertainment/communications, and transportation. Know-how can be transmitted around the world in seconds. Applying the fundamentals of marketing, while realizing that money is not worth the same, static amount in all places at all times, is the next critical success factor in global marketing. People can be transported around the world in hours. Cultures will change, but like many things we have discussed, aspects of them will not change. Understanding those cultures and their evolution is the greatest key to global marketing.

10 Marketing Relationships

The five smartest things to know about marketing

- You must have a plan

- Get close to the customer

- Do your homework

- Remember relationships

- Use the speed and reach of technology

Marketing interfaces

Marketing is the sensory system for a company. It is the eyes, ears, and nose; it is the sense of feel and touch. Marketing is also the communications system that the body of the company relies on to provide feedback from the senses. Woe be unto the company who has poor relationships between its marketing organization and the other parts of the company. And also woe be unto the company that doesn't listen to or trust its marketing feedback.

This is not a perfect world populated with virtuous, honest, and kind people. But it is the world in which we live and work with all its imperfections. A marketing organization is a group of people that touches every part of an organization in one way or another. Marketing similarly influences the external people the organization deals with.

> "The central economic imperative of the network economy is to amplify relationships."
>
> Kevin Kelly

Every part of an organization has a need for and a relationship with marketing because is the eyes and ears of the company with its customers and markets. But the relationship with each constituency is different. Smart readers need to understand these differences. Because of that, there will be brief sections on those varied relationships and their key points.

Sales and customers

This is where the action is. Without customers, there is no reason for being. Without the sales people who deal with the customers, there is isolation from the real world of customers that is intolerable. Marketing must have a close, almost symbiotic relationship with sales. There will always be a friction – a give and take – but it must be focused on making things better for the customer, not at winning or losing internal organizational power struggles.

> "If you want to sell what John Smith buys, see John Smith through John Smith's eyes."

Marketing provides the tools and the instructions, and sales does the work of showing the customer why they need what you have. Then sales brings back the orders, either literally or more often figuratively (electronically) in this wired world. Sales must have input into marketing plans and marketing must have input into sales plans. This input must be respected and well taken, not just a courtesy step.

When marketing does its job well, sales is positioned to succeed. If marketing does its job poorly, sales has a very difficult task indeed. Once sales and marketing understand each other's roles and get closely aligned in their focus on delighting and serving the customer, the business is on its way to success.

Customer service

Customer service is usually the place the customers/consumers communicate with the company after the buying decision has been made and the orders placed or product delivered. It is important that marketing and customer service touch base regularly. This will help customer service understand the rationale behind products and programs, in a way that it can more effectively support and interpret them. More importantly, it will keep marketing grounded in the reality of what customers and consumers are saying.

Since the negotiation stage of the buy–sell relationship is usually over by the time customer service gets involved, the interaction with the customer is much more open and direct. This regular contact also helps marketing understand what does not seem to be working as planned and make adjustments. Adjustments are inevitable – the only question is whether they are the right ones which fix the problems, or make them worse. In fact, other than direct contact with customers and consumers, customer service is often the most reliable and accurate place from which to get customer feedback. Use it!

"It is one of the most beautiful compensations of this life that no man can sincerely try to help another without helping himself."

Ralph Waldo Emerson

The one cardinal sin that I have seen many companies cause their customer service people to commit is lying about performance. Whether it is product performance or delivery performance, too many companies still put the customer service rep in the position of telling small (or large) lies about what the customer (or consumer) should expect. This is bad business and will backfire. As more and more companies get wired (together) this problem will lessen, because the status of things will become transparent, and using lies as temporary shields will become impossible.

R&D, product design and engineering

There is always a debate as to the origin of many new products – do they begin in marketing or in this area? I consider the functions of R&D, product design, and engineering to be the technological idea-ground for smart marketers. Marketing is supposed to get close to the customer and be the senses of the company. If marketing brings this sensory information back to R&D, product design, and engineering with enough richness, and if the relationship between these groups is good, then wonderful things usually result. I had the good fortune to start my career in this area, and later return to it, after learning about how this relationship feels from both directions.

What are the customers who call us complaining about, and what should we be doing differently because of those calls?

The biggest differences a smart marketer needs to understand about the relationship between marketing and R&D, product design, and engineering is that the latter departments are populated with a complex mixture of people and personality types. R&D people are usually dreamers, who may come up with things that won't sell, but are wonderfully unique in their own right. Product designers come in a couple of flavors – the industrial and graphic designers are artists in disguise, and the physical product designers are more like the engineers, whose purpose in life is to make sure these things work and can be built.

Because of these differences, a smart marketing person needs to remember which group s/he is working with and behave accordingly. The marketing person almost needs to be a bit schizophrenic – conservative when working with the R&D folks and creative when working with the rest of them, all the while communicating the nuances of customer needs/wants over and over. Sound like a tough relationship challenge? It is, but get this one started off right and life in marketing can be beautiful.

Just remember, however, that few people take kindly to blunt or brutal criticism of ideas they have originated or things they have designed, so walk softly. Make interpersonal "deposits" in the form of compliments and flattery when you can, because you'll need them when the time comes to make "withdrawals" – when you need to shoot down something or must insist on changes that are not popular. Share the reactions from focus groups or market research, and whenever possible, keep members of this group actually involved in the research process, so they can see and hear consumer reactions first hand.

What is the minimum tooling time including debugging it?

Also, don't be surprised if this group thinks it can do marketing's job better than marketing. That is not unusual at all (and this is not the only group that will think this!). *Just buy them a copy of this book and give it to them. After all, it is better to have an informed critic than an ignorant one.*

Manufacturing and/or operations and office/plant employees

You are probably wondering why I added office/plant employees to this list. The answer is that this group does the work of the business but is often left in the dark as to the plans for going to market and the outcomes of its efforts. Of course it is the job of its management to keep it informed, but few operations executives or managers can

> "…sales and marketing must become more involved in helping a company manage demand in determining how to utilize its manufacturing resources because:
>
> - Customers don't buy according to manufacturing's best guesses, and
>
> - Sales and marketing are close to the customers and, therefore, have the best knowledge of the customers' intentions."
>
> George E. Palmatier and Joseph S. Shull, *The Marketing Edge*

Warning signals (that pain is coming!)

- You seldom meet the first promised delivery date to customers

- Your product availability is worse and delivery times are slower than competition

- You have little or no information for setting good delivery dates

- Consistently poor quality requires frequent field repairs or high warranty costs

- A major portion of each day is spent expediting orders

- Total cost in terms of material, labor, and overhead is high

- Investment in inventory – raw, WIP, and finished goods is high

- Inventory records are inaccurate and unreliable

- Financial and core operating information is ignored – each department keeps its own set of records

- Financial goals are missed often and surprises pop up at end of financial reporting periods

George E. Palmatier and Joseph S. Shull, *The Marketing Edge*

present a new product or an advertising campaign with the style and enthusiasm of the marketing person who created it. Share information with the people – it will help morale, raise some excellent questions and make everyone feel part of the team.

The other group for whom you should buy copies of this book is *manufacturing*, because they are certain they could do marketing's job more effectively than marketing. At least they would not do some of the dumb (or arbitrary) things marketing does to make their (operations) lives difficult. Why do these parts of the organization have this perspective? Because they are not included when the ideas are taking shape and receive them, often in an impersonal manner, when the pressure is on to implement, execute, and perform. Translation: they have little participation, no equity, but are given a lot of responsibility for making things work – on schedule, on budget, and under pressure.

> Do we have enough capacity if we really "hit a home run"? Do our suppliers?

If an investment of marketing time with R&D, product design, and engineering pays off in up-front success, the investment with operations pays off day after day. It is not all that difficult to include all these departments in design reviews, program presentations, and strategy sessions. Believe me, they will contribute. And they will gain equity. You will hear real world issues that will influence the success of the entire marketing effort, and have them as partners instead of critics. Show them your new ads. Involve them with customers to hear things first hand. Share concerns with them early before entrenched positions are set, and the desired win–win collaboration becomes a win–lose confrontation. I guarantee you will be happy you did!

Procurement and outsourcing

In these days of strategic outsourcing and rapid changes in volatile markets, this supply chain part of the business must be fully aware of marketing plans as early as is possible and prudent. Because some supplier may supply competitors, and confidentiality can be a concern, there are times when early disclosure is a risk. There are more times when early partnering with inside (and outside) sourcing people can be the key to success.

> "Let's get all of the department heads together and get everybody on board about what we are planning."

In many companies, marketing dabbles at the job of sourcing, especially when a marketing person sees a new idea and explores how to secure some proprietary rights to it. That kind of cross-functional activity is inevitable. The important thing to know is that you, as marketing person, must get the procurement people involved early and often so they can do "their thing", just as you do "your thing". Procurement – or as it is more often being called these days strategic sourcing – has the job of finding the materials and components (or finished products) you need for your marketing program. Then it is their job to negotiate the "deal", just as sales does with customers. Once the deal has been agreed upon, it falls on their shoulders to see that the material purchased are delivered at the right time, to the right place, with the right quality, price, and specifications.

This is no easy process. While manufacturing has a tough job, most of their involvement deals with people who are employees of your company – not so with procurement. These are outside entities that must be sold on the benefits of giving your company the best deal possible, just as much as customers must be sold on buying your products or services. When the time comes to produce and deliver the product, no one wants to hear that the supplier was late shipping or that the shipment was rejected for some reason.

> "The more I help others to succeed, the more I succeed."
>
> Ray Kroc, founder of McDonald's

If marketing can communicate with procurement early and often, the outcome will normally be a qualified supplier, a good cost, and reliable delivery. Nothing less is acceptable. If marketing goes around procurement, cuts deals on the side, and undermines the efforts of its own sourcing people, the supplier is confused and concerned.

Who can trust a company that has internal conflicts of this nature? If the company people will turn on each other, how quickly might they turn on an outside supplier? Especially when the discussions between marketing and suppliers are highly strategic, the procurement people must be involved or they are uninformed – "left out in the cold" so to speak.

Logistics and carriers, 3PL providers, service contractors

The challenge here is for marketing to be aware of the capabilities that exist in these areas. No product or service is worth anything until it is delivered to where the purchaser can use it. Since these organizations fall in the "supplier" category most of the time, the caveats about dealing with procurement also apply here. More important, the knowledge about what logistics options exist can be critical factors in speed to market and that, as we have covered, is a critical success factor.

Human resources and employees, communities

A simple fact of business is that whichever company has the best talent and leadership will win most of the time. I don't like the term "human resources" (HR) but it is accepted and widely used, so I will use it. Wal*Mart calls it the "People" department. That is more like the truth. Marketing can make a tremendous contribution in this area in two respects. The first is by "marketing" the company to the employees – its people! The second is by being a good partner to the internal HR people (and external ones if used) and helping plan people/talent needs as far in advance as possible.

> "...strategic intent aims to create employee excitement, not just employee satisfaction... excitement often runs roughshod over satisfaction."
>
> Gary Hamel and C. K. Prahalad, *Competing for the Future*

Then all of the basic principles of dealing with people must be taken care of as well – feedback, communications, etc. Too often, marketing or sales may bask in the warm glow of a success in the marketplace when that success was the result of the efforts of many others in the organization. Working with HR to properly recognize all of the contributors to a success is a wonderful contribution by marketing to the overall company's health and future. Do your part in it!

Finance and accounting, Wall Street, auditors, etc.

This is an important constituency that marketing must not ignore. Success in marketing requires resources, and the returns on these resources are not always as immediately evident as on a piece of production equipment. Some of the most successful spin-off companies in recent years have done a great job marketing themselves and what they do, and in turn helped fuel their own successes.

Do we have adequate financing for the growth we are planning?

Marketing can both help this area, and be helped by it. The relationships built as programs and campaigns are being put together will often insulate those same programs from cutbacks in spending during tough times. If marketing shows good fiscal accountability and responsibility, then a strong level of understanding and trust can be built between the functions, which will serve the company well in good times and in bad times.

Information technology and alliances, service providers

"Knowledge is power", or so said Sir Francis Bacon. Information is power in today's economy. If you do not believe that, turn off your computers and telephones for a day and see what happens. Marketing must provide information about the market, the competition, and its own company. By making internal information easily accessible and sorted for use, marketing and IT people build a powerful platform. Create knowledge management web sites, which act as repositories for all of the information needed by and discovered by the people who work in the company. Marketing must take the lead in this, because they have "the most skin in the game".

Corporate executive level and boards of directors

Allies in high places are important to most efforts. This is why marketing must build bridges to the highest ranks of its company. If the executive suite and the board room is filled with people who agree with, support, and buy into the marketing strategy and plans, a lot of good things happen. Resources become easier to get. Decisions are made more quickly.

Of course there is downside to this level of involvement. You'll get a lot of ideas, suggestions, and advice that is hard to turn down. Declining the suggestion of an influential director is a ticklish situation at best. The risk of this is probably worth the benefits of support, but not always. But when (or if) you can bundle any part of such director's suggestions into plans, support is usually forthcoming and immediate.

The other issue that must be addressed with corporate and board level relationships is that these people talk and think in the language of money. Be prepared to state the benefits of marketing programs in both your language (market share, penetration, brand image, etc.) and in theirs (sales revenue, earnings per share, return on investment, etc.). Don't forget to show that you have considered the risks and the downside too – and made contingency plans for dealing with them.

> If we only knew what we already know, we'd be much more effective.
>
> Jim Hawley, VP, Home Solutions, Manco, Inc.

Above all, make sure presentations to this influential group are well prepared, thoroughly rehearsed (and sufficiently vague in hard promises to permit some wiggle room when tough questions are posed). Waffling about answers to questions is bad, so having definitive statements that are not couched as firm commitments is the challenge. Make time or date commitments in as large a time frame as practical (like "during the 3rd quarter" – not specific dates).

Talk in terms of favorable customers' reactions and compare advantages to competitor offerings. This is usually better than discussing either the product or program in the abstract or confronting the much more quantifiable issues of *exactly how much* market share gain, revenue increase, or profit improvement will result. Answering questions with ranges is always better, if you can satisfy the questioner. When you don't know, say so – then agree to get the answer and respond in the near future – assuming the answer is "knowable". Some things in marketing are uncertain and at risk. If that's the case, admit it.

But make sure that the numbers or dates you cite match those in any (financial) resource requests or projections that got the product or program approved in the first place. If they don't, explain why before you are asked. Directors keep track of such things – it's their job.

Conclusion

It all begins and ends with people. Whoever has the best talent and gets them working together the best will win every time – in marketing and in business and in any human endeavor. The bottom line here is that these relationships are invaluable and can create powerful partnerships. It is through these partnerships that everything else gets done – or doesn't. Your choice!

11 The Future: Marketing in the New Economy

The five smartest things to know about marketing

- **You must have a plan**

- **Get close to the customer**

- **Do your homework**

- **Remember relationships**

- **Use the speed and reach of technology**

I know, I highlighted all five of the Smartest Things to Know about Marketing. I did that because in the future, just like in the past and the present, all five are essential. Not four or three – all five! Also, don't look for an order to the topics in this chapter – after all it's about the future! Who knows which of these will come first, second, third, etc. But each one is linked to one (or more) of the five smart things to know about marketing, just to reinforce that whether it was in the past, the present or in the future – those will still be smart things to know.

Marketing at the speed of light – the speed and reach of technology

Where do we go from here? What does the future of marketing hold? Two things are certain: Smart Things to Know about Marketing will grow in importance, and the rollercoaster ride has just begun – but hang on: it *will* be exciting! To consider how marketing will evolve in the future, we must first consider what the future will hold. While no one can predict the future with accuracy, there are some things that can be forecast with directional reliability – because the seeds for them have already been planted and the technology to harvest those crops of the future is at our fingertips and synapses as this is being written. Whatever happens, you can rest assured, will happen faster than ever before. So get ready!

Disposable income distribution – you must have a plan

As Peter Drucker points out, some things are readily tracked and can help planning by leading to some observations about the future. One of these is the distribution of disposable income. Trends in disposable income distribution are critically important to marketers. Such trends signal changes in consumption patterns that may have ominous or wonderful implications for the future of companies, products, and services. What is critical to watch is how this disposable income switches from one part of a market or economy to another.

> "In fact, it is not possible to create tomorrow unless one first sloughs off today."
>
> Peter Drucker, *Management Challenges for the 21st Century*

One most prominent example of this is the huge revenue derived from long-distance telephone services over the past few decades. Bandwidth and the Internet's growth is signaling a major shift in disposable income away from paying exorbitant rates for long-distance telephone services. Telephone network time that sold for $0.25–50 per minute in the US market not long ago is now being offered for $0.05–0.10 per minute, and that figure is dropping by one-half every

> The most profound effect of this (digital) technology revolution...will be that it will make the differences among people more important. As technology adapts to people, our ability to unleash human potential will be the primary source of competitive advantage.
>
> Kevin Kelly

six months or less. Where did that disposable income go? Smart marketers will figure out how to give it a place to go!

Where the money is going – do your homework

How will you find that place? First consider what Drucker categorizes as places where income goes:

- *Government* – whose main function is the redistribution of income – has also become a major consumer of income in the form of taxation, to be spent elsewhere, outside of the taxpayers' direct control!

- *Healthcare* – which is becoming an increasing issue as we face generations with unprecedented distribution of ages – there is no precedent for situations where people past the normal "retirement age" outnumber the younger persons still working for a living.

- *Education* – in what is truly a knowledge economy gains a disproportionate importance – yet is being poorly managed in many developed countries, especially the US primary and secondary schools.

- *Leisure* – becomes a major opportunity for marketers to capture discretionary spending in larger and larger chunks – even in what used to be called underdeveloped countries.

One of the critical issues facing marketers in the future is slowing population growth. Markets that grow with population and its resultant activities become less attractive and more competitive as the growth slows. Thus the premium for high growth will be to, as Gary Hamel so aptly puts it, *"Get to the future first"* and with a revolutionary, innovative, and market-expanding product concept.

His example of just how rife the market is with opportunities is "Lettuce". In the face of a time-starved consumer, the sales of pre- packaged, pre-cut, and assorted types of lettuce in US supermarkets has become a billion-dollar market in just a few short years. A bag of lettuce that contains less than one-third the amount that could be bought in the produce department sells for two or three times the price because it has been chopped up, mixed with different types, and packaged in a readily usable and disposable plastic bag.

> "Problems cannot be ignored. And serious problems have to be taken care of. But to be change leaders, enterprises have to focus on opportunities. They have to starve problems and feed opportunities."
>
> Peter Drucker, *Management Challenges for the 21st Century*

Change can start anywhere – use the speed and reach of technology

In the opening part of this book on history, note that many of the inventions that changed society in the 20th century originated in Europe in the 19th century! How many of the innovations that will change the 21st century will come from "somewhere else" – somewhere where you don't live, and with which you aren't all that familiar? Many marketing ideas originated outside the US, they just matured in the fertile soil of the wealth in the US.

It is no coincidence that a recent *Business Week* ranking of the world's largest companies in terms of stock market capitalization lists 13 US companies in the top 20 and 33 in the top 50. This predominance of wealth and market development means that many marketing ideas (which may have originated elsewhere) will be tested, exploited, and succeed (or fail) first in the US market. But thanks to global communications technology, such failures and the lessons learned to improve on them will spread worldwide, rapidly. Thus the future of marketing will be influenced by what happens first in more developed markets like the US, Europe, and Japan, and then later by what happens in the most populous markets like China, India, and Malaysia. As more and more companies in Europe and the US merge and acquire each other, these two large, developed markets will converge in marketing practices.

The revolution is coming – get close to the customer

I like Gary Hamel's approach in the book *Leading the Revolution* because human nature is to find a safe place and stay there. Maslow's hierarchy of needs has security and safety as is foundations, and so we behave accordingly. But, smart marketers take heed – staying in a safe place may be the most dangerous thing you could do in the future.

Hamel describes it dramatically:

> We now stand on the threshold of a new age – the age of revolution…we know it is going to be an age of upheaval, of tumult, of fortunes made and unmade at head snapping speed….We are witnessing a Cambrian explosion of new competitive life forms. In this new age, a company that is evolving slowly is already on its way to extinction.

I'll go Gary one better. These companies are not on their way to extinction: they are already dead – there are just some residual muscle twitches that look like life still occurring. The dinosaurs were wiped out by a cataclysmic event with which they simply could not cope. Many companies are behaving like the dinosaurs, trying to find a safe place to hide. Still others are like dinosaurs mating: combine one big, dumb, slow organism with another big, dumb slow organism and what would you expect – a quick nimble organism – *not!* You simply get a bigger, slower, and no smarter organism.

> "Getting to the future first may enable a company to establish the rules by which other companies will have to compete."
>
> Gary Hamel and C. K. Prahalad, *Competing for the Future*

Marketing is a wonderful discipline because it can deal with this foolishness if it is allowed to. The answer is getting close to the customer and then using market segmentation, niche marketing, guerrilla marketing, etc., to satisfy and delight the customer with things they couldn't even imagine possible. But this can happen only if the large corporations are smart enough to let their marketers leave those safe places to search for new, better places. Remember Bill Kahl's admonition *"You have to kiss a few frogs if you want to find a prince."* The other problem with revolutions is that if you don't get a head start, or if you fall behind, or if you just don't start moving soon enough/fast enough, it is like running from an explosive shock wave – you just can't run fast enough to get away from obliteration.

The shifts will be profound – get close to the customer

Take demographics of the US market as an example, and consider the figures I cited earlier. In 1950, the US population was 89% white and 10% black, with the remaining 1% a mixture of many minorities. As of 2000, Hispanic population is rapidly overtaking African Americans as the dominant minority. By 2050, 25% of the US population will be of Latino heritage, and adding Asians to that will constitute 33% of the population, and when added to the approximately 12–15% blacks and a smattering of others means that minorities will become the majority. How this will change marketing,

I am not sure. But it will be profound and will require quantum change, not just incremental creep.

The aging of the population will mean that the US will have the predominant part of its white population over the age of 60! Other developed countries will have similar situations. Smart marketers will "bookmark" the US Census web site on their web browsers and spend a lot of time there doing research on market demographic segments. Mass markets may still exist, but they will be amalgams of diversity, based on more socio-economic common denominators than racial minorities. Learn what that is, before your competitor does.

Immigrants go from poor to wealthy countries – remember relationships

Like North America, Europe will incur the same migration of immigrants from its underdeveloped countries into the more developed ones, seeking jobs and a better life, particularly following the European Union's eastward expansion. The range of European languages and cultural differences will make it even more challenging to understand and capitalize upon this migration. Surprisingly, all of the most developed countries of continental Europe have a percentage of immigrant population that is surprisingly close to each other – and the US – around 8–9%! Why? Because these countries all have economic systems that depend on inexpensive labor, yet need inex-

> "Basic assumptions about reality are the paradigms of a social science, such as management. . . . The discipline's basic assumptions about reality determine what it focuses on. . . . They decide both what in a given discipline is being paid attention to and what is neglected or ignored."
>
> Peter Drucker, *Management Challenges for the 21st Century*

pensive labor that earns much more than it would in its own depressed home country. There is a profound message here for marketers. Does the term "two-tier markets" sound appropriate?

Transference marketing – do your homework

What kind of trend does this migration of people show us? It shows that in a free world, people move to places where they can more fully enjoy life. If we believe Drucker's theory that leisure is one of the large recipients of disposable income, then this movement has an opportunity buried in it. For ages, people have made pilgrimages to places of importance. In centuries past it was often to religious sites, or the sites of festivals and gatherings. Today it is in search of new experiences.

Travel around the world has become increasingly easy and less expensive, but air travel, especially intercontinental air travel, is still prohibitively expensive for most people. Yet, marketers realize that people will pay for experiences. If the people cannot go to the experience, then smart marketers transfer the experience to where they can go. If the attraction you want is too far away or too exotic/expensive for you to visit, marketers can bring a replica of it to a location near you.

Disney first exploited this concept with its revolutionary EPCOT (Experimental Prototype Community Of Tomorrow). EPCOT's futuristic exhibits captivated visitors, as did its vignettes of foreign countries complete with restaurants and curio shops. Now, in a burst of gambling-inspired creativity, Las Vegas is doing the same. Luxury hotels on the famed "Strip" have sprung up like weeds in the past few years, each offering a visit to a faraway place replicated with surprising accuracy. The Venetian hotel combines frescoed ceilings with architecture from old Venice, Italy – complete with shops and eateries lining a replica of the Grand Canal with its gondolas and singing

Q: What does this "experience economy" mean?

A: There is a whole book that describes it, but here it is "in a nutshell".

Economic offering	Commodities	Goods	Services	Experiences
Economy	Agrarian	Industrial	Service	Experience
Function	Extract	Create	Deliver	Stage
Nature-offering	Fungible	Tangible	Intangible	Memorable
Key attribute	Natural	Standardized	Customized	Personal
Factor-demand	Quality	Features	Benefits	Sensations

Source: Joseph Pine and James Gilmore, *The Experience Economy*

gondoliers. New York, New York reprises the "Big Apple" with an exterior scale mockup of key points on the city's skyline: the Empire State Building, the Chrysler Building, a Coney Island roller coaster, and much more. Inside, NY–NY even manages to capture the ambience of this famous city's streets and landmarks. Paris–Las Vegas brings a scale model Eiffel Tower, Arc d'Triomphe, and Louvre. Bellagio recalls the decadent splendor of old Rome. Then there are the Luxor's pyramid-shaped hotel, recalling cues from ancient Egypt, the Mandalay Bay, Monte Carlo, Excalibur, and more coming. A trip down the "Las Vegas Strip" begins to replicate a tour of the key experience spots of the world.

Universal Studios in Florida has created a replica of the Italian Riviera city of Portofino. Busch Gardens reprises the African veldt and old Morocco. Smart marketers have built several "Legends" golf courses combining replicas of great golf holes from around the world. Amusement parks, hotels, resorts, casinos, and venues of all types are using "transference marketing "more and more than ever before to bring the experience to where the customer can travel. Expect this trend to continue. Why? Because it works!

Malls rejuvenated – do your homework

This concept of transference marketing is even being extended to rejuvenate shopping malls, an artifact of the past generation of retail marketing. The mall stores reflect the lifestyles of the future with food courts and movie theaters mixed with pure experience venues in the leading edge malls like Easton, in Columbus, OH (instigated by retailer Limited, Inc., founder LesWexner) and the Mall of the Americas in suburban Minneapolis, MN. Major European cities are also catching on to the experience trend, and with "the real thing" in the way of historic architecture. Downtown Copenhagen, Denmark cordoned off many of the streets, creating easy, pleasant walking, shopping, and dining experiences among centuries-old buildings.

Large mall complexes have now become marketing magnets for the area where they are located. South Coast Plaza in Santa Ana, CA is literally surrounded with almost as many stores and dining establishments outside of the mall as are inside it. Going to the mall is not going shopping – it is a recreational experience. Malls will soon sell sponsorships just like athletic stadiums do now – why not?

"The message is the medium."

Marshall McLuhan

Billboards and signage around malls and along highways will be electronically alterable. Messages will vary by time of day and traffic speed. Gas pumps will all have video news updates on them complete with ads. Restrooms will offer instant access to news and communications in semi-private stalls, and any place consumers "pause" will become a marketing venue. Computers now make it possible to project virtual signage on live sports telecasts, and make it look like it is actually part of the venue. Even manhole covers and utility access panels on prominent buildings and heavily traveled streets will contain ads that wear off over time and are resold and reapplied. Advertising on clothing has been common for years, but now consumers are even being paid to display advertising on their personal autos. San Francisco, CA company MyFreeCar.com is paying car owners $350–400 monthly fees to wrap their cars in advertising the logos of many companies from the Library Corporation to *Playboy magazine*. FreeCar.com plans to go one better and *give* people their own ad-wrapped cars. BigStar's fleet of over 200 trucks bearing fluorescent orange and yellow banners have been spotted from planes landing at major airports. What next? The new marketing truth is that the message is everywhere – and the medium is everywhere too.

Resorts, fixed and floating – get close to the customer

Resort towns create experience opportunities within the geographical area surrounding them. Consider just a few of these:

- Jeep tours and balloon rides around Sedona, Arizona, Palm Springs, CA, etc.

- Plane tours over and mule rides into the Grand Canyon or trams to peaks in the Alps

- Helicopter rides over the Waimea Canyon of Kauai, Hawaii or around the volcanoes of Hawaii's big island

- Helicopter rides or horseback jaunts into the Great Smoky Mountains

- White-water rafting on the Snake River, or deep-sea fishing expeditions off Florida's coast

- Small ship cruises up the inner passage to Alaska, or to famed ports on the Mediterranean

- Barges and riverboats cruising rivers in America and cruise boats on Europe's major rivers – like Germany's Rhine

- The ultimate experience nucleus – Orlando, Florida – is home to Disney World, Universal Studios, Sea World and literally dozens more attractions – including a huge convention center surrounded by more and more large hotels, which serve both tourists and business people.

Then there are the growing ranks of gargantuan cruise ships. These floating hotels play to the aging population by providing comfortable relaxation, easy recreation, live entertainment and ample dining all in one great floating hotel – which takes you to a series of interesting destinations. No packing or unpacking, no hassle for arranging travel and lodging, and no problem of food and recreation – they are all bundled into one easy-to-market, plan and buy package.

Tie-in marketing – remember relationships

Each of these experience-based markets is full of opportunities for the growing field of tie-in marketing. Before and during the cruise you need the requisite cruise wear – who better to sell it to you than the cruise line who already knows your destinations, activities and the climate? Golf and tennis pro shops have known for years that they can sell more expensive gear and clothing at higher markups than conventional retailers. Why? Because you are there for the experience and, somehow, economic reality is temporarily suspended.

Tour gear is a glowing opportunity for tour operators. Binoculars and cameras for that Jeep tour or helicopter ride are a must. Where to get them? Right then and there: after all, on a vacation experience, money is not "real" – until the charge bills come in later! Smart malls are learning this and creating their own events – shows, free entertainment, anything to enhance the experience and draw you there, where they can sell you more "stuff ". Celebrity appearances, sporting events, and concerts are another ripe marketing opportunity.

But, what do all of these have in common? The *experience* is the common thread, leading to golden marketing opportunities. Everything in the future from age demographics to ethnic diversity supports this premise. Get on the bandwagon or get left behind.

But what about the Internet? Use the speed and reach of technology

It's hard to believe I got this far without getting into the Internet and technology and how those bombshells affect the future of marketing. Well, now it's time to talk technology. The Internet will continue to grow and the major problems in the future for marketers will be its management, regulation, organization, and capacity. There is no question that the technology exists to alleviate capacity issues – if it is commercialized and implemented as fast as usage explodes – and that's a big *if*!

Let's proceed with a couple of simplifying assumptions:

"A huge tide of information and trust must flow between users and creators in order to create exactly what the customer wants."

Kevin Kelly, *New Rules for the New Economy*

• Somehow, someone will deal with the capacity issue so that capacity and speed will continue to increase as bandwidth increases.

• There is little you can do about regulation, taxation, administration, intellectual property rights, and privacy issues – except stay informed at all times – because these can alter the marketing landscape dramatically. The problem is, we cannot know or predict how.

Now with those massive concerns blithely dismissed by assumptions, let's get on with what may happen and how that impacts smart marketing in the future.

Your web site stinks! That phrase is used often enough, but there is a real possibility that it could be taken literally if new technology for transmitting odors over the Internet takes off. Just to illustrate how technology could impact marketing in the future, imagine you sell cologne. If DigiScents iSmell becomes a widespread commercial reality, your presentation to web-based prospects will be a whole different world. Of course users will have to use a DigiScents iSmell "attachment" to translate the digital scent file into the odor you asked to smell. But how is that so different from adding speakers to listen to digital sound or video cams to send pictures back to others.

Experts tell us that scents trigger more emotional recall than inputs from any of the other individual senses, so why not? Imagine the future of being able to smell things via the Internet. Smell that coffee brewing or bread baking. What an environmental enhancement this could be.We think of brands as being identified with visual icons or names, but why not the scent of real Coach leather and the aroma of fine Kona coffee brewing?

> "Our capacity to dream limits us. Experience has never been more worthless. Most improvement strategies are becoming useless....Size doesn't matter....Linear growth isn't good enough. We must center on new growth, the inventive solution."
>
> Gary Hamel, "Conceptual Thinking", *Executive Excellence*

Brands will matter more – you must have a plan

There are those who would lead you to believe that the Internet will spell the death of brands, because new ones can be created so rapidly and old ones retired with equal speed. Don't believe them. Brands will be more important than ever in the future. Why? Because they offer an easy, convenient form of shorthand and symbolism that encompass a huge variety of information in an era when everyone is (or will be) suffering from information overload. Brands also convey

> "The network economy is founded on technology, but can only be built in relationships. It starts with chips and ends with trust."
>
> Kevin Kelly, *New Rules for the New Economy*

other meanings – trust, reliability, comfort, safety, security, and all those things that human beings long for but always seems to need more of.

Brands save time. Brands compress information. Brands make people comfortable. Brands are very valuable. Brands, done correctly are recognizable, unique, and distinctive. Got the message? Few things are more valuable than a well-known, respected, and valued brand name. If you have one, guard it jealously against damage by over-extension, quality or service deterioration, knock-offs, etc. If you don't have one, get one – fast. If you can't get one, start building one – it takes time, money, and real thought to do this.

Technology will alter the landscape permanently – use the speed and reach of technology

I don't intend to go through all of the technological innovations that will make the subhead of this section true. I will just go through enough to (hopefully) convince you.

Online shopping

This one is old news. Amazon.com is the leader and invented this category. It is easy, fun, efficient, but not for everyone or everything. Pay attention to what works and who likes it, and especially who doesn't. For the right categories, this is a must. For the wrong ones it's a bust!

Digital video recording

Two companies, TiVo and Replay Networks, are out there now, but the blurring of boundaries will make them just the pioneers. Digital set-top boxes in the age of convergence will make TV schedules as easy to rearrange as the sections of the newspapers. What marketers must worry about is that these boxes may zap advertising, changing the decline in TV ad effectiveness from a gradual one to a precipitous one. Permission marketing will then become the key approach. Until or unless that "fall off the cliff " comes, TV ads will still be a prominent and important media choice. But be sure to learn how to shoot with a rifle, because as the number and kind of cable and satellite channels proliferate, TV media selection will become more like choosing magazines and markets to advertise in. Only the wealthiest will be able to afford shotgun blasts of advertising at the whole market to hit just a part of it.

Smart/wired homes and appliances

Are you ready for your refrigerator to tell you the milk is outdated and order fresh milk? Who will it order from? Will you pick it up or will it be delivered? Why do you need a key to open your door?Won't a voiceprint, a retinal scan, or a thumbprint do it? But then who wants to change all the locks? I'd bet that the owners of cars that have built-in programmable garage door openers are crazy about them. Why not the door locks at home?

Subscriptions

Subscriptions (mentioned in permission marketing) work for magazines and newspapers, but why not for toilet tissue, Kleenex, trash bags, dog food, and all of those other staples you consume at a fairly consistent rate – including prescription medications? The problem, say the experts, is delivery costs. I agree. Retailing performs a valuable aggregation and disaggregation function; especially since you pick up the goods and essentially do the disaggregation and delivery yourself. Only when a mega-retailer like Wal*Mart partners with a mega-web site like amazon. com and a mega-deliverer like UPS (or the US Postal Service?) will there be sufficient volume to do aggregation and disaggregation to homes, giving you the choice of delivery or pickup. Delivery can't be free. It's too costly to do. But if your time is valuable and in short supply (whose isn't), then perhaps you will pay a nominal "subscription" fee for deliveries, and make a place for them to be stored until you come home. Remember the milkman?

> "What comes around, goes around."

Of course the days of homeowners being required to detect failures around their homes will slowly disappear. Diagnostic chips in major appliances, HVAC, and even their autos will transmit signals to the selected (subscription) maintenance organizations that will arrange appointments for repairs to be made.

Smart cards and chips – use the speed and reach of technology

Of course, you don't need a wallet full of credit cards, ID cards, driver's license, etc. A single smart card with an embedded chip is plenty. New "cards" that use optical readers are almost ready for the market right now – sort of like a flat CD that is the size of a credit cad and fits in your wallet. It will give your entire medical history and credit ratings to anyone with the right password (s) –which you or your loved ones can give as/when needed. Your smart card will also get you through tollbooths, and could let you start your car, enter your house, withdraw money from the ATM, and lots more.

> "All growth is a leap in the dark, a spontaneous, unpremeditated act without the benefit of experience."
>
> Henry Miller

And if you lost it or it was stolen or damaged, you could invalidate it via your own computer and create a new one – or do so at one of those nearly obsolete financial institutions that are called "banks". Banks are rapidly becoming dinosaurs of a prior era – no longer viable in the era of e-cash and e-stamps, and smart cards. They are

> *"…eventually the wireless web will be as large as the wired web of today, and when that happens, online vendors will connect with mobile millions – once they know where they are."*
>
> Richard A. Shaffer, founder, Technologic Partners

never open when you want them anyway, so the ones that do not close will keep the deposits of the minority of Luddites who distrust technology and provide the service to create new smart cards for the minority who do not have their own PDA computers to do so.

Of course, products will have smart microchips embedded in them or their containers, so checkout lines will move much faster, and electronic funds transfer will take care of payments. A swipe of your smart card past the reader will tell it who you are, and, if you want, show you your account balances to help manage budgets (if you have not already subdivided expenses into categories so it can help you manage your home and personal finances) After all, the use of cash will decline even further, so there will be no pile of coins or paper in your pocket/purse to count.

What do all of these future developments mean to marketers? A lot, but not everything, will change. *People will still make choices based on value* and assumptions of what they get for what they "pay". Your Cell–PDA–PC will tell you what you want to know about buying

> *"I predict that the Internet will continue to grow as a retail device as well as a means to capture knowledge about customers."*
>
> Regis McKenna, "Leadership in the Digital Age", *Executive Excellence*

habits with more accuracy and speed than ever before. It will even let you do instant market research (with permission of course) on your latest and greatest product launch. But will you know what to do with that information? *The basics of marketing will still apply. People will still be people. Maslow's laws of human needs will still be as valid as ever – maybe more so.*

Instantaneous interactivity – use the speed and reach of technology

At the present time, TV broadcasts are encouraging consumers to log into their web sites for interactive experiences. The problem is that many people keep their TV and computer in separate rooms and perceive them as suitable for separate uses. Until this problem is somehow removed, the potential of instantaneous interactivity via multimedia will be limited. With kids, this is not so much the case, thus the early adopters, as usual, will be the new generation.

In the near future, the recording industry must face a very real and immediate problem. Music is cheap on the Internet, if you can find it, if you have an MP3 player, and use low-cost sites such as Napster. The concept of Napster and Gnutella, the file-sharing technology company, depend on broadly available bandwidth in an almost unlimited supply – which may be at odds with our earlier assumptions about capacity vs. demand on the Internet.

> Instability and disequilibrium are the norms; optimization won't last long.
>
> Kevin Kelly, New Rules for the New Economy

Nonetheless, this concept of passing around material protected by intellectual property rights has been brewing on the Internet since its inception. Whether this approach is "outlawed" or not, the Internet will find a way around controls. The ability to get and share information broadly and freely at the click of a mouse will alter the marketing and economics of all forms of intellectual property. E-books and e-zines will continue to proliferate, offering quality information "for free".

Marketers will struggle with this dilemma for the beginning of this decade. How are the creators of content to be rewarded for their contributions? There is no easy answer. As in business today, if someone chooses to give something away at less than its prior value, competitors must play or pass – match the prevailing price – or sit on the sidelines and hope they can wait until the interloper goes broke and goes away, if ever.

New gadgets and new technologies for broadcasting advertisements on the Internet are being dreamed up daily. Marketers everywhere must keep a sharp lookout for where that leads next.

> "Companies will learn about the technologies of real time in the only way they truly can – by adopting them and putting them to practical use. They will deploy them not to predict the future but to live virtually on top of changing patterns and trends affecting every sphere of their business environment, making rapid and continuous refinements in their way of doing business."
>
> Regis McKenna, *Real Time*

Want a stamp to mail a letter?Well, if you still must mail letters, which is rapidly becoming an obsolete way to communicate, you can get one via your computer. Since legislation in the US recently was signed permitting electronic signatures, mailing or faxing signed documents will decline even further than it already has.

As Microsoft jumps on the bandwagon to lead the introduction of XML (Extensible Markup Language) to replace HTML (HyperText Markup Language), web pages will become more and more potent, opening new horizons every day. What will this mean to you? What will it mean to marketing? It will mean dramatically improved ability to reach diverse groups of widely scattered people, or even

"Conventional wisdom has brands becoming less important in the future because 'everybody is going to go online to find the cheapest price'. We think it will be just the opposite. In the future brands will become more important, not less."

Laura Ries, from *The 11 Immutable Laws of Internet Branding*

individuals, in specific ways with customized messages, to gain their permission to engage in interactive dialogues resulting in sales and hopefully profits.Wow. Better figure out what you want to say to them!

Profiling and rifle-shots – get close to your customer and remember relationships

This may sound scary to shoppers, but it is the marketer's dream. As web sites move further and further toward customizing content based on the apparent preferences of visitors, profiling becomes a reality. Profiling means making the offering match the customer's preference profile based on information gained from the customers or their behaviors in the past and present. This technique is potentially so powerful that the US FTC (Federal Trade Commission) already has it under investigation! Companies that do this are often referred to as IRMs (interactive relationship managers).

Broadvision sells software that adjusts web pages content to suit each visitor. Nortel Networks uses Broadvision's software to deliver pages with news and e-commerce options that are matched to the visitor's company, job, and business interests. Of course, the user needs to provide identity information at some point along the way, but once that information is gained, the profiling can start.

> "Introducing Engage AudienceNet™
> Buying Internet media will never be the same."
> Engage – Profile Driven Internet Marketing
>
> Headline from an Engage magazine ad in *Business2.0*

Amazon.com is an IRM, which uses a form of passive profiling by providing shoppers with similar books that may be of interest based on past purchases and current inquiries. Sign on to http://www.amazon.com and see what it recommends for you. Atex Media Solutions goes further by building customization programs that recognize visitors and then use Engage's multi-faceted profiles to decide what to show them (and this is without the need for a sign-up or password!) Predictive Networks offers technology that is capable of profiling individual ISP customers, users of LAN/WANs (Local Area Networks/Wide Area Networks), and enabling intelligent content delivery to those same individuals.

Integrated marketing and communications – you must have a plan

As technology moves ahead in this 21st century, many of the old business models will become increasingly obsolete. Sending photos to be developed, sending materials "out to a printer" are both terms of a prior era's technology. Just as "winding a watch", using "carbon paper" to make copies, or adjusting a TV without a remote control are alien terms to today's youth, tomorrow's business people will wonder why we ever went to such lengths to do such seemingly easy tasks.

The concept that Henry Ford took to its ultimate extent – "vertical integration" – doing everything you need for yourself – is now virtually gone. More likely the future will be an era of "vertical

> "Your customers are invisible. Personalize that."
> Trivida – The Profit of Personalization
>
> Headline from an ad for Trivida in *Business 2.0*

disintegration" in which companies only do what is absolutely "core" to their competitive advantage and that will change daily, weekly, monthly, and occasionally annually. The rest will be outsourced to contractors who are specialists in the latest and greatest methods of doing "whatever". Marketers must be alert for the opportunities this presents. New markets can spring up overnight and be captured in weeks.

Productivity measures, once the province of the factory floor, will come to the service sector. The drive-through lanes of many fast food chains are already closely monitored for speed and accuracy. The world leader, McDonald's, has installed a "custom cooking system" – its version of mass customization. It is now marketing this capability as a unique value, although competitors Burger King and Wendy's have had essentially the same thing for years! Clever move. Who has the high ground doesn't matter unless they hold it in the mind of the customer. Claim that position in the customer's mind and you have it, whether you deserve it or not.

Integrated marketing communications means taking in all of the aspects of the business and using them to advantage to capture the

> "The biological nature of the new economic order means that the sudden disintegration of established domains will be as certain as the sudden appearance of the new."
>
> Kevin Kelly, *New Rules for the New Economy*

mind and money of the consumer. New idea? No – Al Ries and Jack Trout described the essence of it almost two decades ago in *Positioning*.

The great price leveling – get close to your customer and remember relationships

The practice of selling things for prices the market will bear is in great peril. The reason: prices are going to be transparently visible around the world. This will have a profound effect on European companies where country by country pricing and premiums over US prices have been the norm. Customers can now see pricing on the web and in the explosion of purchasing exchanges. Leverage that once belonged to only the largest companies is now spreading. As Gary Hamel so aptly puts it, *"In a web enabled world, there are no more distribution monopolies and no more hostage customers."* This will create

Q: Just how and who are companies building profiling programs?

A: The list below shows some of the players and what they do.

Name	Stock symbol	What they do
Andromeda	MACR	instant psychographic recommendation
BroadVision	BVSN	web site customization
DoubleClick	DCLK	targeted ad services
Engage	ENGA	profile database services
Net Perceptions	NETP	instant recommendation/ personalization
Personify	private	web audience analysis
Younology	private	behavioral modeling of web users
Predictive Networks	private	individual and LAN/WAN surfing habits

Source: *Forbes*

> "...I figured out that investors needed to be fed three bullet points in 30 seconds. Fortunately the three bullet points were always the same. A company needed:
>
> ● A monster market into which to sell
>
> ● An unfair competitive advantage
>
> ● A business model to leverage that unfair advantage
>
> ...Even owning intellectual property is not enough; one must have an innovative business model to maximize returns."
>
> Andy Kessler, *Wall Street Journal*

entirely new marketing challenges. In the markets of the future, competitive advantage must be created by truly superior performance and/or innovation. Or to say it another way, *"Fakin' it is no longer makin' it."*

Whose people are they? Remember relationships

Remember when companies'employees did the work, produced the goods, and delivered the services? Now the work force is an amalgam of regular employees, part-time or temporary employees, and contract employees. The future of marketing depends on knowing how to capitalize on, communicate with, and manage this new-millennium work force. The relationships with these diverse groups of people are critical success factors – for marketing and for all management in the future.

Genomes, DNA, and the future

As the human genome is mapped and the building blocks of life understood, a huge change looms just over the horizon. Are men and women fundamentally different psychologically or is it social conditioning? To what extent is intelligence inherited versus gained over life? These and many other questions have been debated through the ages.

Perhaps we will soon learn the answers, but with such learning comes a series of risks. The institutions of our society, from the family to democracy itself, assume certain aspects of human nature as part of their underpinnings. The potential to change these human aspects through genetic engineering poses questions that are too large and overwhelming for most people to contemplate fully. If biotechnology is about curing diseases and improving quality of life, one conclusion is the result. Marketing can prosper under the rules made for the natural society we live in. If the result is human re-engineering, a whole different scenario is possible.

Whichever it is, marketing will play a pivotal role, because marketing is the eyes, ears and mouth of the company interacting with customers constantly. If you never forget that, and combine it with Theodore Levitt and Roger Blackwell's statements: *"The purpose of a business is to create and keep a customer"* and *"Marketing is having what will sell"*, you will have the basis for a lot of other Smart Things to Know about Marketing.

Now go out there and be a smart marketer and come up with something that will sell!

"Online there's no place for mediocrity to hide."

Gary Hamel

"He who would learn to fly one day must first learn to stand and walk and run and climb and dance; one cannot fly into flying."

Friedrich W. Nietzsche

Smart People to Have on Your Side

Dr Theodore Levitt – Educator and author and former editor of the *Harvard Business Review*, and Edward W. Carter Professor of Business Administration at the Harvard Business School. Author of: *Innovation in Marketing* (1962), *Marketing* (with Matthews, Buzzell, and Frank) (1964), *The Marketing Mode* (1969), *Marketing: A Contemporary Analysis* (with Buzzell, Nourse, and Matthews) (1972), *Marketing for Business Growth* (1974), and *The Marketing Imagination* (1983, 1986).

Dr Roger D. Blackwell – Educator, author and consultant to a diverse group of Fortune 500 companies, a director who sits on the board of at least six companies, large and small, an award-winning professor at The Ohio State University who has taught over 65,000 students in his career. Co-author of the widely used textbook, *Consumer Behavior* (Dryden Press), and author of several books, including *From Mind to Market* (1997).

Dr Sarah Gardial – Director of the MBA Program and an Associate Professor of Marketing at The University of Tennessee–Knoxville, co-author with Robert Woodruff of *Know your Customer* (Blackwell 1996), and has worked with many of America's largest and most respected consumer products companies: Procter & Gamble, Frito-Lay, Gatorade, Saturn, Sea-Ray Boats, etc.

C. K. Prahalad – Harvey C. Freuhauf Professor of Business Administration at the University of Michigan Business School, a consultant to many leading companies author of numerous articles and co-author, with Gary Hamel of the best-selling book, *Competing for the Future*.

Gary Hamel – Founder of Strategos, a strategic consulting firm and on the faculty at the Harvard Business School, and the London Business School. He authored or coauthored (with C. K. Prahalad) many of a series of award winning articles in the *Harvard Business Review* and was co-author of the best-selling book, *Competing for the Future*. His newest book, *Leading the Revolution*, was published in 2000.

Jack Trout – Author of several books including *Positioning – The Battle for Your Mind*, *Marketing Warfare*, and *The New Positioning*, a consultant to major corporations; **Al Ries** and **Laura Ries** – authors of several books including *Positioning – The Battle for Your Mind*, *Marketing Warfare*, and *22 Immutable Laws of Branding*, consultants in marketing strategy to major corporations

Seth Godin – Former Marketing VP of Yahoo!, and author of *Permission Marketing*, consultant and creator of numerous business plans for Internet and e-business companies.

Bibliography

Books

Blackwell, Roger, *Mind to Market*, Harper Business, 1997.

Brower, Charles, *Sales and Marketing*, "First Books for Business", McGraw-Hill, New York, 1996.

Daly, James, Editor-in-Chief, *Business 2.0*, February 2000.

Drucker, Peter, *Management Challenges for the 21st Century*, Harper Business, New York, 1999.

Fine, Charles H., *Clock Speed*, Perseus, Reading, MA, 1998.

Gardial, Sarah and Robert Woodruff, *Know Your Customer*, Blackwell, Oxford, 1996.

Godin, Seth, *Permission Marketing*, Simon & Schuster, New York, 1999.

Hamel, Gary and C. K. Prahalad, *Competing for the Future*, Harvard Business School Press, Boston, MA, 1994.

Heil, Gary, Tom Parker, and Deborah Stevens, *One Size Fits One*, Wiley, New York, 1997.

Hisrich, Robert D., *Marketing*, Barron's Business Library, 1990.

Kelly, Kevin, *New Rules for a New Economy*, Viking, New York, 1998.

Levitt, Theodore, *The Marketing Imagination*, The Free Press, New York, 1983 and 1986.

Mackay, Charles, *Extraordinary Popular Delusions and the Madness of Crowds*, 1841.

McKenna, Regis, *Real Time*, Harvard Business School Press, Boston, MA, 1997.

Palmatier, George E. and Joseph S. Shull, *The Marketing Edge*, Oliver Wight Limited Publications, Essex Junction, VT, 1989.

Pine, B. Joseph, *Mass Customization*, Harvard Business School Press, Boston, MA, 1993.

Pine, B. Joseph and James Gilmore, *The Experience Economy*, Harvard Business School Press, Boston, MA, 1999.

Porter, Michael E., *Competitive Strategy*, The Free Press, New York, 1980.

Ries, Al with Steve Rivkin, *The New Positioning: The Latest on the World's #1 Business Strategy*, New York : McGraw-Hill, 1996.

Ries, Al and Jack Trout, *Marketing Warfare*, New American Library, New York, 1986.

Ries, Al and Jack Trout, *Positioning – The Battle for Your Mind*, McGraw-Hill, 1981, 1986

Ries, Al and Laura Ries, *22 Immutable Laws of Branding*, Harper Business, New York, 2002.

Schmitt, Bernd and Alex Simonson, *Marketing Aesthetics*, The Free Press, New York, 1997

Schultz, Don E., Stanley I. Tannenbaum, and Robert F. Lauterborn, *The New Marketing Paradigm*, NTC Business Books, Chicago, IL, 1993.

Wallace, Thomas F., *Customer Driven Strategy*, Oliver Wight Publications, Essex Junction, VT, 1992.

Periodicals

Aaker, David A., in *Strategy and Business*, 2Q 2000.

Blackwell, Roger D. and Kristina Stephan, "The Retail Paradigm", *Retail Merchandiser*, July 2000.

Blodgett, Henry, senior Internet analyst, Merrill Lynch, in *Fortune*, 26 June 2000.

Branson, Richard, in *Forbes*, 3 July 2000.

Breyer, Jim, Accel Partners, in the *Wall Street Journal*, 14 July 2000.

Browning, John and Spencer Reiss, "For the New Economy, the End of the Beginning", *Wall Street Journal*, 17 April 2000.

Christenson, Clayton and Richard S. Tedlow, *Harvard Business Review*, January–February 2000.

Corporate Branding, in the *Wall Street Journal*, 31 March 2000.

Daly, James, Editor-in-Chief, *Business 2.0*, 25 July 2000.

Dendinger, Martha Jo, CMP from *Meetings and Conventions*, June 2000.

Drucker, Peter F., "Knowledge Work", *Executive Excellence*, April 2000.

Drucker, Peter, *Forbes*, 15 May 2000, pp. 88-89.

Enrico, Roger, CEO PepsiCo, quoted in *Business Week*, 10 April 2000.

Freeman, Matt, Chief Executive, DDB Digital, from the *Wall Street Journal*, 23 June 2000.

GIG, edited by John Bowe, Marisa Bowe and Sabin Streeter, in *Fortune*, 10 July 2000.

Gilder, George, in Gilder Technology Report, *January* 2000.

Gunn, Eileen, "Know Thy Customer", *Business Week's Frontier*, 24 April 2000.

Gurley, J. William, "Startups, Beware: Obey the Law of Supply and Demand", *Fortune*, 29 May 2000, p. 278.

Hamel, Gary, "Conceptual Thinking", *Executive Excellence*, April 2000.

Hamel, Gary, in the *Wall Street Journal*, 6 June 2000.

Ikeo, Kyoichi, Keio University (Japan), in the *Wall Street Journal*, 14 February 2000.

John, Deborah Roedder, "Consumer Socialization of Children: A Retrospective Look at 25 Years of Research", *Journal of Consumer Research*, December 1999.

Kanter, Rosabeth Moss, Professor of Business Administration, Harvard Business School, "Are You Ready to Lead the E-cultural Revolution?", *INC.* February 2000.

Kessler, Andy, Partner, Velocity Capital Management, LLC in the *Wall Street Journal* 18 April 2000.

Logan, Toni, "Marketing VP=VIP", *Business 2.0*, February 2000.

McKenna, Regis, "Leadership in the Digital Age", *Executive Excellence*, April 2000.

O'Leary, Tim, CEO of ad agency Respond2, in *Business 2.0*, 25 July 2000.

Pickering, Carol, citing Tim Draper in "Choking on Cash", *Business 2.0*, January 2000.

Quattrone, Frank, managing director, CFSB Technology Group, in *Fortune*, 26 June 2000.

Raymond, David and Hal Varian, in *Forbes ASAP*, 21 February 2000.

Ries, Al and Jack Trout, from *Rethinking the Future*, cited in *Executive Excellence*, April 2000.

Ries, Laura, from *The 11 Immutable Laws of Internet Branding* quoted on http://www.amazon.com.

Roberts, Kevin, CEO, Saatchi&Saatchi PLC, in the *Wall Street Journal*, 18 May 2000.

Scally, Robert, "Clicks-and-Mortars Have the Right Stuff to Dominate the Internet", *Discount Store News*, 17 April 2000.

Schwartz, Nelson, "Trial By Fire", *Fortune*, 26 June 2000.

Setlow, Carolyn, Group Senior VP, Roper Starch Worldwide, in *Discount Store News*, 8 May 2000.

Shaffer, Richard A., founder, Technologic Partners in *Fortune*, 10 July 2000.

Wilkerson, Phil, Chief Technology Officer, GlobalFulfillment.com, in *Discount Store News*, 17 April 2000.

Index